DISCIPLINE
and the
CLASSROOM TEACHER

DISCIPLINE

and the

CLASSROOM TEACHER

NAOMI F. FAUST

Queens College
of the City University of New York

National University Publications
KENNIKAT PRESS   //   1977
Port Washington, N. Y.   //   London
A DUNELLEN PUBLISHING COMPANY BOOK

Printed in the United States of America

Distributed in United States and Canada by
Kennikat Press, Port Washington, N. Y. 11050

Distributed in British Commonwealth (except Canada) by
Martin Robertson & Company Ltd., London

Library of Congress Cataloging in Publication Data

Faust, Naomi F.
    Discipline and the classroom teacher.

    Bibliography: p.
    Includes index.
    1. School discipline. I. Title.
LB3013.F35   371.5   76-50646
ISBN 0-8046-7091-9 (hard cover)
ISBN 0-8046-7110-9 (paper)

To Roy
who was a source of
encouragement from the moment
the idea for the book was conceived

CONTENTS

PREFACE

A number one concern of teachers throughout the nation is "disciplinary problems." The purpose of this book is to assist teachers in acquiring the secure feeling of being able to establish well-disciplined classes in which adequate learning may take place.

A central goal of the author is to help the teacher meet such needs of youngsters as will encourage these young people to be self-controlled individuals who are willing to take advantage of their opportunities. The author hopes to assist many teachers in gaining the background knowledge needed to work with young people that will assure teachers of healthy survival in the classroom. There is the further hope that through this volume many teachers may be led to the conviction that the teacher's existence in the classroom can be rewardingly productive.

Several chapters are devoted to handling disadvantaged youth in discipline and learning. Much of the book, however, is concerned with the discipline of all types of youngsters.

It has often been said that while all young people present some problems in discipline, regardless of cultural or ethnic background, underprivileged youth—and particularly underprivileged black youngsters—frequently pose more disciplinary problems than others. But there needs to be due emphasis on why the condition is as it is and on how teachers might work to improve the situation. This book offers the unique contribution of delving into the problem.

Many who presently teach in the schools and many future teachers either were originally of middle-class background or have acquired that status. The volume takes these teachers behind the scenes to view and understand what has happened to the less advantaged child, with the aim of enabling them to be more capable of helping to bridge the gap between the less advantaged and privileged youngsters so that all children may more nearly reach their optimum of learning and better behavior.

The book puts great emphasis on using preventive measures for problems in discipline. This approach is of primary importance, for a great many teachers, parents, and others who deal with young people do not amply consider that far fewer disciplinary problems will occur in the first place if due stress is initially placed on preventing them. Numerous teachers and other adults who deal with youth without due regard for these positive, preventive measures actually create trouble, allowing many problems to develop that otherwise would not arise. The fact is that teachers who, for the most part, adhere to the positive, constructive tenets and procedures advocated in this volume should be able to set up classes in which disciplinary problems are at a minimum. These teachers would likewise be expected to achieve success as teachers, for the book clearly shows how the organization and maintenance of classes that are unimpeded by disciplinary problems go hand in hand with an adherence to those principles that make for successful teaching. This volume, however, does not stop with preventive measures, but treats, unstintingly, means of handling disciplinary problems that do occur.

The book has value for a wide audience. It may be of considerable use to every teacher —and that means teachers in all the large cities of the United States and in the smaller communities as well. The content is comprehensive, covering practically all essential aspects in the area of discipline. In addition, the book should be of inestimable value to concerned parents who are responsible for the training and supervision of children. It should be, as well, a highly useful guide for those who conduct courses in teacher training and social work. In fact, the book should be a valuable source in a variety of courses that are concerned with working with youth more advantageously.

Finally, the volume should provide the general public with a look into effective means by which teachers might cope with our youth. What happens to all our young people is of concern to citizens at large as well as to parents and others who must in some way work with the youth of our nation.

An expression of thanks is extended to the many who contributed directly or indirectly to this volume. In particular, the author owes an extensive debt of gratitude to a group of teachers and administrators whose contributions were outstandingly significant: Eddye Brown and May Sheehan, teachers; Eleanor Lovette, teacher and guidance counselor; Howard Seretan, teacher and administrator; William Egger, assistant principal; Dorothy U. Moore, principal; and Nathan Washton and Robert Edgar, college professors and supervisors of prospective teachers. The author extends a special note of thanks to her husband, Roy M. Faust, who was a source of constant encouragement from the moment the idea for the book was conceived. To all who in any way made a contribution to this volume, the author is deeply grateful.

N. F. F.

DISCIPLINE
and the
CLASSROOM TEACHER

ABOUT THE AUTHOR

Naomi F. Faust (PhD NYU) has brought to the writing of this book a
background of teaching experience on each educational level—elementary,
junior high school, senior high school, and college. While teaching in public
school systems, she also served as cooperating teacher responsible for
training college seniors to teach in public schools. Both her public school
teaching and college teaching include experience in cities and communities
in various parts of the country. In the process of performing her duties
as a teacher, she has dealt with a wide range of young people—underprivileged, privileged, advanced, less advanced, disruptive, and less disruptive. In her present position as a professor at Queens College, of the City
University of New York, Dr. Faust is charged with a major responsibility
of helping to prepare students to teach in schools throughout the country.

1

DISADVANTAGED YOUTH AND THE
PROBLEM OF DISCIPLINE

"No thank you. I'll take my chances elsewhere." This was the essence of
the young teacher's reply when she was offered a teaching position in a
highly disadvantaged junior high school in one of our large Northern cities.
She couldn't rightly see why she should get mixed up with trying to dis-
seminate knowledge in what looked to her to be a school for the disorderly.
As she described it, there was pandemonium both in the classrooms and in
the corridors, and throughout much of the building there was limited respect for learning. Primarily, the school consisted of blacks and Puerto
Ricans, with a sprinkling of whites.

It is not to be denied that where the school population is composed
largely of disadvantaged pupils problems are frequently at a peak. Often,
however, too little attention and consideration are given to the conditions
that have caused these deprived youngsters to behave as they do. Teachers
have a need to measure and to know the reasons behind the misbehavior
of these young pupils, a need to understand what has shaped them into the
troublesome youngsters they are.

The truth of the matter is that in large cities where integrated schools
have supposedly been the practice, a great many of the teachers are from
a middle-class background, a large percentage of them being middle-class
whites. Many among the middle-class teachers were born into the more
affluent environment; others have acquired it. In any event, it is important
that middle-class teachers, and other teachers as well, become as knowledgeable about and understanding of the disadvantaged child as possible if
they are expected to become willingly capable of reaching him. Only knowledge and understanding of the deprived youngster will help to bridge the
gap between him and his middle-class teacher.

As it now stands, many middle-class white teachers are reluctant to teach in the schools where the pupil population is largely made up of disadvantaged blacks and Puerto Ricans, and particularly where the student body is almost entirely black. Many of these teachers fear the disciplinary problems posed by these youths.

Recently, a very competent middle-class white graduate refused a regular position in a disadvantaged school attended by blacks, Puerto Ricans, and a few other deprived groups. He preferred to accept substitute work on an irregular basis, where he would be teaching more favored pupils. And there are many young graduates whose reactions have been the same. Besides, there are far too many white teachers of experience and know-how who simply loathe the thought of going into an underprivileged school. Both the proper knowledge and the willingness to work with deprived pupils are important ingredients for successful teaching in difficult schools.

For our purposes, "discipline" will refer to the well-ordered classroom where pupil behavior will lead to appropriate development and learning on the part of the pupils who comprise the class. In this chapter, we shall examine diverse factors that have shaped deprived youngsters and made them so vulnerable to problems in discipline. A variety of insights needed for working with these youngsters effectively will be presented, for despite any discomfort experienced in dealing with them, the sincere teacher who plays a dynamic part in the growth and development of disadvantaged pupils can have the rich and gratifying feeling of knowing that he or she has helped where assistance is urgently needed.

WHO ARE THE DISADVANTAGED?

We may generally consider as disadvantaged the children of lowest socio-economic class—blacks, Puerto Ricans, Mexican-Americans, American Indians, and whites. They are the children who suffer from the chronic unemployment of their parents, insufficient food and food of poor quality, inadequate housing, crowded homes, family instability, and homes with missing fathers. They are the children who suffer the sting of such handicaps as inadequate medical care, insufficient personal attention, insufficient hope, lack of self-confidence, lack of pride, low self-image, insufficient motivation, lack of exposure to cultural activities, inferior educational background, and insufficient achievement.

It is easy to see that the multiple disadvantages from which underprivileged children suffer are not slight. It may also be clearly seen that they are the kinds of disadvantages that easily lead to frustration and hostility that are little amenable to principles of good discipline. It ceases to be startling, therefore, that behavior problems are often very much greater in schools that are largely attended by our deprived youth.

Disadvantaged blacks have suffered from the handicaps we have already indicated, as well as from segregation and discrimination and from a variety of deficits that have been incurred as a result of a history of slavery. Deprived blacks, then, can easily be singled out as the most greatly disadvantaged of all the disadvantaged groups. Therefore, at times in this book, this group will be treated as a representative example, as the conditions of the disadvantaged are elaborated. There is reason to believe that if the plight of disadvantaged blacks is substantially improved, so will there be notable improvement in the conditions of the deprived of other ethnic groups as well.

THE BACKGROUND OF THE BLACK CHILD

Let us take a tour into the past experiences of the black people of our country. Hopefully, such an excursion will cause serious reflection on the deprivations that have been of such magnitude as to subject many black children to what is frequently considered unacceptable behavior and a lack of self-control. The blacks' having been denied humane treatment and reasonable cultural, educational, and economic advantages for such a long time could lead only to patterns and outcomes that have in many ways left much to be desired.

Blacks were captured, brought to America, and forced into slavery. They were largely deprived of their own African culture; yet segregation, discrimination, and restrictions kept them from taking on the basic cultural and behavior patterns of those in the mainstream of American society.

In slavery, blacks, for the most part, were denied the opportunity to learn to read and write. Some masters were relatively kind, but many slaves were often brutally treated. Black men were in many ways stripped of their manhood. Forced to slave for their masters, they did not have the opportunity to work for a decent salary and proudly provide for their wives and children. Men in particular had to watch their behavior, lest they be accused of being insubordinate. The cruelties of slavery forced the black into submissiveness, and many of the brutal effects of the slave institution have lasted long after the Emancipation Proclamation.

After emancipation, blacks were allowed education, but it was separate from that for whites, and inferior. Having been born in the South and having taught school both in the South and in the North, I am well acquainted with the patterns of the nation's school systems. Until the more recent efforts to desegregate Southern schools, the black schools of the South were, in many instances, provided with whatever books, materials, and equipment the white society gave them. The books were often discards from the white schools. The variety of books was often limited, in comparison with the offerings in the white schools. In rural black schools, taught by blacks who had managed to become teachers, a single teacher often had to teach many grades, all in the same classroom. It was not uncommon to find one teacher teaching three or four grades. A great many of the black children could afford to have only five or six months of schooling per year, for in early fall and in the spring they had to help their parents work on white men's farms. As a consequence of all of these debilitating factors, learning for the black child was greatly curtailed.

Becoming unbearably confused, frustrated, and hopeless, many blacks began to take refuge in places outside the South. Naturally they took with them the culture they had, an impoverished culture that had been imposed on them, yet the only one they had to pass on to their children. These blacks fled the South in search of better living conditions, including a brighter educational future for their young ones.

The majority of blacks who came north settled in the segregated slum areas, sections of cities from which whites fled as blacks began to move in. For the most part, white people who took flight settled elsewhere in a city or in the suburbs. In the meantime, the black ghetto areas grew larger and larger and more and more isolated from the mainstream of the city's culture, until they resembled the areas from which the blacks had come. As the whites left the areas and the blacks moved in, financial and moral support of the neighborhood schools that blacks had to attend was greatly diminished. For the most part, however, blacks were forced to remain in these Northern ghettos because discriminatory practices in housing and lack of economic means would not allow them to move into more favored neighborhoods. As a result, de facto segregation subjected blacks to the inferior schools of their own ghetto areas.

Some black parents began to protest the plight of their children. They began to demand that their youngsters be allowed to have access to some of the better schools attended by whites. As their requests were fulfilled, the flame spread. Blacks from other urban areas made similar demands. Now black men and women all over the country are proclaiming their right to be first-class citizens, as documents of our nation have decreed they should be. The right of black children to a proper education is among those citizenship rights.

It is easy to see that the fair and proper education of the black child should be a foremost issue of national concern. Blacks of the nation await their country's atonement for the many deficits they have incurred.

The deprivations of the black people, over the years, have naturally affected the reactions of black men and women and in turn the attitudes of their children. This fact perhaps helps explain why some black youngsters who have become aware of their deprived state sometimes go overboard in their reactions, mistreating a deserving white teacher in a manner that says: "Show us that you are not among the whites who are really not concerned about us; prove to us your worth." And it must not be surprising either when some black children give a worthy black teacher a hard time, for some young people have not been sufficiently removed from a nurtured idea that "to be right is to be white," an image that a racist society so long perpetuated. It is not really the color of the teacher's skin that matters in the long run, but rather the development of certain necessary teacher qualities. Despite ethnic background, the teacher who develops a real understanding of deprived youths, honestly accepts them, and seriously teaches them in such a way as to meet their needs will, in time, not only be able to reach them but will be able to maintain discipline as well.

A look at the background of black people perhaps can make it clear to the classroom teacher how the black child's history of impoverished educational and cultural exposure generates the lack of hope that leads to hostility, belligerence, or indifference; the lack of self-control or finesse that leads to impudence or boisterousness; and the lack of feeling of self-importance that leads to anxiety, withdrawal, or the seeking of attention. Yet despite all his impairments, the black child will both learn and struggle to behave himself if a concerned nation will make learning conditions adequate for him and if teachers will be accepting and encouraging and willing to teach him properly.

A REVEALING COMPARISON

The disadvantages of the deprived child as compared to the advantages of his middle-class counterpart are factors that work against all low-socio-economic-class children—lower-class blacks, Puerto Ricans, Mexican-Americans, American Indians, and whites. All underprivileged groups suffer from such deficits as economic handicaps, substandard living conditions, and poverty of educational and cultural background. The following comparative account of disadvantaged blacks and middle-class whites has much insight to offer the teacher in understanding and dealing with deprived pupils of all races and nationalities. Having considered the double deficit of the majority of the black children resulting from their heritage of slavery and history of segregation and limitation because of color, we have used the plight of these lower-class black children to serve as dramatic contrast to the lives of middle-class white children. Our reasoning is this: A great majority of our teachers are middle class and need substantial understanding of the disadvantaged children with whom they are presently working or with whom they will work in the future. Our comparison indicates to the middle- or upper-class teacher the major differences between lower- and middle-class pupils and implies essential steps that may be taken to reach deprived youth and help bridge the gap.

Approximately 70 to 80 percent of the black population in our large cities may be termed lower class. The situation with respect to the white middle class is just the reverse: from 70 to 80 percent of the white urban population may be considered middle or upper class (Thompson, 1963). In the pages that follow, we shall see that to ask ill-equipped, disadvantaged youngsters to compete with their favored middle-class counterparts without the proper teacher understanding and guidance and without necessary compensatory education to fill gaps is to beg for school-hostile clientele among our disadvantaged pupils. We shall see from the academic, social, cultural, and psychological deficiencies of the underprivileged child why he is so prone to misbehavior. The teacher must work diligently to help fill his needs. Only then will the deprived youngster begin to have the tools for proper self-control.

Two reminders are in order at this point. First, though it is perfectly clear that compensatory education for the disadvantaged pupil must be used to secure a substantial foundation upon which basic learning may take place, it is expected that the teacher will move the deprived child along the path of progression as efficiently and rapidly as it is possible to do so. Second, it is to be emphatically stressed that the deprived state of the black disadvantaged child is not justly to be considered a reflection on the youngster himself, but rather a consequence of what oppression, limitation, discrimination, and segregation have imposed.

It must be emphasized that the deprived black child can learn if conditions are made right for him. Unfortunately, a great many teachers still act as if they think black people are innately inferior in intelligence to whites. Sufficient studies, however, clearly substantiate the fact that the blacks are not inherently less intelligent than the whites. Rather, it is the impoverished heritage or environment that society has imposed on black people that causes them generally to score lower on intelligence tests than whites.

We have just stated the capacity of the deprived black child for learning; yet we have previously pointed up the less than favorable lot that blacks have had to bear. Through a comparison of the circumstances of disadvantaged blacks and middle-class whites, let us look at major deficits black youngsters have amassed as a result of deprivations. Helpful suggestions are offered for coping with the deficiencies in such ways as to improve the pupils' chances for learning and for greater self-control.

INSECURITY VS SECURITY

In the middle-class white home, there is, for the most part, economic security and stability. The breadwinner is frequently the father, although increasingly a larger number of wives work, too, particularly after the children have gotten off to a good start in school. The family income is sufficient to afford comfortable living, and the homes and neighborhood are usually attractive and well kept.

Today there are a great many job opportunities for blacks who are well trained or highly skilled, and many fields once closed to them are now open. In lower-class black homes, however, there are still a number of men who are unable to get decent jobs. Naturally the children feel the effects of this economic deficiency. Unfortunately, too, in far too many under-privileged homes fathers have left because they were ill prepared to get and maintain jobs sufficient to provide well for wives and children. The lack of a father image in the home is a deficit for the young people of the family. And in many urban places where integrated schools are supposedly the pattern, black male teachers who could serve as surrogate father images are few in number. Teachers might help, however, by trying to encourage the young people to join organizations sponsored by black men, such as Boy Scout groups and other organizations; and teachers might invite successful black men to appear as speakers at assemblies and in the classroom.

MOVING VS STABILITY

There is often, too, a great amount of shifting or moving among deprived family members. Frequent changes in home conditions create in children anxiety and a sense of instability, just as a constant teacher turnover causes a lack of security in the school setting. The new student should be sincerely welcomed; and, if possible, the teacher might find something the youngster can do, however small, that can be brought before the group for recognition and praise.

UNWHOLESOME SURROUNDINGS VS NICE NEIGHBORHOOD

Many lower-class urban black families live in slum areas where homes are usually run down and shabby and where illness, alcoholism, drugs, and violence frequently prevail. Recognition of these conditions will allow the teacher to realize that sometimes when the child is sleepy and inattentive and perhaps cranky, he may have experienced a harrowing night. At least a teacher will know not to take such a child's acts of insult or obstinacy as being purposely directed toward the teacher. Teachers, of course, need to make the classroom a place where the disadvantaged pupils may live in a wholesome atmosphere of acceptance. The child spends a great amount of time at school. If his home is less than desirable, an inviting classroom and understanding teacher can certainly help to make up for the environmental deficiency.

UNEDUCATED PARENTS VS EDUCATED PARENTS

Middle-class white parents are usually very much better educated than parents of lower-class black children. Their background has usually made them aware of the importance of keeping themselves apprised of what goes on in the schools that pertains to their children's welfare and progress. There needs to be, however, an all-out teacher-administration effort to get the parents of disadvantaged pupils into the schools, in large numbers. More of these parents are taking an interest in the school affairs of their children than in previous years, but the number supporting parent-school relationships is still much too small. Parents of less fortunate youths should be especially welcomed to the schools at times when they can come, since it is so easy for them, like their children, to feel that they don't count. Teachers may make these parents aware of the ways in which they as teachers are attempting to help the children, and they may help to raise the sights of the parents for their young ones. Additionally, teacher contact with the parent often gives the teacher important leads on how to work more effectively with the various children, with respect both to teaching and to disciplining them. Even if some parents aren't able to do very much with their youngsters in matters of control, it gives both the parents and the children a better sense of well-being to know that teachers are concerned enough about parents and their offspring to form parent-teacher relationships.

LOW EXPECTATIONS VS HIGH EXPECTATIONS

For the most part, middle-class white parents have high expectations for their children. The youngsters are generally expected to avail themselves of higher education and to achieve occupational success. The children, then, become motivated from a long-range point of view. Accordingly, a great majority of them may be depended upon to achieve a reasonable level of classwork, and to behave at least reasonably well. On the contrary, since many disadvantaged youngsters receive from home very little, if any, stimulation to achieve, teachers are called upon to motivate these children at school, through outstanding teaching and through content, methods, and materials that meet the pupils' needs and make sense to them.

It has been seen that in the families of many deprived blacks, in contrast to the situation in most favored white families, there has been a lack of tradition of getting ahead, a lack of aspiration. Accordingly, teachers should at every available opportunity show underprivileged pupils what avenues are open to them with regard both to work and to post-high-school education. Teachers should bring before the youngsters job opportunities and descriptions of qualifications and the means by which they may be met. Pupils should be made aware of the offerings of higher education and of other special training beyond the high school years so that pupil goals may be set, toward which the youngsters may direct their efforts. Certainly not all pupils will take advantage of these aids, but some will. Of course, it goes without saying that disadvantaged pupils need well-equipped guidance services that can give expert assistance toward helping them make the most of their potentials; yet an extra boost from teachers is unquestionably meaningful. Instruction regarding job opportunities and advanced training should come early in the child's school life, though the information is better late than not at all. One student teacher of English was particularly proud of the manner in which she helped a class of disadvantaged twelfth-graders think of their future.

She made arrangements with the guidance department to supply her class with necessary information on a variety of vocations or careers. After the reading had been done and there had been discussion of requirements for various jobs and careers, she prepared interviewers and corresponding interviewees among the class members to role-play interview sessions pertinent to acquiring some of the types of jobs about which the class members had studied. The students considered the unit one that was extremely worthwhile for them. The practicing teacher was particularly pleased when two of the boys who had potential but very little aspiration decided they were going to college. Incidentally, all of the student teacher's pupils loved her; for the regular teacher had done very little to conceal his opinion that the class was completely uneducable.

Often in many disadvantaged homes, the parents have not prodded the child about what he will be since a great many of them don't expect him to be anything special. As a consequence of a low self-image, many youngsters of such parents haven't had high expectations for themselves.

POOR SELF-IMAGE VS FAVORABLE SELF-IMAGE

Certainly teachers are in an ideal position to help build the child's ego or self-image by letting him know that they have faith in him, by letting him know that he can succeed and that they expect him to. Teachers can help build the self-image of black youngsters by diligently teaching them in such a way that they can see they are making progress. The work should be geared to the pupils' achievement level or they will become discouraged. The children should be allowed to realize some success daily so that they will continue to be heartened. Teachers should be patient with them, and should praise and reward them for their efforts and achievement. One teacher of beginners is to be noted for the stand she took regarding her beginning pupils.

She was a black teacher of a group of all-black disadvantaged first-graders. On the particular day in question, she was having her class members write in their notebooks such statements as: "I am clean. I am neat. I am beautiful. I do my work well." The teacher explained that she makes sure these things are true, on the part of her pupils. She emphasized that she was beginning early to build within her pupils a worthy self-image.

INADEQUATE PARENT ATTENTION VS SUBSTANTIAL PARENT ATTENTION

Middle-class white mothers who remain home with their offspring while the children are young generally make far better use of their time with the youngsters than do lower-class black mothers who remain home. This situation is true because of the more substantial educational and cultural background that has been the good fortune of the middle-class parents. Unlike the average lower-class mother, the typical middle-class mother reads to her children, talks to them, answers their questions. She corrects faulty pronunciation and expression, and the children learn to speak well. The youngsters are encouraged to be observant and to develop keen senses.

In the lower-class black home, older children are frequently charged with the responsibility of caring for younger siblings. On the other hand, preadolescent boys, in particular, are often at liberty to go and come as they wish. Such premature assignment of responsibility and undirected activity can make these older children less than easy to control at school. Generally, middle-class children of the same age are sheltered and very much under the wing of the parents. It is particularly essential that teachers try to make school followers out of the disadvantaged pupils we have described, through an atmosphere of concern and superior teaching.

INSUFFICIENT HELP WITH HOMEWORK VS SUBSTANTIAL HELP FROM PARENTS

Unlike middle-class parents, lower-class parents often do not have sufficient background, interest, and know-how to give their youngsters the kind of help needed with homework. Because of this deficiency in the home and the generally impoverished state of the disadvantaged child, teachers are enjoined to teach hard and to cover the bulk of the work in the classroom under teacher supervision, where they may motivate, inspire, explain, and make relationships wherever these techniques will be helpful to the pupils. When homework is given to the children, the teacher should be sure that pupils know specifically what to do and can do the assignments themselves.Teachers should make certain that homework is of such high interest for the students that it will bring desirable returns.

A further reason for making the classroom the place where the primary part of the work for the disadvantaged takes place is that lower-class homes, unlike the homes of the middle-class, are often too crowded to provide a place conducive to study. Some schools have attempted to make provisions for after-school study within the school buildings. Often, however, many of the underprivileged pupils who are most in need of this assistance somehow fail to take advantage of it. This negative pupil response is perhaps disheartening for concerned adults who have made possible the provisions for study. It is understandable, nonetheless, that youngsters who have accumulated so many shortcomings over an extended period of time sometimes require considerable time to become sufficiently stimulated and responsive even to offers that are designed for their own improvement.

MEAGER EXPOSURE TO BOOKS VS BEING READ TO

Unlike their typical middle-class counterparts, disadvantaged children, for the most part, have not had the privilege of hearing their parents read bedtime stories to them. This is a primary reason that many deprived junior high school youngsters listen with great satisfaction to fairy tales and legends and stories that were read to middle-class children during their early years. Teachers would do well to supply these deprived pupils with this intriguing material that they missed at an earlier age, if they seem to enjoy it. It must be remembered, too, that these youngsters who, for the most part, missed being read to, often enjoy having their teacher read to them. Teachers would do them a service by seeing to it that they get a healthy share of this delight. A matter of concern, however, is that the teacher try to understand the youngsters' desire to enjoy what they have missed, that the teacher refrain from scorning the interest in material that may not be on a par with the pupils' chronological ages.

In general, little reading is done in the homes of the disadvantaged. The children have therefore missed opportunities to identify with heroes and heroines and to pick models whom they would like to imitate. Except for textbooks, there is usually a dearth of books and reading material. In middle-class homes usually there are picture books and brightly illustrated reading matter for the younger children. There are supplies of reading for the older children as well.

One has only to observe in order to be aware of the large number of middle-class parents who accompany their children to the library, help them find and select books, and allow their youngsters time for reading and browsing. Many disadvantaged pupils do not have public library cards unless they were obtained through some means other than through the initiative of the parents. Teachers may help by scheduling class trips to the public libraries. Arrangements should be made in advance so that librarians will be prepared both to display suitable reading material for the class visitors and to whet the pupils' appetite for the reading by giving partial synopses of the material.

INSUFFICIENT GENERAL CONVERSATION VS INTERESTING CONVERSATION

Conversation at the dinner table, in which the children participate, has helped to make the middle-class child self-confident and articulate. Often, a topic for discussion at mealtime is what went on in the school day of the children; or the topic may concern a general subject of moment, in which family members take part. This type of family exchange is not the typical pattern in deprived homes. Recently, however, a teacher based a beautiful lesson on the slang expressions used by class members as compared to the slang locutions students' parents used when they were youngsters. The class of deprived pupils loved the lesson; class members were live wires and very much enjoyed culling the necessary information from their parents. Projects that help deprived youngsters to express themselves are to be welcomed, for it must be remembered that many lower-class children are not verbally oriented.

Generally, disadvantaged pupils hear poor speech patterns in the home. As a rule, the youngsters lack facility with words, a deficit that stems largely from insufficient reading and limited free conversation. All these conditions make it particularly difficult for underprivileged pupils to express themselves fluently and effectively. Teachers must plan a variety of experiences that will help the deprived child gain ease with words and the ability to express himself adequately.

Taking trips is an excellent way for less privileged youth to gain greater facility of expression. Aside from the general educational and cultural value of these excursions, trips give the youngsters something concrete and worthwhile to talk about. Many parents of disadvantaged children do not take their youngsters on excursions outside the neighborhood. In contrast, a great many middle-class white parents accompany their young ones to libraries, museums, zoos, and to other points of educational and cultural significance. These parents describe, explain, and answer questions as the tour proceeds. The importance of teachers' taking deprived pupils on such excursions cannot be overemphasized. The wealth of knowledge and experience to be gained through trips would greatly advantage the disadvantaged child.

FORCE VS REASON

Middle-class white parents, too, are far more likely to talk to and reason with their misbehaving offspring than are parents of socioeconomically deprived children. As a general rule, middle-class parents exhibit a greater amount of patience to cope with their usually healthy, active, and inquisitive youngsters. Often harassed with the exigencies of day-to-day living, underprivileged black parents have frequently been known to strike their misbehaving youngsters out of shortness of patience in dealing with them. Male teachers have testified to the fact that when some disadvantaged youngsters are misbehaving, they are begging to be whipped in the manner they have become accustomed to in the home. Some of these teachers report, too, that they oblige these children with the punishment they are begging for; whereupon they go along their merry way. But teachers must learn to control the child in ways other than flogging. They must let the youngster know at the outset that they are not there to box him. The pupil must be led to understand reasoning, and he must always thoroughly understand the logic behind whatever regulations are set to help him toward better self-control. Additionally, it might here be pointed out that many black youngsters who live in slum areas and are accustomed to seeing violence get the idea that to be male they must prove their masculinity through being daring. This tendency often leads them to fight easily. Teachers must get them to see that their maleness is safe in the eyes of the teacher and fellow pupils without the need to fight.

IMMEDIATE AIMS VS LONG-RANGE GOALS

Characteristic of many disadvantaged children, as well, is their preoccupation with immediate goals. Coming from a family that barely keeps its head above water, if indeed it fares as well as that, the youngster is not surrounded with a great amount of hope. This sort of hopelessness causes him to resort to satisfying more proximate desires, with limited attention directed to the future. The middle-class white youngster, on the other hand, has been trained in a number of ways that make it possible for him, when this procedure is advantageous, to forego the present for the future. For instance, the middle-class child usually has access to money of his own. He is expected to spend some on immediacies, but is frequently encouraged to put some money aside for a future time. He knows, too, that he is expected to do well in school and to work toward some future goal. Having had ample emphasis on more distant views, in school the typical middle-class pupil is able to do a representative job with subjects and phases of subjects that he doesn't necessarily like, for the sake of working toward an ultimate aim. In a great measure, if the cooperation of the disadvantaged child is to be nurtured, it is initially important to gear lessons or content as closely as possible to immediate experiences and interests since the youngsters have learned to honor the immediate. Again, however, the teacher must not forget the responsibility of raising the sights of these youngsters as rapidly and efficiently as this may be done.

HELPING TEACHERS OF THE DISADVANTAGED

We have noted that economically, educationally, culturally, socially, and psychologically, the gap between middle-class white children and disadvantaged youngsters of all ethnic groups is immense. The assistance of educationists, schools, society, and the government is needed to help remove blocks to the teacher's doing an effective job of training and instructing as first-class citizens all deprived youth. And assuredly, teachers must work hard to fill gaps and eliminate deficiencies of disadvantaged pupils, if adequate learning and resulting good behavior are to be achieved.

Governments—local, state, and federal—and diverse institutions, foundations, and other organizations have funded and sponsored a number of experimental programs for the disadvantaged, throughout the country. The programs were designed to raise the sights and aspirations of culturally deprived pupils and to accelerate their adjustment, growth in achievement and ability, and readiness to make better use of their education. The reported outcomes of many of these pilot programs have indicated that there has been substantial improvement in learning and behavior on the part of the pupils who have been reached by the projects, and the sponsoring bodies must be recognized for this contribution. The very crucial need, however, is for effective far-reaching programs for the disadvantaged of all ethnic groups, ones that are extensive enough to reach the masses of deprived pupils on a continuing basis. This section will examine some of those urgent needs which, if supplied, would have a major impact on the learning and, concurrently, on the behavior patterns of our disadvantaged youth.

SMALL CLASSES

Classes comprising primarily disadvantaged pupils should be small and controllable. Adequate guidance services within the school should be available for the care of pupils who are so disturbed as to be unmanageable in the classroom. Special out-of-school services, as well, should be available for pupils who need them. Our nation is given to taking care of diverse needs. Manageable class sizes and manageable pupils are needs of the first order among our deprived young people. Two special-project elementary schools where some adequate provisions are being made for disadvantaged pupils have illustrative value here. The first school consists of a primarily middle-class white population, but with some deprived black and white pupils in attendance. The second school is made up of a primarily disadvantaged population.

Recently, in the middle-class school, one remedial reading class for disadvantaged pupils was observed to consist of around a dozen pupils. Materials were appropriate; teaching was competent; and reading levels had been considerably raised. And scattered here and there throughout the school were regular classes of disadvantaged pupils, but in no case did the deprived classes exceed fifteen pupils. The rooms for these children were gaily decorated, and at various places in the rooms children's work was on display. There was real teaching being done, and the teachers viewed their work with the pupils pridefully.

In the school of primarily disadvantaged youngsters, there were some classes that were out of hand. But the concern here was two classes of eight students each. One class was taught by a guidance teacher; the other by a regular teacher. The guidance instructor explained the details of her eight-member class. The pupils had been only behavior problems in their regular classes. In fact, they were so unruly that they had been put into this small class where they could be handled without keeping other pupils from progressing, and where they could receive the individual attention they were desperately in need of. In this class they were given a feeling of well-being, for often they had been told they didn't know how to behave, and they had acted as if they should prove it. In her class of eight pupils, the guidance teacher showed that she believed they could both learn and behave. The procedure worked. She praised the pupils lavishly for their improvement in schoolwork and in conduct. The guidance counselor of the school assisted, too, by keeping in close contact with the parents of these pupils. All in all, the eight pupils were making progress. In a large class, they would merely have helped the class resemble an institution for the emotionally disturbed.

GUIDANCE SERVICES

We have already implied how crucial is the need for adequate guidance provisions. Schools where there are large numbers of disadvantaged pupils should have very effective guidance services. They need to be properly equipped with competent guidance counselors, and with the services of social workers, psychologists, and psychiatrists.

TEACHER AIDES

In classrooms of disadvantaged pupils, there is great need for teacher aides. An assistant teacher's working along with the regular teacher makes it possible for deprived young people to get at least a representative amount of the individual attention they need. Assistance from an aide promises much greater teacher success in meeting the needs of the pupils in such areas as individualized attention, self-expression, basic academic skills, and behavior. Teacher aides need to be extended as far up into the grades as they are needed. In most cases, they are greatly needed to help at least through the elementary years. In some schools áides are being used rather freely, especially in the first few elementary grades. Yet there are some systems that have not yet begun to use these assistants in any grade.

BILINGUAL TEACHING

It might be stressed here that bilingual teachers for Puerto Rican and Mexican-American students who have not mastered the English language well enough to travel in comfort with regular English-speaking classes may serve as a bulwark in helping these practically non-English-speaking youths cope with their language necessities with dignity. Such a bilingual program has the additional feature of offering the parents of these youngsters an opportunity to converse with their children's teacher in their native language. The bilingual program, then, is to be highly encouraged for promoting a spirit of self-worth among children and parents who have a very limited background in the English language. Certainly a sense of well-being promotes greater propensity for learning and better behavior.

SPECIAL TEACHER PREPARATION

Another crucial need is the enrollment of teachers and administrators in college courses that train educators especially to teach and arrange for the education of underprivileged children; in fact, there is much need for college curriculums that lead to degrees in the teaching of disadvantaged pupils. Programs designed to help administrators, teachers, and teachers-to-be to work with culturally deprived youth should stress, among other things, the psychology of working with disadvantaged pupils, effective means of teaching reading to deprived pupils, and means of exercising skill in the use of audiovisual aids to make learning more effective.

It is important that teachers fully recognize the ability of lower-class children to learn when they are properly taught; and it is equally important that teachers convey to the underprivileged child their faith in his ability. Deprived youngsters need much in the way of ego boosts; they need self-confidence; they need to know that someone cares; they need to be given a sense of belongingness. It becomes clear that a program geared to assisting those charged with the responsibility of teaching underprivileged boys and girls should incorporate essential background knowledge pertaining to the disadvantaged as well as humane ways of working with these young people, so that these youths may be given the chance to turn their potential to good account.

Reading is the gateway to mastering almost all other subjects in the schools, as well as a key to acquiring the type of culture that makes for social mobility. Colleges that accept the challenge to assist teachers and administrators in working with disadvantaged pupils will be remiss if they fail to place abundance of stress on successful ways of teaching culturally deprived children to read. That underprivileged youngsters can learn to read if they are properly taught has been adequately substantiated by a number of studies. James Farmer (1968) cites, for instance, a project of the Bank Street College of Education in New York City that uncovered revealing information regarding the ability of disadvantaged youth to learn to read. Twenty black and Puerto Rican school dropouts ranging in age from sixteen to twenty-one and ranking from zero to third-grade level in reading skills had the benefit of a remedial reading program at the college for one summer. They worked with programmed instructional materials. At the end of the summer of work, not only were those young people reading on a sixth-grade level and above, but one youngster had written a play; another was writing poetry. It was interesting to note that previous to the summer project, the group of youths had been pronounced uneducable (Farmer). Adequate sums of money are needed both for purchasing appropriate reading materials and for training teachers to help youngsters to read.

Because disadvantaged pupils usually have had a poor background in reading, they do not generally have the competency to cope with abstract ideas that middle-class children have acquired. The copious use of audiovisual aids is an excellent way to help underprivileged youngsters move from the simple to the more complex or from the concrete to the abstract. For instance, what a child views in films or on slides, what he hears on a tape recorder, and what he sees in photographs or pictures are concrete experiences which he may use as a basis for forming opinions or judgments

He may also use these concrete aids as a foundation for discussion or as motivation for writing or reading. These enriching experiences promote achievement. Besides, audiovisual aids have an inherent motivational quality that is appealing to youngsters. These aids, then, have great possibilities for stimulating learning among culturally deprived pupils.

OUTSTANDING LEARNING EQUIPMENT AND BOOKS

It cannot be overemphasized how crucial the need is for the best learning equipment and supplies for our disadvantaged pupils. Not having acquired from home a great drive to learn and often having felt hopeless in his unwholesome plight, the average deprived child is not likely to make a great deal of effort to bite unless the learning is made appetizing for him. It is ironical that so often in classes largely composed of disadvantaged children where top equipment and supplies are needed most, they are least in evidence.

Books, as we know of course, are our most common equipment for teaching. Those provided for deprived children should be appropriate for them, and highly palatable. Unfortunately this is often not the case. All too frequently, in classes for disadvantaged pupils, it has been customary just to bring sets of books out of the closet to be used irrespective of whether they are the best books for the already deprived children. This is a particularly odious practice where reading skills need to be strengthened, where respect for proficiency in reading needs to be promoted, and where blocks against reading need to be removed.

One young teacher complained vehemently about the inadequacy of the reading material for his highly disadvantaged sixth-graders, whereupon the administrator brought from the bookroom at least one set of very appropriate reading material that got the pupils fruitfully involved. The set of books had been in the closet for weeks without even an effort on the part of the administrator to supply the young teacher with adequate materials, though the pupils were running wild in misbehavior, largely because their needs were unmet.

Disadvantaged children need to be offered highly appetizing books and other printed materials so that they will desire to taste and digest them. The materials should be colorful, attractively illustrated, and readable. There should be a variety of books on reading levels appropriate for the various groups of pupils who will use them. Deprived children need all the encouragement they can get to learn to read.

It is to be recalled, too, that underprivileged children, and particularly black ones, frequently suffer from a low self-image. Readers are currently being published which place pictures of black people alongside those of whites. Social studies books are now recognizing contributions that have been made to the nation by black men and women and by members of other minority groups. Various textbooks are now portraying blacks. Though there is yet ground to be covered in the featuring of blacks and other minority groups in printed school matter, what is already being done is a welcome gesture to help curtail the minority child's feeling that he is nobody with no possibilities; and these types of materials need to be made available to children in all schools. In addition to the boost the integrated publications furnish children from minority races through identification and inspiration, the wide use of these urban materials will allow youngsters from the majority groups opportunities to get to know and respect minority people as citizens and contributors. Certainly as disadvantaged minorities come to have greater respect for themselves and to be respected by others they will have the kind of increased pride that is favorable to more fruitful learning and to better self-control.

TEACHER INCENTIVES

One way of making work with the disadvantaged a prestigious aspect of teaching is to pay higher salaries to the teachers and administrators who work acceptably with large numbers of disadvantaged youth. Justification for the higher salaries would be the immediate need to salvage groups of our pupils from an education that so grossly fails to meet their needs, in addition to the fact that there are a goodly number of openings for those who wish to give of themselves, sincerely and constructively, for the cause of disadvantaged pupils. And finally, working with the underprivileged may gain prestige through a liberal offering of scholarships to those who wish to further their education in areas that are preparatory to teaching disadvantaged pupils.

SUPPLEMENTARY EXPERIENCES IN EARLY GRADES

As it now stands, studies and reports have for some years indicated that, for the most part, disadvantaged children in de facto segregated schools retrograde in achievement and intellect from the time they enter school to the time they have been in attendance for several years. On the basis of reports by Martin Deutsch, two educators, Hilda Taba and Deborah Elkins (1966), noted that both the intellectual and achievement differences between lower-class and middle-class children are smallest at the first-grade level and tend to increase through the elementary grades. They observed that the interaction between school and an early environment of deprivation has had a negative effect rather than a facilitating influence. The authors uncovered further factors that should be mentioned here. Disadvantaged children, because of their culturally deprived background, are frequently labeled uneducable. Little is expected of them and they give little in return. Comparatively speaking, they get "dumber," until by the fifth grade they are three grades behind. The meager achievement causes them to have even less self-esteem and promotes hostility toward the school, teachers, and the whole institution of learning. By the time these deprived youngsters reach the fifth grade, they have become the ones described as alienated, withdrawn, angry, passive, apathetic, and just plain troublemakers (Taba and Elkins).

Because of the impoverished economic, cultural, and social background disadvantaged children bring with them to their first school experience, they lack facility in a great many skills essential for effective learning. As Taba and Elkins have observed, these deprived youngsters enter the first grade already behind their middle-class counterparts in a number of skills necessary for scholastic achievement, and the gap between the two groups has been allowed to widen as the pupils progress through elementary school.

Project Head Start is to be extolled for its efforts to cope with the unreadiness of disadvantaged youngsters to enter the schools formally. And yet, to see the deprived pupils safely through the grades, the momentum of preschool training must not be extinguished; or else one might rightly ask with Fred Hechinger, editor and writer for *The New York Times,* "Head Start to Where?" (Taba and Elkins).

Taba and Elkins have very perceptively observed that disadvantaged first-grade children who report to school enter with simultaneous burdens: (1) the handicap of an acculturation problem, the problem of acquiring both the concepts and the language skills necessary for future reading, and (2) the hardship of trying to master the new skill of reading, for which they are not ready. To avoid dealing with acculturation problems and school learning at the same time, early supplementary experience seems necessary. This experience could be supplied by ungraded sequence in the first few years, by the addition of a preschool year for filling in gaps in the children's experience, or by postponement of reading instruction. It is possible that such measures would prevent the development of negative attitudes toward learning and the lowering of self-esteem. It is also possible that separating acculturation and learning to read may be the single most important measure for improvement in achievement (Taba and Elkins). Whatever measures may be used, it is clear that taking care of the deficits of our disadvantaged children and helping the youngsters reach their potential must be an issue of utmost concern.

2

DISCIPLINING DISADVANTAGED YOUTH
THROUGH EFFECTIVE TEACHING

The seventh-grade social studies class consisted of around twenty-five pupils of low socioeconomic background. The majority of the pupils were blacks and Puerto Ricans, but there were a few others of white descent. It was a rowdy group, to say the least. The regular teacher was to be absent that day, and a substitute teacher, Miss X, had been asked to take her place. Having known a day ahead of time that she would take over the class, Miss X brought in several lessons she thought would be suitable. After the class had entered the room, she pulled from her attaché case the lesson "Countries That Make Up the United Nations," so that she could begin teaching. She moved into her carefully planned motivation for the lesson; but a few students were chasing each other around the room; several were hitting each other; some argued; a few banged on desks. She tried moving into her lesson proper, but still she could not get enough attention to proceed with her plan.

It became clear to Miss X that if she intended to get control of the class, she would need to produce a lesson more fitting for the group of pupils she faced. This time, she pulled out a book that contained a mysterious adventure story that took place on a secluded island. Talking over the noise, Miss X informed the class members that she was going to read them a good story. Still talking loudly, she told them just a few of the fascinating highlights of the story, enough to whet their appetite for the reading. Then she moved rapidly into the reading of the mystery that was of surefire interest. Gradually, but surely, most of the noise makers settled down, focused their eyes on the teacher, and began to drink in the story. There were a few, however, who continued to fool around; actually, several of the pupils in the class were greatly disturbed children. But at least the class as a whole had become attentive, and some of the boys who had been among the worst troublemakers had moved as close as they could to the teacher in order to be sure not to miss any of the details of the story.

After the reading had been completed, the children were allowed to ask whatever questions they wished and to discuss the parts of the story that held a great amount of interest for them. Since it was a story of Russian background, the teacher talked a little about Russian customs that were peculiar to the story, and she drew a map on the chalkboard to explain where the mysterious action took place. When the bell rang for dismissal, there were some students who wished to remain a few minutes with the teacher, to talk further about the story.

The lesson wasn't perfect; neither was the discipline. But the incident clearly points up the relevancy of appropriate teaching materials and methods to desirable discipline.

AREAS OF DEFICIENCY

READING

One teacher of a group of fifth-grade disadvantaged pupils confessed to having requested a class member to read from a blackboard a few sentences of extremely easy directions so that fellow classmates could collaborate on means of carrying out the instructions. In apparent fury, the student who had been drafted yelled to the teacher, "I don't want to read." To keep from fanning the flame, the teacher ignored the comment and pointed to another pupil to read. To the teacher's astonishment, the second draftee shouted to the teacher, with even greater aggravation than the first youngster, "Read it yourself." The instructor was finally able to find a few volunteers who were willing to attempt the reading.

Of course the obvious reason for the two pupils' explosions was that they couldn't read, yet were ashamed and humiliated that they had reached the grade they had with such little competency. No mistake should be made, however; most youngsters would like to know how to read, even those who go to great lengths to cover up their shortcomings with blatant defense mechanisms. What is more, a great majority of the youngsters can learn to read if teaching conditions are made adequate for teachers and the teachers throughout the school years will actually teach. It is unfortunate that so many disadvantaged youngsters pass through school from year to year and grade to grade not learning how to read. This is wrong. The inability to read is one of the most crippling states that a child may experience. Reading is the basic class tool, which, unmastered, will preclude the child's taking his place in the educational sun, but rather promote feelings of incompetence, inferiority, indifference, and hopelessness that keep close company with hostility, belligerence, and other behaviors that give rise to problems in discipline.

It cannot be overemphasized that each time a teacher makes a reader of a pupil, that teacher has filled a child's life with a permanently rich blessing. In a world that professes to be cultured, what can surpass the acquisition of the basic tool to success? The child who is taught to read adequately is equipped to cope effectively with the demands of the classroom. Besides, the child who learns to like reading has hours of enjoyment and constructive endeavor in store for him. He is able to live vicariously in diverse times and climes; he may have his imagination stimulated; he can identify with youthful characters, some of whom are suffering from some of the same hurts of growing up as he himself and can afford him solutions to some of his problems; he is able to choose, from his reading, characters and personages who inspire him; and he is able to explore and formulate moral and ethical values. Very important, still, he will have acquired a pleasurable and constructive pastime for life. It is pathetic to observe so many people who are at a total loss when they have a little free time at their disposal. And not to be discounted is the fact that lovers of reading stand a chance of keeping themselves out of a great amount of trouble by virtue of their involvement in a gratifying activity.

Once teachers of beginners have gotten the young pupils off to a good start in reading, all teachers at all levels and in all subject areas must accept responsibility to help the children continue their progress. This assistance includes helping them extend their vocabulary; helping them spell better; and helping them with pronunciation, word analysis, and comprehension. The importance of all teachers' lending a hand with reading very seriously poses the legitimate question of whether at least a one-year, competent undergraduate reading course shouldn't be required of all future teachers regardless of level of concentration or of subject area, before those graduates are allowed to enter the schools to teach.

On the matter of reading comprehension, all teachers must be alert to lacks in understanding. For instance, frequently when class reading is being done in the various subject areas of concern, teachers will need to backtrack, to see if pupils are following. They will need to question the pupils and allow them to ask questions to be sure that meanings are clear.

With respect to vocabulary building, teachers are reminded that firsthand knowledge of words may often be gained through places and things. The child, for instance, who takes a worthwhile trip adds word meanings from what he sees and talks about. The youngster who manipulates objects and asks and answers questions about them enlarges his vocabulary through firsthand contact. And it should be remembered that to get the youngster both to like to read and to read is a powerful way to enrich the vocabulary, through context. On a cautionary note, teachers are reminded that, for the most part, using key words that are over the head of class members can be disheartening, to disadvantaged pupils in particular. Difficult words must be clarified through the use of synonyms, through definitions written on the chalkboard, through further illustrations of how the words might be used in context, or through some other means that brings about necessary clarifications.

Finally, in many of the subject areas such as reading, English, social studies, and science, free reading through self-selection may go a long way toward strengthening the children's ability to read well. It has often been said that to learn to read, a child must read. Since many disadvantaged youngsters have very little, if any, motivation from home to want to achieve, it will often be helpful, in the beginning stages, to allow pupils much freedom for selecting reading material that appeals to them. Permitting this choice is better than their not reading at all. Sights may be raised, with respect to selections made, after the deprived youngsters have become less reluctant readers. An additional caution of importance is that the reading material for the particular pupils of concern should not be too difficult; or else disgust and discouragement are sure to set in.

SPEECH

In terms of achievement, disadvantaged children perhaps suffer the greatest disabilities in reading. But deprived pupils, unlike their middle-class counterparts, also suffer greatly from poor patterns of speech and from the lack of ability to express themselves fluently and effectively.

Let us now consider disabilities in speech. First it should be emphasized that non-English-speaking students should be kept in classes for pupils speaking English as a second language until their mastery of English is sufficient to insure success in regular classes. This caution is particularly pertinent in the case of Puerto Rican pupils, since time after time members of this group have been known to travel with regular classes with only the faintest ability to speak English. It is obvious that such children have no background to cope with the content of their various subjects when they are unable to master English as a working tool. This type of unwarranted placement begs for an attitude of defeat and resulting poor behavior.

There is a need to make disadvantaged pupils aware of the kind of speech that will be needed for social mobility without causing the youngsters to feel ashamed of their parents' speech or of the speech patterns they as off-spring have acquired as a result of their roots in a low socioeconomic environment. The children need to be taught the type of language that will help them get desirable jobs, further their education, and move with ease among the classes of people who set the standards for our use of the English language.

Observation and prognostic tests, formal and informal, must be used to discover the phases of language in which disadvantaged pupils need assistance. Because of the circumstances of a limited and impoverished background, many black children, for example, frequently fail to add necessary *ed's* and *t's* to the ends of verbs. They often make gross errors in the agreement of subject and verb. They make quite a few grammatical mistakes with reference to the use of the verb in the third person singular: "My *teacher come* early on Mondays" or "When *he get* a job, we'll move." Such errors in principal parts of verbs as "You know you *rung* the bell" or "He's already *drank* the water now" are common. In the area of pronunciation, very often whole syllables which should be pronounced are omitted; a great emphasis on phonetics is needed, throughout the grades, for the self-improvement of these deprived pupils. Moreover, many disadvantaged whites and other lower-class students use glaring double negatives, such as "I *don't* have *no* pen."

In language skills, as with reading, teachers must continually diagnose and uncover the practical needs of the various disadvantaged groups. The teacher should use ample drill and lively situations for teaching the correct forms. At the hands of a diligent, concerned teacher who won't blame the youngsters for the deficits which years of deprivation rather than inferior mental ability have imposed on them, the pupils can come to love their concrete remedial studies. Teachers must not be impatient with slow progress made by disadvantaged pupils. It has taken some years to formulate unacceptable speech patterns as well as the faulty habits and deficiencies in other areas. Middle-class children, black and white, have learned acceptable speech forms from the home, but in the case of the lower-class child, the important thing has often been just making himself understood, not a matter of how he expressed what he said.

SELF-EXPRESSION

Self-expression is another area in which disadvantaged pupils need training and practice. This has often been true of blacks who were reared in the South in an open atmosphere of oppression, where they had very little contact and communication with middle- and upper-class whites. Here again, it is easy to see that it is not a lack of intelligence or of ability of blacks to compete favorably with their white counterparts, but rather a situation which came about as a result of black people's feelings of suppression and of their limited exposure to open and free expression. There are now signs of changes for the better. The outlawing of discrimination in the Southern schools and in the use of public facilities has given many black people the confidence to speak up and express themselves freely, even though the antidiscriminatory directives may not always have been obeyed. If many of the more fortunate blacks have frequently found it difficult to express themselves, it can be understood why less fortunate blacks in elementary and secondary grades have often been frustrated when their level of performance in discussion or conversation has been measured by the level achieved by middle-class whites, who from the outset are trained and encouraged to speak out. Oftentimes the meagerness of general background, lack of training and practice in self-expression, and lack of skill in formulating what is to be said in more than single words or several-word phrases make deprived youngsters unwilling to participate in discussion. Fortunately, some members of the various deprived ethnic groups are now being seen on television and are being allowed a chance to take active part in discussions. This is a step in the right direction, even though considerably more of this type of opportunity is needed. Those who are participants are helped in self-expression and viewers of similar background are encouraged.

Let us further consider obstacles to self-expression. Lack of self-confidence, fear of not measuring up to the level of expression of more advantaged youths, fear of not having answers that compare favorably with replies which might be offered by more fortunate classmates, fear that if he has a worthwhile contribution to make his words will be inadequate to express it, and fear of being criticized are types of blocks that keep the disadvantaged child from expressing himself effectively.

Teachers must help underprivileged children to achieve adequate expression, for with this accomplishment comes a healthy boost to the ego, a sort of pride that helps youngsters think better of themselves. The better these young people view themselves, the better behaved they're inclined to be. The teacher must set the tone for acceptance, must encourage and praise youngsters for their efforts, even for slight improvements in self-expression. The teacher should see to it that he, as well as the various class members, exhibits the attitude of willingness to help those who might be struggling to achieve satisfactory expression. In the beginning, it is helpful to give reluctant speakers something to talk about that is directly out of their experiences and observations and interests and to leave more remote topics until later. Student interest in self-expression will increase when pupils see that they are making progress; then they may be led into worthwhile discussions less immediately associated with themselves. Guidelines will help toward effective expression, particularly before the pupils have loosened up and are willing to respond freely. One type of helpful guide is an outline on the chalkboard from which the pupils may talk. Another kind of useful aid is a list of points on the topic which the teacher allows each individual pupil to jot down on paper. This kind of prop gives the youngsters the security of having something right before them on which they can rely as they engage in conversation.

Again, the assistance of educationists, schools, society, and governments is needed in making classes small enough for teachers to be able to work more advantageously toward helping disadvantaged pupils express themselves effectively. Teaching deprived children not to talk all at one time when they have finally opened up, getting them to know that the teacher can't listen to all of them at once, getting them to be constructively helpful to each other, and even to listen to one another, are all difficult tasks to achieve when classes are large.

AREAS OF INTEREST

Helen F. Storen (1968) has revealed important findings on types of content that will appeal to disadvantaged early adolescents. The findings are based on a three-year project in a junior high school in a Northern city. As invaluable as the information is, however, Professor Storen does not conceive of it as being definitive. Teachers are enjoined to experiment continually on further learning experiences that may be organized and used to the advantage of the underprivileged child.

This discussion is geared to the findings in Storen's three-year project. Teachers will find the results very helpful in involving deprived children in the learning process in such a way as to obviate the need for a great amount of misbehavior that becomes rampant when the content offerings are inappropriate. The teacher will likewise discover that even though the study was made in connection with underprivileged junior high school pupils, many of the findings are suitable for lower-class pupils of other grade levels as well.

PEOPLE

Disadvantaged early adolescents have a lively interest in the lives of people, what people look like, how they feel about each other, why they are angry or afraid, and how they were able to achieve success. In schools that will allow teachers to adapt the course of study to meet the needs of deprived pupils, teachers will find it useful to take optimal advantage of pupil interest in people. In social studies, for instance, it is sound practice to capitalize on student interest by first studying the colorful lives of the historical figures and afterward tying in the movements or organizations for which these people were responsible. In short, in dealing with disadvantaged youngsters, it is important to use their areas of interest as points of departure and to proceed later to material that is remote or complex. Middle class children, too, are interested in people, but having been conditioned to an academic orientation, by the time they are junior high school pupils, they have already begun to turn their attention to principles and to abstract ideas. They have learned to accept the remote and complex whether or not they are interested in them (Storen).

The disadvantaged child's fascination with people may serve as a point of departure for literature as well as for social studies. Biography is highly effective in both subject areas. It is to be remembered, nevertheless, that the lives of people alone will not engender a great amount of student enthusiasm; interest will center on action and feelings. The greater the feeling and drama in the story, the greater is the impact (Storen). Teachers who work with disadvantaged pupils in any subject area will do well to investigate the possibility of using the "people approach" as one means of incorporating student interest and of getting across meaningful content at the same time.

FANTASY AND MYTH

The project also revealed that early adolescents of deprived backgrounds love fairy tales, fantasy, myths, and legends. The youngsters probably enjoy the works of fancy partly because they involve people, even though the characters are not real (Storen). Reading being perhaps the most important area in which disadvantaged pupils need help and improvement, teachers will do well to capitalize on the youngsters' interest in tales and fantasy by giving them a generous amount of fanciful reading. The important thing is that the teacher thoroughly understand the deficits in the children's background that would cause them to be fascinated by certain readings that more favored children of the same age enjoyed earlier. With this knowledge, teachers should be able to supply the youngsters with the reading they crave without looking down on them for desiring it.

The study revealed that it does not matter to the deprived child whether the time is past or present or whether the setting is far or near so long as the content deals with people. The important factor is pupil understanding of the human relations involved (Storen).

Teachers make a mistake by not using a great amount of fiction. The drama of events, as emphasized in fictional work, is particularly fitting for reluctant junior high school pupils. It does not matter if some facts are omitted or some exaggerations included. Needed corrections or refinements may come at a later time (Storen). Teachers must exploit fiction, in a great many of the subject areas, as an interesting and rich means of putting across basic subject matter.

THEIR OWN PROBLEMS

Disadvantaged early adolescents were found to be intensely interested in themselves, in solving their own problems. Teachers should capitalize on this self-interest by selecting for the children pertinent human relations materials that meet these personal needs; but providing for the pupils' vicarious involvement with content is perhaps a better approach than dealing specifically with the children's problems. In time, the pupils' attention may be directed to more complex social relations that are not so heavily steeped in personal interests (Storen).

PHYSIOLOGY

In science classes, the children involved in the project liked the biological aspects of science, with emphasis on physiology. More specifically, the youngsters liked studies dealing with the human body, health, and sex. These were perhaps great points of interest because these children, coming from impoverished homes, had missed a great amount of important medical knowledge. Accordingly, "The pupils showed an intense desire to get information about the bodily functions, accidents, disease, pregnancy, alcoholism, dope addiction, and mental illness." These were topics on which the pupils had not had systematic study in the elementary grades (Storen).

Though the interests of deprived children may not be used for selecting all content material, it is wise to make the most of their interests as one criterion for selecting material. Some phases of various subjects hold decidedly more interest for the children than others; where such interest may be utilized as a beginning point, the youngsters learn better (Storen).

Many times the courses of study advocated for disadvantaged youngsters are grossly inadequate. When they are so, they should be adapted to the children's needs or, if necessary, simply abandoned. To do less than give the youngsters the types of learning they demand is to compound the injuries already inflicted upon our underprivileged youth.

SUITABLE TECHNIQUES AND METHODS

At the beginning of this chapter, we noted how a substitute teacher was finally able to do a relatively adequate job quieting an unruly class through the use of content, techniques, and methods that were suitable for the class at hand. Again, teachers must continue to uncover the kinds of content and procedures which offer disadvantaged children learning experiences that are meaningful and engaging. Reaching the class through pupil involvement that is the result of superior teaching is one of the surest means the teacher has to achieving desirable discipline in the classroom.

There follows here a discussion of selected techniques and methods that have proved to be highly successful in working with the disadvantaged child. Teachers are challenged to uncover others.

CONSTRUCTING A UNIT

In their book *Teaching Strategies for the Culturally Disadvantaged* (1966), Hilda Taba and Deborah Elkins reveal invaluable knowledge regarding models for constructing units. The information is based on successful experiments with classes of culturally disadvantaged junior high school pupils, but the models may be used as patterns for constructing helpful units of work for pupils of any grade level. The following explication of the models is based entirely on the work of Taba and Elkins as presented in their book.

Let us begin by considering the design of the models for constructing units. The idea is to have a broad topic or theme from which a series of short sequences may stem. For instance, Taba and Elkins use as a broad theme "The Family of Man." Then grouped around this topic are the sequences entitled "Human Hands," "Walls in Our Life," and "Aspirations," all related to the broad topic. The sequences are in reality models of processes of teaching and learning. A very strong point regarding these model sequences is that they stress factors important to meeting the learning needs of deprived children. The sequences, for instance, start with the concrete knowledge or experiences of the child and gradually move him to the abstract and impersonal through the use of enriching content and procedures; they tactically employ challenging comparisons and contrasts that cause the pupils to think or formulate ideas, as the youngsters move along at their own pace.

Let us consider in some detail the sequence "Human Hands," which was taught to classes of sixth- and seventh-graders by a group of beginning teachers under the supervision of Deborah Elkins. The parts of the body being a point of interest to all youngsters, the pupils of one class were asked to trace the outlines of their own hands on a piece of paper. A discussion followed regarding the beauty of hands and the similarity of hands among all people. The pupils were then asked to write about important things their own hands could do. The answers were categorized on the chalkboard under "Play" or "Work." After the tallying had been done by a small group of students, each pupil was given a copy to be included in his notebook. The following day the teacher read a chapter from Mary Medearis's *Big Doc's Girl.* There was discussion of what happened and of why a smaller child refused to accept punishment from an older sibling who was left in charge. Pupils used their tally to compare what they did with their hands to how hands were used in the story; and, in addition, the category of "What Other People Do with Their Hands That We Don't Do" was added. Some of the teachers, however, made use of the original tally by having the pupils discuss the relative importance of each category. The various teachers, of course, had the option of using different teaching techniques to achieve their objectives.

The literature that had been read and the tallying caused the formulation of ideas as well as heated discussion among class members. As a homework assignment, the children were asked to observe, for one half hour, what adults do with their hands, and to take notes on their findings; some of the teachers divided their classes in two, asking some class members to observe how adults use their hands and others to note what uses babies make of theirs. A large number of students did their homework. The reports, from the children's notes, were shared and then tallied. Afterward, each child summarized his observations in a paragraph. The paragraphs were rexographed and made into a booklet, with the title "Hands Do" or "Observation of Hands." The students worked hard to correct their errors, for they were highly excited over being authors and having their work represented in a publication. The youngsters requested that each fellow classmate read his own creation. Interest in the reading and listening was sustained for a full period. During the time the excitement lasted there were no discipline problems.

The teacher provided each student with the committee's tallies, to be used as a summary in the booklet. Pupils used a textbook as a guide to making a table of contents. It is needless to describe the pupils' excitement over seeing their names listed in the "Contents" section. Some pupils showed off their completed work at home, but because some students had no interested adult to whom they could show their work, it was agreed that a copy of the booklet should be placed in the guidance office where waiting parents could read it. The pupils agreed, in addition, that a copy of the booklet should be given to their various churches.

The teacher read a chapter from Carol Brink's *Caddie Woodlawn* in order to help the children both to interpret their findings and to gain perspective on the results. The chapter reveals the fact that Caddie was punished, the younger boys allowed to go free. The children were called upon to understand the abstract manner in which hands are used in this story as opposed to the physical or concrete use of hands in *Big Doc's Girl.* The pupils observed, for instance, that when Sis carried the tray to the culprit's room, hands pleaded for forgiveness; that when the child drew on the wall of her room a picture of her missing mother, hands cried out in loneliness.

Professor Elkins has described a number of other stimulating processes of teaching and learning that the teachers and their pupils engaged in, in connection with the sequence "Human Hands." In addition, the sequences "Walls in Our Life" and "Aspirations" are replete with provocative gems for reaching underprivileged pupils.

PROVIDING "HIGH INTEREST / EASY READING" MATERIAL

In her book *Reading Improvement in the Junior High School* (1963), Deborah Elkins describes her ingenious project that required below-level readers of junior high school to compile and publish an appropriate list of little children's books that could be used as a guide for parents of preschool children. Since the regular vocabulary of much of the junior high reading material was too difficult for the junior high youngsters, children's books gave the junior high pupils extensive reading practice at levels where practice was greatly needed. To test the suitability of various selections for the children's list, the junior high school students very frequently read the material to younger siblings or to neighbors' children. In short, the youngsters did their reading and evaluative work with pride. The project was an ego boost, for the pupils were serving in the grown-up capacity of being critics, with the exalted responsibility of evaluating reading material that would be profitable and enjoyable to younger children.

The idea implicit in the Elkins project may be adapted both for use with disadvantaged pupils of various grade levels and for use in diverse subject areas. And, very important, the project may be used to generate ideas on similar activities that will give reluctant readers a great amount of reading practice on the levels that are appropriate for them, yet practice that is clothed with a sense of dignity.

A great amount of "high interest / easy reading" material should be used for disadvantaged pupils in the various grades and subject areas. This type of content, which has high interest appeal but is of low reading level, can help to make readers out of deprived pupils who might throw up their hands in disgust if offered repeated doses of reading that is too difficult for them. Fortunately, even mystery stories on the third-grade level are now available.

Increasingly, "high interest / easy reading" material is being published for disadvantaged pupils of different grade levels. Scholastic Book Services, for example, publishes material of this nature for the various grades and subject areas. The company also sponsors Scholastic's Action Reading System—a high-motivation reading skills program for secondary students with reading levels from 2.0 to 5.0. With respect to serial books, the "Merrill Mainstream Books" by Charles G. Spiegler comprise a series that offers "high interest / easy reading" content for reluctant readers.

USING THE TAPE RECORDER

The tape recorder is a rich resource for providing learning experiences. It would be good to have a recorder in each classroom, and particularly in the classrooms of disadvantaged pupils. Teachers have only to be imaginative in order to create, with the recorder, a wealth of meaningful and exciting activity, in any of the subject areas. For instance, one teacher of a group of deprived pupils of an upper elementary grade reported having set the stage for valuable reading results through the use of the tape recorder.

The teacher had carefully selected highly interesting reading material and had taped it at a pace that was appropriate for the class. As the tape was played, the pupils were asked to follow the reading until a stop signal was given. At the signal, pupils who were able to find, on their copies, the point at which the reading was stopped were asked to raise their hands. The teacher circulated about the room taking inventory of the pupils who could point to the correct place. Discussion followed the reading that had been covered, before the teacher resumed the playing of the tape. The youngsters enjoyed the tape-recorded reading and gained much from it.

Another teacher taped exciting fiction for his eighth-grade English class. And although the underprivileged youngsters were ordinarily considered to be tough customers, they were well behaved during this exercise.

In taping the fiction, the teacher gave due emphasis to highlighting the drama of the events. The taping was done in an expressive tone that would admit of no lag in interest. Prior to playing the tape, the teacher made a few preliminary remarks in order to establish the setting and to whet the pupils' appetite with an appropriate inkling of what the plot was about. As the tape was played, the pupils followed the reading on rexographed copies. At prearranged points, the teacher stopped the tape to ascertain the students' comprehension of the selection and to conduct lively discussion based on the plot. At the conclusion of the lesson, the pupils' reaction indicated that the activity had been both engaging and fruitful.

And Helen Storen has noted that the tape recorder may be an aid to certain disadvantaged pupils who are reluctant to write. A group of such students were asked to talk into a tape recorder on the topic "What I Would Do If I Won $1,000." The pupils did their recording, then, following instructions, listened to what they had taped, and wrote it down. Thus it was that their reluctance to write was overcome through the use of the recorder. The paragraphs the pupils wrote down gave the teacher insight into the children's desires and feelings and made the teacher aware of the pupils' errors in spelling and grammar as well.

STRUCTURING WRITING EXPERIENCES

With writing, it is good practice to have a fair amount of oral work or conversation before culturally deprived children are asked to write on the type of topic that requires free expression or an opinion or critical evaluation of a situation, person, or character. The prior discussion helps to give the pupils the feeling of engaging in an activity that is of importance to all; it gives the child who had no ideas or thoughts on the topic a pool of information which can help him formulate his own opinions; it gives a child greater self-confidence through his awareness that he too has something worthwhile to contribute.

In correcting the writing of culturally deprived children, teachers must be careful not to discourage them by marking their papers with too many red marks. In fact, in the case of very reluctant writers, it is sometimes advisable to postpone the correcting of spelling and grammar until the pupils have opened up considerably and are willing to express themselves freely. Before formal correcting begins, comments with reference to the content of the writing will frequently be effective for highly reluctant students. It is good policy to praise the youngsters for their strong points before entering into suggestions of what might be done better or into negative aspects of criticism. Even in the worst papers, there is usually something that can be found for which the youngster may be praised, however small the finding may be. It should be remembered, too, that even negative comments may be stated in an encouraging manner. The point in question here is how negative criticism may be made in such a way that the child will not be discouraged but rather will want to improve. For instance, the comment "I like the way you say your dog watches over you, but next time let's see if you can stick more closely to your topic, 'Why I Like Mary as a Girl Friend,'" is kinder and more encouraging to the pupil than the curt comment "You didn't stick to the subject."

It must be remembered, however, that there are classes of disadvantaged pupils who are far enough along not to be discouraged by the teacher's simultaneous correction of what is said and how the pupil says it. And there are other class members who though not immediately ready for the concurrent correction of content expression and structure move into readiness fairly quickly.

When the papers of disadvantaged pupils are ready to be graded for grammar and spelling, teachers are reminded of the disparaging effect of throwing the book at the students. Usually, culturally deprived pupils make a great many glaring errors. For example, they make mistakes in spelling, in the use of small and capital letters, and in the agreement of subject and verb; and they write fragments, run-on sentences, and stringy sentences. To correct all of these types of errors would be to embellish many a paper in red. Generally, a much more satisfactory procedure is marking by the cumulative method, that is, the method of adding only one or two types of errors at a time as targets for correction. If, for instance, spelling should be the first target, then the drills, lists of errors anonymously culled from student papers as practice work, and other exercises would be largely concerned with spelling, and the pupils' papers would be corrected in terms of spelling, insofar as formal English is concerned. If the next formal target should be fragments, then the drill work and other exercises would be devoted to the writing of complete sentences rather than fragments, and student papers would be marked down for mistakes in spelling and for the inclusion of fragments.

The cumulative method seeks to take learning in steps small enough to avert frustration. However, when pupils are engaged in a special project such as making a booklet that will be displayed in school or given to the principal or when they are engaged in such activity as writing letters to favorite entertainers with expectation of receiving a reply, there is extra and sustained incentive, among the pupils, to correct all errors readily. And the value of having readers to whom a fair portion of the pupils' writing is directed cannot be overemphasized. Yet, in connection with the ordinary writing activities of deprived class members, the teacher is justified in accepting the position that taking care of the most glaring errors or those that would hamper the students most in social mobility is better than setting unrealistic goals.

GOING ON TRIPS

Trips furnish children with a tremendously rich background both for oral expression and for writing. Without school-sponsored trips, a great many culturally deprived pupils have very little opportunity, if any, to venture outside their immediate vicinity. In addition to providing youngsters with firsthand experiences about which they may talk and write, trips are highly recommended for academic and cultural advancement.

Some school projects that have been designed to raise the sights of disadvantaged pupils have used trips as one of the main ingredients. These elementary, junior, and senior high schools have taken pupils on frequent trips to such places and activities as zoos, museums, plays, musical concerts, libraries, newspaper establishments, industrial centers, historical buildings, and other points of interest. Pupils were provided with appropriate background knowledge for visiting these places or functions; and teachers prepared in advance basic ways in which they would help the pupils use information gathered, to the children's advantage. Reports on the results of these projects have been highly favorable. Aside from the academic and cultural gains from the trips, these excursions allow pupils from minority groups to see some adults of their own ethnic background in a variety of jobs. This kind of observation should serve as inspiration for these youths by letting them know some of the opportunities that might be available to them.

The following special elementary-school project in connection with taking trips should be noted. Although the classes involved did not consist of disadvantaged youngsters, the project will, nonetheless, point up the impact that trips may make.

At one of the favored elementary schools of an urban neighborhood, tests had shown that Group X ranked very much higher than Group Y in achievement. For the balance of the school year, Group Y was fed a diet of trips. The greater part of the schoolwork was tied in with constant excursions to cultural, educational, and industrial centers and to performances. Group X, the control group, was given the regular school fare but was not permitted to go on trips. At the end of the school year, Group Y had not only gained tremendous ground, in achievement, but had surpassed Group X.

Teachers must always remember to turn trips to the children's best advantage. Pupils in lower grades, for instance, might be allowed to make little booklets about their trip. The content could be used as one source of reading matter, and there could be an interchange of the books among classmates. Youngsters generally very much enjoy reading what they themselves and their peers have written.

MEETING CHILDREN'S NEEDS

Work with disadvantaged youngsters can be most rewarding when the teacher merits the children's confidence, helps to release their hostilities, and can see fruitful returns for the efforts expended. As the teacher works with disadvantaged youth, there are a number of general principles that should be kept in mind.

The teacher must continue to administer pretests and diagnostic tests in order to uncover weaknesses; and content, techniques, and methods must be used that will best supply the children's needs. Achievable goals must be set for deprived youngsters; to do otherwise is to frustrate the pupils and cause them to amass further hostilities. When it becomes obvious that a particular lesson, activity, or technique is not commanding the pupils' attention, the work or technique must be discontinued in favor of profitable endeavors that do hold attention. And teachers must be careful not to make the portions of learning too large. It is best to work with a few ideas or concepts at a time and to add new knowledge only as the children are able to handle it successfully.

The attention span of disadvantaged youngsters, in particular, is not long. Teachers must therefore be prepared to vary the classwork sufficiently to prevent boredom and inattentiveness. It is true that underprivileged children need a great amount of drill on certain fundamental principles, but the drill exercises need not be monotonous. There must be much repetition in order that less privileged pupils may grasp certain basic knowledge or tools, but it is possible to have variety in work that is repeated. If the target material to be learned consists of items to prevent glaring errors in the agreement of subject and verb, for instance, the items under question may be incorporated into a number of different exercises. They may be used, for example, in rexographed seatwork for all pupils, in a seat game between boys and girls, in some form of oral lesson that requires the use of the items in conversation, or in a lesson that requires corrections in these items by means of the overhead projector. Thus, there may be creativity in repetition.

All children need to be given clear directions, but underprivileged children may become disheartened and refuse to put forth effort when they don't understand what is expected of them. Teachers must spot-check and double-check to make certain that instructions are understood by all pupils.

In general, a teacher's use of methods and techniques that actually reach the pupils and meet their needs makes a real difference in how much the students learn and how well they behave. Effective teaching and a well-disciplined class go hand in hand.

3

SPECIAL HANDLING
OF THE DISADVANTAGED CHILD

Dorothy was a twelve-year-old underprivileged black girl who repeatedly reported to school late. Requests from her teacher that she come on time merely brought from her lackadaisical stares and a whole attitude of indifference, but continued lateness. Her teacher, Miss J, simply could not get through to her. Interpreting the child's reaction as acts of defiance, Miss J resorted to scolding and shaming her before the class. This proved to be an erroneous way of handling Dorothy, because she withdrew and became obstinate, but didn't improve. Finally Miss J called Dorothy in for a private conference to ascertain why she had to be late almost daily. Miss J discovered that there was no legitimate reason. The child simply got up too late in the mornings and, in addition, was slow getting dressed. Dorothy's teacher tried to reason with her by pointing out to her how much classwork she was missing by reporting late and how a habit of lateness might hamper her in life, but in addition Miss J assured her that she would be highly pleased with her if she'd consent to come on time. Very important, Miss J made the decision that since scolding and shaming Dorothy hadn't brought results she'd try praising Dorothy for the few times she did show up on time. From then on, nothing was said to Dorothy when she was late, but each time she came to school on time, Miss J gave her a broad smile and the first opportunity she got she praised Dorothy sincerely for being on time. Dorothy was more than pleased with the attention and praise she received, and although she didn't improve miraculously overnight, a vast amount of improvement gradually but surely came about.

When the background of underprivileged children is thoroughly understood, the fact that some of them do not have the drive and sense of optimism to get to school on time ceases to be astonishing. As a whole, middle-class children have a reason to value time and punctuality. They have been oriented to education by their parents. Their parents expect them to achieve or to get ahead and to go to college. Generally, then, whether they like it or not, middle-class children will do pretty much what is in line with helping them to achieve the goals that have been set for them. Being punctual is a trait that will help them to achieve their goals. On the contrary, culturally deprived children frequently have not had substantial orientation in some areas generally well mastered by middle-class youngsters. Punctuality, respect for time, speed, and orderliness are some areas in which the habits of disadvantaged children often do not measure up to the demands in the classroom. Generally, the youngsters simply have not had ample training in these areas. Teachers who have not become knowledgeable about the deprived child's background might easily consider failings in the areas designated the result of indifference or stupidity rather than habits that have been learned in deprived homes and neighborhoods.

Generally, then, because of middle-class children's substantial orientation to school and achievement, they will respond with favorable results to check-ups, pointed questioning, and reprimands regarding frequent lateness; with underprivileged children, teaching the value of punctuality and extending praise and rewards will often bring better results.

It is of essence to note here, too, that some disadvantaged pupils are late coming to school because they have to play parent roles to young siblings. Such pupils have to dress younger brothers and sisters and get them safely to their school areas before they themselves can report to school. In such cases it is not surprising when these young parent surrogates are frequently late to school. These types of cases, of course, warrant meeting with parents to try to get their cooperation in making the types of family arrangements that will allow the children to arrive at school when they should so that they may take full advantage of the school's offerings.

It is not unlimited license but understanding and awareness that are wanted for the underprivileged. Disadvantaged children want to feel that they count too. They want to know that the teacher cares. They want to know that the teacher is interested in them and that he has their welfare at heart. Deprived children also want the security of being given limits, of knowing what is expected of them. They are less confused and anxiety-ridden when this is the case.

Since more is being said now than previously about the rights of disadvantaged children, and about the rights of black disadvantaged pupils in particular, some white teachers of black youngsters are concerned over how they should treat them. A portion of these teachers have been known to go overboard in a frantic effort to show that they are not among those white teachers who administer ill treatment to black pupils. But this action, too, is unacceptable. The surest way for a teacher to treat a black youngster as he should be treated, of course, is for the teacher simply to be human and to be able to treat the child as a human being without thinking of him in terms of being white or black. For teachers who find it difficult to treat the black child in this natural manner, however, certain suggestions may be helpful.

POSITIVE APPROACHES

As a black woman, I think I can safely say that a vitally important ingredient in handling black youths is that the teacher offer them equality in interest, treatment, opportunity, and teaching. When a black youth shirks his responsibility or obligation, however, he should be helped to see in what way he is being irresponsible and should in some way be made to realize that he is expected to mend his ways. And, very important, he should be led to realize that when doors have been opened for him, he must work in order to attain.

In general, while the methods of dealing with the various disadvantaged groups may at times vary from those needed for other children because of deficiencies in the background of the underprivileged, the major objectives are the same. Teachers must remember that ultimate goals for all children are optimal learning and acceptable behavior.

PRAISE

For the most part, disadvantaged pupils need a great amount of praise. There are, of course, those among other children who sometimes need more than an average share of praise as well. For instance, the middle- or upper-class pupil who is suffering from sibling competition that makes him feel inferior to a sister or brother, or the culturally advantaged child who has feelings of worthlessness because he is unable to bring his class achievement in line with parent expectation, may be in considerable need of teacher praise as a containment against emotional strain that impedes progress. But, as a whole, disadvantaged pupils need more lavish praise than their more favored counterparts for effort and improvement shown in classwork and conduct. This is true because the underprivileged youngster is frequently in need of ego boosts and a sense of self-confidence of which he has had a far too meager share. Often disadvantaged children need teacher praise as a buffer against the hopelessness and feelings of worthlessness that limited and depressed surroundings have imposed.

REWARDS

Youngsters of all groups like rewards, and generally profit from them. But the culturally advantaged child, who has been inspired to make getting ahead his ultimate goal, can forego tangible rewards with far less damaging effect than is true in the case of the deprived child. This condition exists because many disadvantaged children, with their rather precarious motivation and hope for the future, have come to respect immediate gratification. The long-term motivation of middle- and upper-class children, however, should not preclude their receiving a portion of the rewards. And certainly the disadvantaged child must receive a goodly share of them, for they encourage him to work and behave better. Gold stars, emblems, commendation cards, extra credit, school supplies such as pencils and paper, a chance to be a leader or monitor, and an opportunity to display classwork are only a few of the types of rewards that may be granted.

SENSE OF SUCCESS

Teachers should make certain that disadvantaged children achieve a fair amount of success each day. They have already suffered too much from a feeling of defeat. A sense of success makes the child feel that he is worthwhile and accomplishing something. Some sense of achievement makes youngsters more amenable to improved behavior.

AFFECTION

A teacher must remember that it is well to be aware of the pupil who craves the love of the teacher and to show approval of the pupil through some gesture of warmth or kindness. It becomes less difficult to handle a child whose clamor to get adult love and approval is duly recognized. Besides, perhaps the youngster may be one of the many pupils who have failed to receive an adequate amount of attention and affection in the home.

MONITORIAL DUTIES

Disadvantaged children, for the most part, have a propensity for doing little monitorial jobs in the classroom. They like such duties as distributing and collecting books, passing out supplies, erasing and washing the chalkboard, helping with attendance, writing announcements on the chalkboard, and assisting with the arrangement of bulletin board displays. These youngsters are usually appreciative that these duties have been turned over to them. They should be both helped and encouraged to perform them efficiently and with pride. Success in performance helps to build in these young people a sense of responsibility and an improved self-image, both of which are favorable to better behavior.

STRUCTURE

All children need to be taught respect for organization, but disadvantaged youngsters need a great amount of structure. These children have a tendency to show anxiety and to become confused when the organization is too loose. They wish to know what is wanted of them, and they are happier and far better controlled when there are recognizable rules for governing them. It works well, for instance, for them to be aware of the regulations they must obey and the reasons they should respect them; it is well for each of them to know where he will sit and how he will line up for dismissal; and it is essential for the pupils to know how books, paper, and other supplies are to be distributed, where the name and other parts of the heading are to be placed on a page, and where pupils are to record each type of information in their notebooks. In short, the routines and work of the classroom should be unmistakably delineated for our underprivileged pupils.

EFFECTIVE TEACHING

Throughout the book we have pointed up the invaluable role effective teaching plays in averting and diminishing problems in discipline. It only remains to be said here that since circumstances have made it so that the greatest number of disciplinary problems occur among underprivileged pupils, it stands to reason that exceptionally good teaching should be provided for our disadvantaged youth.

LAUNCHING THE VERY DIFFICULT CLASS

Children who have had training and have benefited from it may be depended upon to respond favorably to the teacher's cue to cease talking and activity when it is time for class proper to begin. But some classes of highly underprivileged children have little respect for the teacher's signal. In some classes of from twenty to thirty very disadvantaged, unruly pupils, if teachers were to wait for perfect quiet before beginning the classwork, they could be waiting endlessly.

Unlike the procedure for ordinary groups, then, in the highly difficult classes, classwork must often begin in the midst of din. Since it is frequently futile to wait for complete quiet, work should commence immediately. If one or two reliable monitors can be found among the group, they might help the teacher by distributing necessary materials and tools, preferably as the class members enter the door; they then have less opportunity to mill around the room in diverse horseplay. Extra pencils should always be available, for these are children who often come unprepared to work without a prick of conscience. Notebooks that are to be passed out to the youngsters daily may be made from construction paper and kept in the room if the class members can't be relied upon to bring notebooks to school each day.

We're speaking now about the types of children who, to almost the fullest extent, will receive whatever motivation and general training they realize not from home but from the teacher, for many of the parents of these children might not respond readily if sent for, while some wouldn't show up at all. Among those parents who would report to school to consult with the teacher about their children, a sizable number would almost certainly let it be known that if the teacher could do anything at all with the youngsters, that would be more than they as parents could do. Teachers should try to have conferences with the parents of these pupils, however, for there are always some parents of highly difficult youngsters who might be able to make a contribution toward better control of their children; besides, the parents, as a whole, can furnish important clues into the background of their youngsters, even if only unconsciously.

Work for these extremely difficult classes should be of unmistakably high interest. Much of the printed matter should be "high interest / easy reading" material. Work in the form of puzzles and games should be offered, conveying the idea that schoolwork can be fun. But much of the pupils' work should be done at their seats, using duplicated lesson sheets, to minimize the chance for milling around the room. Adequate provisions should be made for variety in work. And there should be liberal use of engaging and appropriate audiovisual aids. For the most part, teachers will succeed in getting these children to buy only what is made interestingly and appropriately salable to them.

Not all disadvantaged classes are as difficult as the one we have been describing, but far too many of them are. Here again, let it be said that the interest and support of educationists, schools, governments, and society are greatly needed toward helping to make these types of extremely difficult classes quite small and toward having greatly disturbed children in such groups referred to the proper specialists for adequate care. These adjustments should be made so that the teacher of difficult youngsters doesn't remain in a state of perpetual tension, fighting for mere survival. Very difficult classes should be cut to manageable size and to controllable caliber if teachers of these classes are to give the best they have to the classroom and if the pupils are to reap rich profits.

MANAGING UNUSUAL DAYS AND PERIODS

Teachers may reduce problems in discipline by being appropriately prepared to meet the exigencies of unusual school days and periods. These are times when class routines are interrupted by an out-of-the-ordinary environment or event. During these times, pupils are often overly stimulated or highly excitable. These reactions are apparent, for example, on days when the student body is to see the important play production of the year, on days when there is a strike that affects the school and upsets regular organizational patterns, on the day before an extended holiday, and on Fridays. Similarly, there are special periods during the day that are more difficult than other times of the school day. Many children show unusual excitement in the periods before and after lunch and before dismissal for the day.

It is important that teachers prepare lessons that will minimize confusion during the times designated. Teachers will have their own ideas about the nature of the lessons that will meet the exigencies cited. And this is as it should be. In many instances, however, instructors will use good judgment in selecting for the exciting times mentioned exercises or work of a quiet nature. This would include seatwork rather than activities that give pupils the opportunity to mill around the room and compound confusion. Some teachers might wish the class to join in with them in the reading and discussion of some surefire material pertinent to the particular subject area under consideration. There are instructional leaders who will use rexographed games or puzzles that cover important work interestingly. Others will have the pupils take a teaser test on people in the news, a written exercise that will be graded by each individual pupil but with the knowledge that the grades will not be recorded. Some teachers will have pupils supply matching answers for a list of vocabulary items or missing letters for a list of spelling words. The essential matter is that the teachers be fully aware of the importance of being equal to the task of taking care of the exigencies of unusual days and periods.

WORK-STUDY PROGRAMS

A sizable number of teachers have testified to the success of the work-study program in meeting the needs of some underprivileged youngsters of high school age. The program provides for the pupils' spending a portion of the day in school studying the major subjects and the other part of the day working on jobs in the community or in the school. The plan makes school bearable for some poorly prepared youngsters who, except for the plan, would feel hopeless and disgruntled over the school's failure to meet their needs and interests. But with part of their time spent in the realities of acquiring job skills and experience and with only a portion of the day devoted to acquiring the academic work, the pupils have the feeling of at least getting something tangible from the school "deal"; they are consequently more willing to behave and to strive for the completion of school.

GRADING

In issuing grades to youngsters who have so many gaps and deficiencies, teachers must take into due consideration limited backgrounds and the amount of effort expended by the pupils. This position does not mean that teachers are justified in taking the attitude that there is little to be gotten from underprivileged pupils. Rather, teachers should teach diligently and try to encourage the pupils to put forth their best efforts. The stand taken regarding grades really means that youngsters who have been passed from grade to grade without having mastered the previous year's work may not suddenly be marked by an absolute scale. A teacher, for instance, may not justifiably fail all fifth-grade youngsters who fail to achieve average fifth-grade level if the schools have passed the pupils along without having seen to it that they reached earlier grade levels; such failings are not possible unless school systems discontinue mass promotions and refuse to allow any pupils to advance to the next grade level before they have actually mastered the work of their current school year. What we are concerned about is fairness in grading. Teachers who mark with a sense of fairness help to gain for themselves the respect and confidence of the pupils and minimize the chances of resentment and hostility over grades.

DEALING WITH EMOTIONAL REACTIONS

In the course of bringing discipline to classes of disadvantaged children, the teacher inevitably arouses resentments and hostilities. The pupils' reactions must be understood and then dealt with calmly and rationally within a consistent framework of expectations.

THE FEELING OF BEING PICKED ON

Black children have been known to accuse teachers who reprove or punish them of picking on them. It is not unusual for a black youngster to inform the teacher, "You wouldn't do that to me if I wasn't colored" (Noar, 1966). In a nation where many injustices have been perpetrated on the black man, it is understandable that a black pupil, particularly one who has been soured by many deficits, can easily arrive at this opinion. Gertrude Noar (1966) has offered for the fair-minded teacher one very perceptive solution to the problem at hand. She notes that the teacher will benefit by remaining calm while quietly saying to the child who has made the accusation: "I know how you feel. I understand why you feel that way, but let us look at the facts. Yesterday Andy, who is white, did the same thing you did today. How did I treat him? The same as I am treating you now." This kind of calm effort to help the youngster face reality and refrain from being unduly conscious of race will need to be repeated until the child has had enough experience with the teacher to know that the teacher is not given to practicing race prejudice (Noar).

THE CORPORAL-PUNISHMENT BEGGAR

We have previously noted that some youngsters from disadvantaged homes virtually beg to be hit or slapped by the teacher, in return for their misbehavior. We observed that, for the most part, these are the pupils who have become accustomed to being handled by slaps and blows, at the hands of impatient, depressed parents who use little, if any, of the method of reasoning or talking to the children about their misconduct. Because of the possibility of becoming involved in legal suits or in outright combat with some belligerent youngsters who might not be at all hesitant about striking back, the teacher must refrain from accepting these pupils' challenges to administer to them corporal punishment. Teachers must let a youngster know that they are leaders who accept him, care for him, and expect him to behave, but without the use of the rod. The teacher must set up rules and regulations for governing the pupils at the beginning of the term; and the students should understand thoroughly the reason for each rule. Some penalties should likewise be set for designated acts of misconduct. It is helpful to have the pupils give as much assistance with the establishing of regulations as they are capable of giving. Pupils are more willing to abide by regulations which they helped to formulate and which they consider to be just and reasonable. Additionally, it is wise for the teacher to mention from the outset that time will be set aside at intervals for the discussion of ways by which better behavior might be achieved, and specifically of ways in which specific acts of misconduct might be corrected. Teachers must also have private conferences with pupils who misbehave and reason with them about their conduct. They must help the youngsters learn how to behave, but are enjoined to refrain from the use of any form of corporal punishment.

RUNNING AWAY

A number of disadvantaged pupils have a tendency to withdraw or run away in the face of conflict or difficulty. For instance, certain children are prone to run out of the classroom for reasons such as being questioned or reprimanded by the teacher or having words with another student.

In dealing with a runaway pupil the teacher might have a private conference with him, help him to understand that he is running away from his problem, and try to show him how he might handle his difficulty in some way other than through withdrawal. At an opportune time there may be class discussion of ways of meeting problems similar to the one that caused a particular pupil to leave the classroom. An additional way of dealing with pupil difficulties is through reading and discussing fictional selections in which the characters undergo problems related to the ones encountered by members of the class. An evaluation of the solutions these young characters find to their problems should give pupils greater insight into handling their own problems.

The teacher should, of course, report the incident of the runaway pupil to the appropriate administrator of the school. This action will prevent the teacher's being held liable should the youngster become ill or involved in some delinquent act while out of the room.

STEALING

Some privileged youngsters have been known to steal. Yet middle–class children usually own a great many things of their own and have been taught not to take articles that belong to someone else. Often the underprivileged youngster has not been given such instructions; nor has he had the opportunity of having a large number of his own belongings. It is not difficult to see, then, that the stage is more perfectly set for stealing on the part of the disadvantaged than on the part of the more fortunate youth. Frequently, the underprivileged youngster simply wants the good feeling of possessing something of his own. Many times, however, when a child steals, it is out of the need for a relationship that is of utmost importance. In general, children steal because they want the security of possessing something of their own, because they are in need of a relationship, or, in the case of very young children, because they are not aware of the fact that they are stealing.

In classes where stealing is likely to occur, teachers must continually caution pupils to keep tempting belongings safely out of view of classmates, and particularly should this be done in classrooms where stealing has already occurred. Teachers themselves may need to keep a vigilant eye on pupils' coats, hats, and overshoes, in an effort to try to prevent pupils from stealing from each other.

In the case of the child who has stolen an object, it will be helpful for the teacher to have a private conference with the youngster. If he denies having stolen, he might be asked to prove his innocence. Should proof be established that stealing has taken place, the pupil should be required to return the stolen goods. The teacher must, of course, ascertain whether or not the child is aware of his stealing. If not, the act of stealing should be thoroughly explained to him, including results to which the act may lead. The child should be cautioned that stealing makes one highly unpopular with fellow classmates. It would be helpful, too, to elicit the youngster's future cooperation in refraining from stealing. If it is a matter of a relationship that the child is seeking, he might be seated next to someone who is congenial and with whom he can get along well. At an appropriate time, stealing might be made a subject of general discussion—why it should be avoided and how class members might help to keep each other from engaging in it. If the youngster in question continues to steal in spite of measures used to prevent him from doing so, it may be necessary to seek the cooperation of his parents in breaking the habit. Further trouble from the youngster would possibly require a referral to the proper school administrator or to the guidance office.

OBSCENITY AND PROFANITY

Low socioeconomic areas are usually breeding places for obscenity and profanity. Children hear obscene or profane expressions tossed around as freely as if they constituted highly acceptable language. It is natural for youngsters to bring with them to school what is a dominant part of their environment; and thus it is that in their classrooms many lower-class pupils use four-letter words and swear at the teacher and fellow classmates. The younger children sometimes do not even know the meaning of the words they use, and older pupils frequently use distasteful language simply out of habit even though they are aware of the meaning. It is important that teachers realize this language background of culturally deprived children. The realization should preclude an inclination to become angry and retaliate. Instead, teachers are called upon to expend their time and energy toward helping the youngsters rise above their background.

In the initial class meetings devoted to setting up rules and regulations, in the periodic class discussions that are held regarding behavior, and in private conferences with individual class members, the use of obscene and profane expressions may be one of the issues of concern, in accordance with the demands of the situation. At these times, the pupils must be helped to understand why the undesirable expressions are unacceptable and why the use of them will not make for social mobility. The youngsters should be given illustrations of the type of language that is acceptable. They must come to know that obscenity or profanity offends some classmates and makes the users of it unpopular with these class members.

Inviting to the classroom speakers who might serve as an image for under-privileged pupils should be helpful. These speakers might talk briefly on the matter of appropriate language and on any other matters of conduct that might be beneficial to the youngsters. Additionally, trips should be immensely helpful. Such tours would allow the children an opportunity to see what some of the other part of the world is like, how other people talk, and how they act.

Teachers should know, however, that while some of the younger children of lower-class background don't know the meaning of the distasteful language they use, there are those among the older ones who may try to bully the teacher through the use of obscene or profane expressions. Gertrude Noar made some observations that are germane to the case in point. Teachers, she cautions, must not suffer from self-derogation because a youngster swears at them or calls them names. Neither should they ignore the pupil's impulsive or deliberate attempt to dominate them. Often a first procedure is to determine whether or not the youngster knows the meaning of the expression he has used.

The following examples are ways various teachers treated the use of bad language. Playing with a toy, a kindergarten child suddenly used the oath, "You blank ─────" When called upon to give the meaning of the expression, the small child smilingly explained, "It means the car won't start." Naturally the case demanded no action on the teacher's part. One teacher was attempting to correct the behavior of a difficult pupil. He, in turn, called her a liar. She answered calmly, "No, I'm not." Still another teacher threatened to inflict dire punishment if the youngster continued to disturb the class. The youth muttered, in exasperation, "Aw, go to hell." The teacher responded without perturbation, "I don't have to" (Noar).

Other children of the class listen to the types of exchanges we have described. A defeated protagonist is subject to losing face; later when the teacher gets him off to himself, he is receptive to a private conference where his actions may be corrected. Teachers can remain in possession of the classroom—and thereby defeat the attempt of the youngster to get control and make a scene—by using a calm manner and quiet voice and by making it obvious to the pupil in question that his attempts at bullying and insulting the teacher and at dominating the classroom will not work (Noar).

It should be remembered that fighting is not a trait peculiar to under-privileged youngsters; other children fight as well. But in the case of the culturally disadvantaged, fighting is a way of life because of circumstances to which the youngsters have been exposed.

Teachers sometimes find it difficult, however, to understand the deprived child's propensity for fighting. We have previously noted the tendency of segments of disadvantaged pupils to feel that in order to prove their mas-culinity they must exhibit their physical prowess. And having come from a background setting of limited wealth, overcrowding, violence, alcoholism, and drug addiction, as many lower–class youngsters have, they have often been driven to fighting for themselves. It is not unnatural, then, that these culturally deprived youths transfer to the schools their tendency to fight.

Again, the sessions at the beginning of the term where limits are set and rules made, the intermittent class discussions on behavior, and the pri-vate conferences with individual class members are convenient times for discussing the hazards of fighting and for trying to set the tone for consider-ing fighting a type of classroom action that is not "in" behavior. The fact that the pupils as a whole play some part in making rules and in discussing how behavior might be improved, and why it should be, should go a long way toward setting a desirable tone. Pupils as a whole are not happy about disregarding the stand taken by the peer group. If under the guidance of the teacher, then, the majority of the class members come to consider fighting a type of behavior they should seriously avoid, their decision bears weight with fellow classmates.

With respect to dealing with a fight, the teacher is sometimes able to detect when a fight is brewing. Often the teacher may prevent the fight from materializing by moving near the antagonists and reasoning with them or by changing the seat of one of the youngsters.

When a fight does occur in the classroom, some of the larger boys are quite willing to separate the persons involved when there is a desirable re-lationship between teacher and pupils. It is frequently advisable that the teacher arrange to meet with the fighters in private. Each child, of course, should be given a chance to tell his side.

In the private conference the teacher should make it clear that fighting is not necessary in order to prove oneself masculine. If the teacher has reason to believe that a youngster feels the need of proving himself, the teacher may be helpful by discovering something constructive the pupil can do well, however small, and by bringing the youth before the class in a favorable light, so that he may experience the type of praise that makes him less dependent on shining in a negative way. In a conference, youngsters might be reminded of pertinent points made regarding fighting during the class sessions on behavior. At the time of the teacher-pupil meeting, the teacher may also find it necessary to arrange to change the seat of one or both of the youths involved in the fight in order to make certain they are seated near classmates with whom they get along well.

If the offenders should not discontinue their fighting after the foregoing measures have been exhausted, the teacher would be called upon to use whatever penalty may have been set for persistent fighters. With some children, it may be essential that the teacher go so far as to bring in the parents to try to enlist their cooperation in putting an end to the fighting; and with still other children, there may be the need to refer the case to the proper administrator or to the guidance office. Teachers are reminded, however, that if the pupils involved in arguing or fighting have in their possession knives or other dangerous instruments, they should be restrained from using the weapons, and the case should be referred to the proper administrator immediately. Similarly, if there is violent fighting, even without weapons, appropriate referral should be promptly made.

In general, it is to be remembered that the disadvantaged child has many deficits, and one of them is a shortage of knowledge on how he should behave. Much patient and encouraging teaching is needed in the department of behavior. It should be remembered, nonetheless, that underprivileged youngsters will have far less need to misbehave if the teacher makes it possible for them to learn and if they can sense that the teacher understands them and accepts them as human beings.

4

MANAGERIAL ANTIDOTES
FOR DISCIPLINARY PROBLEMS

Preventive techniques play an inestimable role in countering disciplinary problems as a whole. This chapter and the two chapters that follow present basic tenets for warding off behavioral problems on the part of the students. The tenets are based on the principle that if the school life of young people is sufficiently filled with positive, constructive measures, there will be very little room for problems in discipline. Naturally, some problems are to be expected. But where disorder is sufficiently minimized by positive means, there can be a classroom climate that is favorable for learning. Actually, the tenets presented here and in Chapters 5 and 6 may be described as preventive, for they stress preventing the majority of the anticipated behavioral problems from occurring, through a program that is replete with positive approaches and activities.

The importance of the preventive approach to classroom control cannot be overemphasized. Far too many teachers get off to a poor start in their classrooms only to find themselves overwhelmed by problems. Pupils who are permitted to become disorderly or unruly are difficult to retrieve. Teachers must work hard and fast with positive measures to keep the students from getting out of hand at the outset. And let us not be the least bit mistaken. When we speak of warding off trouble from the pupils at the outset we refer to ways of preventing problems from all types of children. We refer to offsetting many of the possible problems from the advantaged as well as the disadvantaged; from upper, middle, average, and lower classes; from whites as well as blacks. While it is recognized that the numerous deficits of ghetto children will generally cause them to act out more obstreperously than the more advantaged youngsters, when means are not appropriately established for avoiding the storm, even well-brought-up kids may cause the teacher a great many headaches if he doesn't plan ably to prevent them.

The preventive measures are not, of course, a panacea for misbehavior; nor have they been presented as such. But adherence to them can unquestionably make the classroom surroundings livable and promote a wholesome base from which the teacher can work to advantage with individual problems in discipline. Certainly readers will wish to know what might be done regarding disciplinary cases that occur despite a program filled with constructive measures. Chapters 9, 10, and 11 will deal with such problems.

The basic positive tenets in this chapter are managerial in nature. They are positive, constructive measures that stress ways teachers may organize and manage the class and classroom environment so that numerous behavior problems may be prevented.

ANNOUNCING EXPECTATIONS

During the first few sessions with your class, let your pupils know what will be expected of them. To do so makes for good organization or management. Letting the students know what you will require them to do in class, what you hope to achieve, and, in general, how the class will be run also relieves the pupils of their anxiety.

You would be wise to overprepare the lessons for the first days. Your readiness to cope with a class, whatever the required pace, brings you the security of being able to manage your group. Besides, you want to impress upon your students, from the outset, that in your room classwork is business. What you do during those first days will help to establish student expectations with respect to the value of your classroom.

It is wise, then, to begin some of the classwork on the first day. Plan some surefire lessons that will interest, challenge, or pique your pupils' curiosity. You will be wise to convey to them the idea that your class will not be a drag. Get your pupils involved immediately.

During the first days, some teachers may wish to require a written assignment that will give them insight into pupil needs, interests, and background preparation. This type of getting-acquainted lesson may often serve the teacher the useful purpose of determining what successive steps to take with the class.

Although it is not desirable that the teacher attend to records during class time, the fact remains that on the first days of class teachers are sometimes called upon to do clerical work. In the event that this situation cannot be averted, teachers might have available for the students challenging mimeographed exercises which pupils may do with minimum supervision, reasonable quietness, and a high degree of interest, while the teacher is doing necessary paperwork. In general, the classwork should get off to such a live, constructive start that disciplinary problems will not arise.

With respect to behavior, remember that the youngsters, from first grade to twelfth, will be sizing you up on those first days, determining what type of person you are and deciding what they will and will not be allowed to get away with. For the most part, pupils are relatively mild or tame during the time they are scrutinizing you as a teacher. If not given something better to do, however, your students will naturally resort to antics and acting out. The teacher is discerning, then, who works rapidly within those first days to try to get ahead of the artifice of the pupils in order that a well-organized classroom may be established, in which gainful activity may take place.

FORMULATING RULES

As early as possible within the first few days, it is good policy to set certain limits with regard to behavior, limits that are reasonable and that you expect to keep. Key behavior rules that are essential to a reasonable level of conduct should be set. However, the list of regulations should not be formidable, or the pupils will become discouraged and uncooperative.

It is of very great moment to have pupils join in with you, as teacher, in formulating the rules of behavior for the class. While the members of a few classes may be too young to engage in this activity and though some class members may be too unstable, a great many of the classes may take part in this function to great effect. As a rule, pupils who feel that enough confidence has been placed in them to allow them to have some part in setting up the rules by which class members are to be governed are less reluctant to adhere to the regulations. Additionally, when the class as a whole has worked on rules, under the leadership of the teacher, regulations get peer acceptance; and the pressure of a group on a potential problem maker can be a powerful deterrent.

A basic understanding of why the rule is necessary or of what function it will serve toward the advancement of the group and of individual group members is central. When the pupil has this knowledge, he no longer needs to feel that to obey a rule is merely to satisfy the vagrant whims of a teacher; rather, the child comes to know that the regulation has a true reason for being. As some authorities have aptly noted, getting a child to respond with good behavior requires teaching, just as the subject of a curriculum must be taught (Green, 1965; Hymes, 1955; Sheviakov and Redl, 1956). Teaching, interpreting, and explaining are, without question, necessary to achieving desirable discipline. And certainly teaching the reasoning behind rules that are set as behavior limits is fundamental to establishing a well-ordered class.

ASSIGNING SEATS

Assign seats to the members of your class at the beginning of the school term. The assigning of seats makes it possible for the teacher to devise a seating chart which may be used for a more ready association of names and faces. Besides, having a seat that he can call his own usually adds to a pupil's sense of well-being and security.

The typical elementary teacher who is to have a single class throughout the day will often find it helpful to study the records of incoming pupils and perhaps to consult with the previous teacher regarding class members. This procedure may furnish the current teacher important clues on how to devise a seating plan prior to meeting the class, a plan that will best take care of potential disciplinary problems. For instance, the teacher may discover some pupils who will be better behaved seated near the teacher, other pupils who should not sit near each other if numerous problems in discipline are to be avoided. The high school teacher, however, will not generally find such a prior effort at devising a seating plan practical, since he would usually have records for four or five classes to examine and many teachers to consult.

In secondary schools, especially, an alphabetical seating arrangement may generally be satisfactory, since such a plan emphasizes an objective pattern. And particularly in junior high school the objectivity of an alphabetical plan may be helpful in breaking up cliques of pupils who after having traveled together in the same neighborhood over a period of time might, if permitted, be inclined to be talkative and troublesome. The alphabetical arrangement would of course assume that the teacher would make exceptions for pupils who because of poor vision or out-of-the-ordinary height need to be placed in a different spot from the one the alphabetical pattern might dictate. Similarly, a teacher may need to make some exceptions in the alphabetical scheme in order to achieve a desirable pattern of integration if indeed the attempt to integrate the various ethnic groups doesn't cause the teacher to abandon completely an alphabetical attempt.

There are of course teachers who, from the outset, prefer to let students choose their own seats and remain in them as long as the youngsters can control themselves properly. This arrangement, too, may prove successful if the teacher is diligent about making changes in the seating when pupils seated near each other begin to misbehave. There are, nevertheless, some schools that have special set policy on the type of seating design that is to be used.

A main point to remember is that the careful management of seating arrangements is a technique that may, in itself, take care of a sizable number of potential problems in discipline. The teacher, therefore, must not be hesitant about making changes in any type of seating plan in order to promote better behavior. Some teachers, in fact, may find it highly desirable to plan for a regrouping of the pupils during the school year.

In most classes, teachers will generally avoid a great amount of noise and confusion by insisting that pupils keep their regularly assigned seats. Each pupil should then be encouraged to become proudly responsible for the control of himself within his own assigned domain; in this way, the teacher does not become tortured by numerous annoyances resulting from a promiscuous change and exchange of seats.

LEARNING NAMES

Make a special effort to learn the names of your students quickly. A typical James or John may be observed to give a startled jump when the teacher calls him by name within a very short time after a new term has begun. The reaction of such a typical pupil is as if to say, "Oh, the teacher knows my name!" The teacher's ability to identify him not only gives the youngster an increased sense of well-being because the leader has shown sufficient interest to know him as an individual pupil so early in the new term but usually gives him, as well, the feeling that the responsibility will hereafter be his with respect to the type of conduct he exhibits, now that he has been identified in person.

BEGINNING CLASSWORK

Make a practice of beginning classwork readily and in a businesslike manner. At the beginning of the term, there may be stragglers who seem never to be able to report to the classroom on time. But as you continue to convey to your pupils the idea that they are being held responsible for work that begins promptly and as you firmly and consistently question latecomers with regard to the causes of their lateness, class members will get the idea that in this classroom we are expected to begin on time and in earnest. Pupils should be convinced that the teacher is there to work, to offer them something for their welfare, not to stall or waste time. And the majority of the students should be relatively easily led to understand that the caliber of their schoolwork will suffer greatly if, through lateness, they continue to miss work for which they will be held accountable.

Teachers must realize the importance of being persistent and consistent, from the outset, regarding the enforcement of such routine regulations as reporting promptly to the classroom and leaving the room in reasonable orderliness, regardless of any inward pain the teacher may suffer from the demand for firmness on these matters. Pupil resentment and other difficulties are the result when a teacher seeks to change behavior once the pupils have been allowed to establish their own haphazard and disruptive patterns of conduct.

PROVIDING PRECLASS WORK

If your area is junior or senior high school teaching which calls for a change of class members by the period, provide for your various classes some phase of preliminary or preclass work on a special section of your chalkboard that you have reserved for prework purposes. This practice encourages class members to settle down and puts them in the frame of mind for work. Although the students need not be perfectly quiet before the lesson proper begins, the preclass work should assure reasonable orderliness and at the same time allow the members of the class to accomplish something worthwhile before the lesson proper begins. In addition, the preliminary work affords the teacher a few minutes of free time to take care of essential routine matters before beginning the actual lesson for the day.

Pupils should come to know, through some form of checkup, that they will be responsible for prework, in addition to their regular classwork. The prework should help to teach the students a sense of responsibility, should advance their knowledge, and should substitute constructive activity for what could very well become a number of behavior problems.

While the prework may in some way pertain to the lesson for the day or to the lesson of the previous day, it is not absolutely necessary that the preliminary work fall into either of these two categories, so long as it is work of a constructive nature. The prework could consist of several technical vocabulary words, for example, with the requirement that class members guess the meanings of the words through contextual clues. The prework could be a proverb, the meaning of which class members would be required to determine. Still further, the pre-exercise could be a special problem that calls for the pupil's applying knowledge gained from a previous lesson. Each teacher, of course, would want to determine the best types of preliminary work, in accordance with the particular subject area and class needs. The prework exercises may play a dynamic part in helping to bring about a well-organized class where behavior problems are constructively controlled and where the classroom atmosphere is favorable for learning.

MANAGING MOVEMENT AND TRANSITION

Make your management of activity movement conducive to desirable classroom behavior. In connection with this tenet, studies made by Jacob S. Kounin (1970) may be of particular assistance. In his chapter "Movement Management: Smoothness and Momentum," Kounin records the degree to which a group of elementary teachers managed "smoothness" and "momentum." His studies, however, have important implications for both elementary and secondary teachers, since movement management is inevitably a duty of the classroom teacher. The studies revealed that the two categories of movement, smoothness and momentum, correlate significantly with children's behavior.

Smoothness (anti-jerkiness) referred to the avoidance of sudden starts and stops during the transition from one subject to another or during an ongoing recitation. Momentum referred to the avoidance of slowdowns or of behaviors that actually make the pace of the recitation activity slow or draggy.

Kounin's study revealed that the following types of mistakes in smoothness have a negative effect on young people's behavior: (1) the teacher's deflection from a goal by some minutia, such as the interruption of explanations concerning a notebook assignment, for a noticeable amount of time, to question a pupil regarding a piece of paper on the floor; (2) sudden interruption of pupils' activities with an order, statement, or question; (3) lack of pause or sensitivity to group readiness to receive message, for instance as soon as the last person in Group I finishes reading, the teacher's closing her book and, without pausing or looking up, ordering Group II to the reading circle; (4) leaving an activity "hanging in mid-air," then returning to it, as the teacher's requesting Mary to respond to an arithmetic problem then leaving the reply hanging in the air in order to go into details regarding a pupil's absence, prior, of course, to the return to Mary's response; (5) leaving an activity hanging and not returning to it; (6) termination of one activity (for example, spelling), then the initiation of another activity (for instance, mathematics), followed by a return to the terminated activity (spelling).

The study by Kounin showed that the following slowdowns or mistakes in momentum have a negative effect on students: (1) Overdwelling or dwelling on an issue by engaging in action or talk that exceeds a point necessary for most pupils' understanding or inducement to act. For instance, the teacher asked one pupil to stop talking. Then she directed her talk to the entire class, naming some children who were cooperative as well as a student who wasn't. Following this, she reminded the students that the place was not a playground but rather a classroom. She informed them that it is difficult to try to learn when there's a great amount of noise. The behavior was considered overdwelling because it would unnecessarily slow down the activity. It was assumed that the pupils knew the content of the talk; thus, the teacher's preachments were considered nagging. (2) Fragmentation or unnecessarily breaking down an activity into subparts, when the activity could be performed as a single unit. For example, the teacher had just finished with one group at the reading circle and was ready for the second group to move from seatwork to reading. She had the target group put their seatwork away and stand. Then she called each child, one by one, to take his seat at the reading circle.

Kounin found smoothness and momentum to be significant factors in successful movement management. The two dimensions are conducive not only to better work involvement but also to better behavior of children.

BEING ALERT AND OBSERVANT

Be observant of and attentive to what is going on in your classroom and convey this alertness to your pupils. In his studies of groups of elementary students, Kounin found that a teacher's having "eyes in the back of the head" is a quality that is conducive to better classroom control. He called this attribute "withitness."

On the matter of "withitness," it is important to remember, for example, that many classes particularly require teacher alertness while the teacher is writing on the chalkboard. In a class inclined to be unruly, for instance, the teacher would be wise to assume a position at the board that will allow for turns and, in general, a see-out-of-the-corner-of-your-eye stance and alertness, in order to be ready to deal with disciplinary cases should they arise. The important matter is that the teacher seek to convey to the children an awareness of what goes on in the classroom and the judgment to act when action is required.

Kounin likewise found the quality of "overlapping" to be conducive to a higher level of disciplinary control in the classroom. This attribute is essentially the ability of a teacher to take care of two necessary functions almost simultaneously. For instance, the teacher who is able to attend to the initiator of trouble in the seatwork circle and at the same time remain with the reading circle and show cognizance of the progress of a child who is reading, through such things as appropriate praise or comment, is managing an overlapping situation. An ability to handle simultaneously more than one classroom detail communicates to the pupils the kind of teacher alertness that makes for better discipline. In summary, demonstrated "withitness" and manifest "overlapping" contribute to greater managerial success.

REQUIRING NOTEBOOKS TO BE KEPT

The keeping of an effective notebook teaches orderliness and organization, worthwhile accomplishments for any youngster. Certainly for those
who eventually go on to college, the extent to which they can take adequate
notes and organize their material properly will, in many instances, determine
the degree of success they will have in certain of their courses. But even for
the students who will go to work after their high school years, good training in the keeping of notebooks is important. Businesses often complain
about the incompetent, lax, and unorganized work of young people. Proper
training in orderliness and organization, then, should also pay dividends
in the workaday world.

Students, however, must be helped to take notes properly. For a period
of time they will need assistance with regard to the taking and arranging of
notes and with respect to determining what notes are essential to record.
For the most part, the brighter pupils and students in the higher grades
will gain proficiency in taking notes more quickly than the slower pupils
and the younger children. Of very great importance is the allotting of time
for notebook training in accordance with the needs of the particular group
in question. And let it be stressed that the keeping of notebooks should be
emphasized from the lower elementary grades through senior high school.

It is good procedure to have students feel that careful note-taking is an
important aspect of their work. This may be done in several ways or in a
combination of these ways: (1) There may be formal notebook inspection
before each marking period. (2) Students may be questioned orally on specific materials that they should have recorded in their notebooks. (3) When
students are asked to give certain information, such remarks as "You must
remember recording these essential points in your notebook" or "How does
your notebook read?" may be made. (4) Essential materials that have been
recorded in student notebooks may be included in quizzes and examinations.
(5) And occasionally students may be given open-notebook tests.

As long as notes are legible, well organized, and accurate, students should
receive ample credit. Pupils should be discouraged from feeling that it is
satisfactory to copy someone else's notebook the night before notebooks
are to be inspected, if there is to be an inspection. Such last-minute scurry-
ing about to meet requirements defeats much of the real purpose of notebook keeping. Pupils should be trained to look upon the keeping of a
notebook as an aid that is cumulative in procedure. These young people
must be made to realize that the primary purposes for requiring the keeping
of notebooks are (1) to help each individual pupil exercise discriminatory
judgment in selecting and recording essential content of a particular course,
(2) to help pupils gain proficiency in organizing and arranging important

subject-matter material, and (3) to help the pupils realize the pertinency of good notebook keeping to effective learning and to being successful in responding to oral and written tests or examinations. But also, a major point of stress is the very essential part notebook keeping plays in promoting good discipline. Effective note-taking and notebook keeping not only help to promote a sense of organization on the part of young people and greater competence in classwork but also help to keep students constructively busy. And pupils who are gainfully engaged have far fewer opportunities for misbehavior.

SCHEDULING A VARIETY OF ACTIVITIES

In scheduling the activities of the classroom, allow your class ample opportunity for the release of suppressed energy and emotions. It is not wise to hold the youngsters tightly for long periods of time. Your pupils need some time to let off steam or to get rid of pent-up energy and emotions. If legitimate provisions aren't made for these outbursts, emotions will continue to well up until they result in explosive behavior problems.

In elementary school where pupils remain in a single classroom, excess energy may be released in a variety of ways. For example, highly concentrated activity like the study of problems in mathematics and of difficult issues in social studies may be interspersed with less demanding activity. Pupils may at times gain ample release through such appropriately scheduled activities as role playing, the establishment of identity with characters in language arts, creative writing, music, dancing, and arts and crafts. In some of their various classes, secondary students too will have access to some of these forms of release. But in the junior and senior high school where pupils change classes by the period, the change of periods itself serves as a type of release. Additionally, prework that precedes the classwork proper is free from excess tightness, since the presession requires only reasonable orderliness but not a high level of quiet. And on all levels, audiovisual aids, demonstrations, and other illustrative devices as well as the use of varied teaching techniques may serve as planned means of keeping the pupils from becoming bored and restless. Finally, teachers of all levels should be encouraged to have their classes engage in brief physical exercises as a means of releasing class tension and pent-up energy. Let it be emphasized that exercising is a powerful type of release.

KEEPING THE ROOM ATTRACTIVE

An attractive room helps to make the students far more receptive to learning than does a drab, untidy room. A classroom that appeals to youngsters helps to add the warmth and mood that are favorable to positive or constructive endeavor. With respect to an appealing room, it is to be remembered that students are favorably affected by attractive bulletin board displays. These exhibits may consist of display work which relates to the immediate work of the classroom, to a pertinent subject area in general, or to some special occasion or event of great moment. It is to be borne in mind, too, that students get a great amount of satisfaction and encouragement from helping to make the classroom educationally appealing through a display of their own classwork.

BEHAVING WITH DECORUM

Avoid distractive dress, and behave with decorum. A teacher who is neatly and attractively dressed is easy for youngsters to look at and therefore plays an important role in making the classroom climate inviting. On the contrary, attire that is not in good taste or is too farfetched can draw pupils' attention away from the work of the class.

Women, in particular, will be wise to avoid wearing clothing that is too provocative, overly tight sweaters and skirts being one example. In the upper classes, the female teacher's wearing of provocative attire, sitting atop desks in a careless manner, and nestling too close to the boys when giving them assistance have been known both to distract attention from the teaching and to incite the ire of girls of the class who consider the teacher to be flirting with the boys. The male teacher who uses his position to put the girls in a romantic dither is likewise begging for the type of familiarity that leads to problems in discipline. Teachers as a whole, male and female, need to be observant and to exercise discretion in matters of dress and teacher decorum.

AFFECTIVE ANTIDOTES
FOR PROBLEMS IN DISCIPLINE

The term "human relations," in a broad sense, characterizes the focus
of this chapter. The tenets that are advocated pertain to the feeling or emotional relationship. The precepts are positive, constructive ones. In essence,
they are affective principles which seek to build in pupils such sense of
self-worth as will aid them in being receptive to learning, but antagonistic
to adverse behavior. Taking the welfare of students to heart and establishing
rapport with these young pupils are important considerations of this section. The affective tenets outlined below may play the positive or preventive
role of minimizing and counteracting numerous problems in discipline.

SETTING LIMITS

Remember that your class members want the secure feeling of knowing
that limits have been set. In the preceding chapter, the part that setting
limits plays in good management was elaborated. It now remains to be said
that youngsters expect teachers to be on their toes in proposing guidelines
that will make for a well-ordered class. Setting limits gives your pupils a
sense of security. That students like the secure feeling of knowing what is
expected of them is demonstrated in this report of quite a conscientious
fifth-grade teacher.

When she failed to set behavior limits for her class, her very uninhibited
group of youngsters notified her, "Teacher, you too easy." This alert teacher
reminded herself that if those young pupils were insightful enough to voice
their need for limits and security, she should certainly be enterprising
enough to change her tactics. When the teacher, following her students'

suggestion, set and announced sound limits which her pupils could plainly see she intended to enforce, her outspoken class members did not fail to inform her, "We like you like this."

The following report exemplifies youth's respect for limits from both the school and the home. It is the case of a youngster who lacked limits in her own home.

Three ninth-grade girls suddenly began to cut certain of their classes to hang around in the lavatories and smoke and to misbehave in other unbecoming ways. Two of the young girls were from superior homes, and seemingly well reared. These two girls were very much hurt when the assistant principal requested that their parents come to school in connection with their misbehavior. One of the two girls cried so profusely and promised so faithfully not to give trouble in the future that both her teachers and the assistant principal were sympathetic toward her. The third young girl, unfortunately, was her own little woman. Her father and mother were separated, and neither parent exercised very much control over her life. She went where she pleased and when she pleased, and acted as she wished. She was quite impudent to most of her teachers. But she felt it a very great honor to be associated with the two girls from the superior homes. As the three girls returned to one of their classes after having been in conference with teachers, the assistant principal, and the parents of the first two girls mentioned, the third girl, whose parent had not reported to school, announced loudly: "You just wait until I get home. My mother's going to kill me about my behavior."

Of course, it was obvious that the third girl's mother would do nothing of the kind, and that, in reality, she was powerless to do anything to her young daughter. It is indeed pathetic when a youngster has to pretend that there is enough parental love, concern, and control to set for her proper limits and accompanying security. Most assuredly, young people both expect and need limits and the security that such limits promote.

MAINTAINING FIRM CONTROL

Be relatively firm at the beginning of the term, relaxing the reins only as you find that you may do so without losing control of the class. To be firm means to be sufficiently strict, or reasonably free from laxness. To be firm means that you must have the determination or steadfastness to carry out standards and rules that make for a well-disciplined class.

The need for firmness in classrooms of the various grade levels and of the diverse age groups is readily observable. The following case, for instance, is indicative of a type of situation that demands firmness if the class is to be saved from fast deterioration.

The members of a first-grade class were reassembling at a rectangular table for a repast, after having had a brief break that followed a regular recitation session. One youngster refused to be orderly enough for the serving of food to proceed in a normal manner. He was roaming about from place to place at the table tampering with various pupils' plates and spoons and in diverse ways pestering classmates. The regular teacher asked a little boy whose seat was next to her own to take another seat in order that the misbehaving youngster might sit next to her. The disorderly child not only refused to sit where he had been requested to sit but moved first to one then to another of the vacant seats that were farthest away from the teacher. She continued to repeat her request to the child in a tone that made it obvious that she knew her attempt to have the boy take a seat near hers was in vain. It was only when the teacher aide pointed to the seat next to the regular teacher's seat telling the youngster to sit there where he had been told to sit, in the tone of "I mean do nothing short of that . . . now," that the boy took the designated seat and behaved himself. It is not difficult to visualize how the group as a whole could get out of hand if a teacher repeatedly failed to exercise necessary firmness in connection with various individual members of the class.

On the matter of what constitutes firmness, there are certain kinds of teacher action that communicate to the child the idea of firmness. The following list is inclusive of some of those actions. It may be clearly noted that the list is made up of two important main ingredients: an emphatic request for action and a follow-through on the request (Kounin, 1970).

In giving an order, make a clear break from the activity in progress in order that the stress may be on the request made.

Use an emphatic voice which implies that you expect compliance, rather than a casual, hesitant, or uncertain voice.

Look at the person while issuing the order (as if to give the warning signal "In a moment, I'll . . .")

Use the tone of voice "I mean do this" or "I intend for you to carry out this request now," and pause and wait until the pupil acts appropriately rather than go on to another activity, as if you have left it with the child to comply or not according to his own decision.

Repeat the order for emphasis, but not in the tone of failure.

Move in the direction of the child with "I mean it" eyes fixed upon him.

Direct the pupil to the requested place or position (by the hand, if a small child and if necessary; or by such action as pointing or signaling) while giving the youngster the stern eye of "Do as I say," until he responds.

Teachers must come to realize their remissness in duty when sufficient firmness is not exerted to prevent individual deviancy from having a demoralizing effect or when the reins aren't taut enough to keep the action of class members as a whole from destroying the class. The importance of this tenet cannot be overemphasized. To be assured of a productive class-room, it is indeed wise to be relatively firm at the beginning of the term, relaxing the reins only as this may be done without loss of the control of the class. A failure to observe this tenet may cause teachers to encounter numerous and unnecessary disciplinary problems. It is well to mention here, too, that it is better to be too strict in the beginning stages than to be too lax, since youngsters are oftentimes resentful when a teacher attempts to take away liberties which were formerly granted them, if indeed it doesn't become utterly too late to retrieve such unwarrantable freedom. With some classes, a teacher can conveniently begin to loosen the reins sooner than with others, as the different class groups vary considerably with respect to potential troublemaking. And finally, by way of further pointing up the importance of this tenet in providing for good discipline in the classroom, it is of significance to note the following case of a student teacher who be-gan class with far too much laxity only to regret later the dilemma he found himself in when his twelfth-grade students began to take advantage of what they considered to be a teacher too lenient.

Previous to doing his student teaching he had asked, "What is all this business about discipline?" This young man had a false sense of the part permissiveness should play in the classroom. In his opinion, rules, regula-tions, or limits were taboo and undemocratic. "Let the students be natural," he felt—which, in his mind, was synonymous with saying, "Let the students be free to act as they see fit." During the semester he did his student teach-ing, his class was in a turmoil. In reality, his group was comprised of rather good-natured youngsters. They simply misused the practically complete freedom they had been granted; and the student teacher was unable to retrieve the class where matters of discipline were concerned. Answers were continually shouted out by groups of students. The most serious classwork was transformed into jokes, and the student teacher was treated as just one more peer. This student teacher had failed to keep the reins taut until he could judge the degree of freedom the class could safely handle. It was far too late to retrieve class liberties when he came to realize that the failure to observe this basic tenet was causing him countless heartaches.

BEING FRIENDLY BUT NOT FAMILIAR

Be warm, kind, and friendly, and show that you have the students' welfare at heart; but don't be familiar. It is indeed possible to show warm, kind interest in the children's welfare and yet not be familiar. In short, it is not necessary to be "buddy-buddy" with pupils to show that you are a regular guy or gal. The respect and real love of the students may not be purchased in this manner. But a genuine interest in the well-being of your pupils will help them to respect you and to have confidence in you as a teacher. It is a fact that even very small children can sense the warmth and real concern of a genuinely interested teacher.

It is altogether possible for a teacher to be sufficiently firm or strict at the beginning of a given school term and yet be warm, kind, and friendly at the same time. The teacher who patiently helps the student who is struggling to answer a question or the teacher who gives extra help or individual attention to the pupil who has fallen behind in classwork is expressing warmth, kindness, friendliness, and concern without any lowering of disciplinary standards. In short, it is appropriate for a teacher to be warm, kind, friendly, and interested in the students' welfare while remaining sufficiently firm until reins may be safely relaxed without the loss of class control.

INJECTING A SENSE OF HUMOR

Generally, students look very favorably upon the teacher who, in the process of executing classroom duties, can inject a sense of humor. To the student this is an assurance that the teacher is alive and human. In fact, one study which revealed high school seniors' reasons for choice of "best" teacher placed sense of humor second on the list of teacher traits liked by the selected group of students (Riccio and Cyphert, 1962). A similar study made of junior high school pupils revealed sense of humor as fifth on the list of teacher traits admired by pupils (Riccio and Cyphert). And two educators listed sense of humor among seven qualities of a good teacher (Cutts and Moseley, 1959). Indeed, a warm sense of humor on the part of the teacher may often play a vital role in strengthening the teacher-pupil relationship. Yet a teacher must judge carefully as to when the time is ripe for employing a sense of humor in a given class. Very early in the term, some classes can accept the teacher's sense of humor without responding by taking undue liberties. In dealing with other groups, the teacher may need to wait until it is safe to relax taut reins considerably before employing a sense of humor freely without unwholesome repercussions from the students.

KNOWING YOUR STUDENTS

The idea of being well acquainted with one's pupils might well be referred to as "knowing one's customers." A teacher who knows his customers well has a firm foundation upon which to establish rapport. Needless to say, the more wholesome the relationship between pupils and teacher, the greater the chance for curtailing problems in behavior. Following are some of the diverse means of gathering important information regarding your students.

Initial survey of the students' environment. It would be helpful if before meeting the new students for the term the teacher would survey the socio-economic and cultural conditions or surroundings from which the pupils come. This study would allow the teacher to bring to the classroom more realistic ideas of what to expect from the youngsters and of how to establish with them meaningful relationships.

Cumulative records. A cumulative record is a comprehensive record of a student, which is compiled over a period of time. This record travels with the pupil from elementary to junior high school, then from junior high to senior high school. Unfortunately, too many cumulative folders are distressingly incomplete. Ideally, it would certainly be expected that the cumulative record of a student would include full information on such matters as scholastic grades; reading scores; results of I. Q., achievement, aptitude, and personality tests; the student's health record; record of special commendations, of awards, and of services rendered; anecdotal records; and record of the pupil's family background. Despite the frequent incompleteness of cumulative records, however, teachers should consult them, for whatever information is available will be of some help in dealing with the particular pupils in question.

A prior scrutiny of the cumulative folders of students whom a teacher will be teaching should normally be of very great help to the teacher in terms of gathering information on what may reasonably be expected of the students, on how to meet student needs, and on how to cope more effectively with group and individual problems. There are those, however, who strongly feel unable to make a prior investigation of class members' cumulative folders without being prejudiced by negative findings. And perhaps it should be said that such teachers should refrain from making the suggested prior study, for the sake of justice. It is to be remembered, nonetheless, that the ideal goal is that the teacher be able to use the varied information from cumulative records as clues to working with pupils to greater advantage.

Direct observation. Much helpful information needed for working advantageously with students may be gathered through the watchful eye of an interested and discerning teacher. For the pupils' benefit, the teacher should endeavor to be increasingly more observant.

Oral and written reports. Likes, dislikes, special interests, capabilities, ambitions, problems, frustrations, and a wealth of other data may be revealed through oral and written reports. At times, a teacher may wish to structure the required report so as to obtain from the students a special type of information that would be particularly helpful in working with them.

Private talks. As is true with oral and written reports, varied information may be gathered through the private conference. In fact, many of the kinds of information obtained through reports may likewise be gathered through private talks. The private conference, of course, has the additional attraction of the one-for-one relationship between pupil and teacher. Such a conference is an outstanding morale builder, because it gives the pupil a feeling of importance in being able to meet with the teacher face to face.

A study of the characteristic behavior of young people. In studying the behavior that is characteristic of youth, the teacher will need to give close attention to situations that provoke negative reactions or misbehavior. A teacher should become fully aware of danger signals that could possibly erupt into trouble, in order to work toward what may be done to try to offset the storm.

Some youngsters may not be able to adjust readily at school and stay out of trouble because of difficulties that are the result of such handicaps as physical illness, physical or emotional needs, poor home environment, or negative qualities that are characteristic of the age group with which the teacher is dealing. The teacher is challenged to observe carefully a pupil's difficulty and to instigate appropriate steps for diminishing or correcting the unwholesome situations. The child who is constantly inclined to misbehave or defy regulations has a problem which should be discovered and treated.

In some instances, ill health or a physical handicap may interfere with the youngster's learning and cause him to become helplessly aggressive as well. Very frequently, children with physical defects come from homes where the parents have not sought treatment because they are victims of poverty, low intelligence, ignorance, indifference, or a combination of these factors. When a teacher suspects a physical disability to be the source of the pupil's disorderly conduct, he should remember, however, that he is a teacher and not a physician. He should neither attempt to diagnose the case nor prescribe any form of medication, lest he seriously err in trying to do so. Instead, it is the obligation of the teacher to do everything possible to secure the professional medical help the youngster needs and to obtain any professional guidance that may be needed for handling the behavior of the youth.

When a teacher takes a peep behind the scene to determine what factors may lead to misbehavior if not given proper attention, he would do well to take into full account certain basic physical and emotional needs which should be supplied. Physically, all children are in need of adequate food, clothing, rest, and shelter. Where any of these needs are seriously deficient, the youngster lacks the physical and mental vitality and emotional stability to respond as he should in the classroom. Instead, he easily succumbs to the type of irritability that is fertile ground for problems in discipline. The wise teacher will do what he can to improve the adverse circumstances through efforts to have the pupil's basic needs fulfilled.

With respect to the emotional aspect, every child wants to love and be loved. He wants this reciprocal relationship with family members, teachers, and peers. Each youngster wants the security of knowing that he will be well cared for, now and far into the future. Young people desire to be sufficiently recognized, in the home, among their peers, and in the classroom. When any of these emotional needs substantially lack fulfillment, the deficiencies could become the source of a whole spectrum of behavioral problems. Ideally speaking, parents are the main fountainhead for satisfying their youth's needs in all areas. Teachers, of course, are certainly expected to play a major role in supplementing parental efforts; and where parents virtually fail to supply the physical and emotional needs of their children, teachers will do well to strive relentlessly to fill the void if they expect to diminish the pupils' chance of becoming behavior problems and possibly maladjusted youngsters. The teacher who can show pupils who crave love that he sincerely likes them has an excellent chance of reaching the youths and establishing a warm relationship with them. Similarly, the teacher who observes youngsters to be in need of recognition and helps them find a respectable and praiseworthy place in the class and peer group can help to satisfy the pupils' yearning and pave the way for wholesome teacher–pupil relations as well.

The conditions that could make for a youngster's unhappy home life are many. There may be constant bickering between the parents, or perhaps there may be a divorce or desertion. It may be that the family is stricken with poverty, or there may be chronic illness on the part of one parent. Perhaps there has been a death in the immediate family. In some instances, one parent may be mentally ill or an alcoholic. The mother may be a prostitute or the father or mother a criminal. The neighborhood may be one in which fights frequently occur and gangs hang out. One parent may be overprotective, the other too strict; or it's possible that one or both parents may be inconsistent in handling the child. There may be insufficient time to spend with the youth, a lack of love for the youngster, or even a rejection of him.

Though most of these situations are far more prevalent in ghetto areas than in the more advantaged neighborhoods, it is clearly evident that a great many of the conditions take their toll among middle- and upper-class families as well. Any one or any combination of the conditions noted, if not given adequate attention or appropriately compensated for, could lead to a child's frustration and subsequently to his inclination to misbehave. In many instances, if youngsters from the kinds of surroundings we've been describing are not given sufficient attention in the home, they try to obtain the love and security they've missed by being overly aggressive showoffs at school. This bid to gain attention makes them continually more obnoxious and less likely to get the accepting audience they seek.

In attempting to acquire a clear understanding of what the possible behavior patterns of young people are, parents as well as teachers might well benefit by reading references that will help them see the whole sweep of development of our young Americans. Under the headings "Public Affairs Committee" and "U. S. Government Printing Office" in the Bibliography are listed a number of inexpensive pamphlets of great value.

A teacher who is well versed in the developmental patterns of growth would, for instance, be expected to be sensitive to the yearnings of children of late childhood to be accepted by the gang. With thoughtful guidance, such a teacher may be able to help an unhappy isolate replace unacceptable behavior with that which is more likely to be approved by the group. Perhaps, for example, it can be brought to the awareness of the striving youngster that his tendency to argue so much, to make unpleasant remarks about fellow classmates, or to talk too much about himself decreases his chances of being approved by the group to which he strives to belong. A child who feels accepted is less likely to become a noisome problem in discipline. The teacher who is aware of the state of fatigue and listlessness brought on by rapid growth and bodily changes during puberty is in a position to be appropriately considerate of youngsters in this stage of development and to be certain not to pile on them such large assignments as to embitter the youths and cause them undue strain. And the teacher who observes that an early adolescent is being overlooked because he is colorless and has so little to offer is at a vantage point to help the youth put the best he has on parade.

SHOWING INTEREST IN YOUR STUDENTS

Inquiring about a student's relative who has been ill, complimenting another student for rendering some type of service to the school, informing still another student that you heard about his performance at a basketball game, and good-naturedly showing interest in various concerns of the pupils can go a long way toward helping a teacher establish the rapport, respect, and student cooperation that make for a well-disciplined class. Youngsters welcome the interest and concern of the teacher so long as it is not a nosy delving into their private affairs.

One young man, for instance, was extolled for the warm rapport that existed between his students and himself, for the great amount of respect the youngsters had for him, and, in general, for the success he had achieved in handling his class. When asked to what he attributed his favorable results, his response, in essence, was that to a great extent he gained his students' respect, love, and cooperation through his warm expression of interest in his pupils' individual affairs or concerns.

BEING FAIR AND GRADING FAIRLY

Anonymous questions and comments submitted by groups of prospective teachers have indicated that high on the list of disciplinary concerns is the teacher aspirants' anxiety over being respected by the pupils. It cannot be overemphasized that being fair is one of the very effective means of helping to assure a teacher of the respect and goodwill of students. And teachers who can convince their pupils that genuine efforts are being made toward the achievement of fairness can make great strides toward the realization of a well-disciplined class, so great is the students' respect for what is just.

It is a fact that some students are far more likable than others. Nonetheless, it is incumbent upon each teacher to refrain from favoritism and to strive, in every way possible, to be fair. Youngsters are quite sophisticated in sensing the sincere efforts of a teacher toward fairness.

Being fair, however, does not always mean treating every person in exactly the same way. This point may be amply illustrated through an account of one college professor's method of assigning prospective teachers to public schools, for an Observation-Participation program.

One prospective teacher who was to be assigned to a school for the Observation-Participation activities was a woman sixty-five years of age. Before the assignments had been made, the sixty-five-year-old college student informed her professor that she could obtain the consent of a principal to observe in his school, which was only a few steps from her home. Although it was the policy of the college instructor to assign the future teachers to schools rather than let each student seek his own placement, the instructor laid aside the regulations for this one student. It was the feeling of the professor that if that student, at sixty-five, had the will-power to work for her degree with a view to becoming a teacher, she deserved special consideration. The other members of the college class gave evidence of being very much in favor of the professor's decision, even though some of them had hoped to arrange for their own placement but had been denied the opportunity. Obviously, it was the feeling of the younger prospective teachers that if any of them had been sixty-five, they too would have received the special consideration. And so it is with elementary and secondary pupils as well. If they can get the feeling that the teacher will make a sincere effort to handle their cases according to the particular circumstances involved rather than in accordance with the extent to which the individual student is liked, the pupils will consider the teacher to be fair.

All teachers will find it valuable to keep a record book that is indicative of a conscientious effort to grade all pupils fairly. It should be possible to make the record available to any student who questions a grade at the end of a marking period. Usually, students who question the fairness of a grade at the end of the first marking period go away well satisfied, never to return with a question of impropriety in grading, when they are allowed to inspect a record book which shows that the teacher has put forth a great amount of effort to work out a marking scheme that is honest and impartial. And it is altogether possible for a student to see his own grade in relationship to the teacher's total marking scheme for the class without his being permitted to meddle with grades given to other pupils.

The following additional points pertinent to fairness in grading are offered. The issues raised should at least help the teacher grade pupils with a greater sense of confidence.

The teacher may bring a greater amount of objectivity to subjective evaluation by determining specifically what content is to be evaluated. If essay questions are to be graded, for instance, it will be helpful for the teacher to prepare for each question a key of the content that is expected as an answer, together with the weight or points to be given to each part of the expected content. By this method, the grading becomes more objective and fairer, in the provisions made to grade all pupils as nearly on the same basis as possible.

There is no final answer with respect to what factors should make up a grade. Usually, however, such components as "achievement," "effort," "improvement," "cooperation," and "extra work" are the ingredients on which pupil grades are based.

How much weight the various ingredients of a grade should receive or how the weight should be distributed within a single ingredient is another matter which is not at all conclusive. For instance, whether or not the teacher will wish to give one third for the final examination; another third for daily response, effort, and special oral and written work; and a final third for improvement, extra work, and cooperation; or whether the teacher will wish to use some other division of the factors that make up the grade must be left with the ingenuity of the teacher. The important consideration is that the teacher devise a method of grading the students that will convince them and their parents of genuine teacher effort toward fairness. *Grading pupils fairly is not synonymous with grading them in accordance with the Normal Curve of Distribution.* Since the Normal Curve was standardized on very large random samplings, it does not justifiably apply to the groups of from about twenty to thirty-five pupils one finds in the average classroom. Besides, most classes give some semblance of a homogeneous grouping, and it would not be reasonable to insist that a bell-shaped grading pattern come out of relatively homogeneous groups. Thus, when a teacher is ready to make up grades for a particular subject, it is not reasonable to expect him to determine how many pupils will receive A's in order to reach a conclusion on how many F's must be given. Neither is it logical for the teacher to work diligently to give the same number of B's and D's. And finally, there would be no justification in the teacher's insisting that the majority of the students must make C's in a class that consists of pupils of similar rank.

COMING TO TERMS WITH "RINGLEADERS"

To the reader who questions including "ringleaders" with positive or preventive measures by reason of the fact that these persons have already been identified as potential troublemakers, it might be said that the focus here is the attempt to prevent such leaders from spoiling the whole tone or atmosphere of the class through their detrimental influence on fellow classmates. Many teachers can perhaps call to mind potential ringleaders who, by words or action, even by the mere flicker of the eye, can command a following among the class members that can produce demoralizing effects in the classroom. A major aim, then, is to try to direct a leader's negative inclinations into positive, constructive channels. In order to effect such direction, it is necessary to win the goodwill of the belligerent youngster.

The following means have worked well in winning goodwill or in establishing rapport with the potential leader: (1) giving the student monitorial responsibilities that bring pride to him, (2) giving the pupil special recognition for improvement in an area where he has previously had difficulty, and (3) helping the young person to gain class-wide recognition through encouraging him to make worthwhile contributions to the class, based on his own special interests, aptitudes, or strong points. The efficacy of a teacher's establishing rapport with a potential ringleader may be clearly illustrated through the following case of a secondary pupil.

X was a very pronounced potential spoiler in most of his classes. However, his English teacher had the foresight to attempt to establish rapport with him through capitalizing on his outstanding ability and interest in spelling. He was allowed to help both with the compiling of spelling lists and with the administering of spelling lessons and tests. He gained such a sense of well-being over his responsibilities, which he executed with pride and proficiency, that one could virtually see his chest protrude with pride. He really liked the teacher for making him feel important. Needless to say, he saw to it that his classmates didn't give that particular teacher any serious trouble, for where his eyes had formerly signaled the class members to join him in his antics, his cues were now for them to behave themselves, which they did.

Two cautions, however, are in order. First, it must not be construed that it is possible to establish rapport with potential ringleaders in one hundred percent of the cases, but success with channeling the potential negative behavior positively or with gaining the goodwill of the potential leader is certainly frequent enough to give the method a fair trial. Second, in trying to gain the goodwill of a potential ringleader, it would not be wise to bend over so far as to lose the respect of the class. Sound judgment must at all times be exercised.

BUILDING A HEALTHY ATMOSPHERE

It is the responsibility of the teacher to set the proper tone in the classroom, which should be a pleasant one where pupils, by virtue of the climate, are encouraged to assume appropriate demeanor and to work. It must not be forgotten that, over a long period of time, a student spends a great amount of time in the classroom. It is the professional duty of the teacher to help to make this time palatable for all types of students. What a credit it is to the teaching profession, for instance, when pupils who come from various types of unwholesome home surroundings can at least look forward in eager anticipation to attending school where the atmosphere will be inviting and devoted teachers will welcome them warmly and with interest and concern. To build such a healthy classroom environment, however, a teacher must have due regard for the essential directives that follow.

Treat all of your students humanely, or with proper regard. It is a sad state of affairs but nonetheless true that there are some nonprofessional teachers, and far too many, who belittle certain of their pupils vilely, and many times in the presence of the students concerned. Such words as "stupid," "dumb," and "silly" and such statements as "This class can't learn" and "This class is not all there" flow freely in the classrooms of these unkindly teachers. And what is more, frequently when the teachers in question do not verbally utter such thoughts they clearly indicate that they bear the feelings toward their pupils that the derogatory terms suggest. It is no wonder that young people who are the victims of such treatment are oftentimes belligerent or hostile and lacking in feelings of self-worth. Fortunately, however, it has been shown that a great many of these student sufferers can make great strides in the caliber of schoolwork done and in resulting behavior, if given a fresh chance to prove themselves, through the genuine encouragement and help of discerning teachers.

Perhaps we should stress here that information regarding a student which one teacher passes on to another in a spirit of sincere helpfulness may be valuable for the pupil's future growth, but the willful derogating of a pupil on the part of a teacher is to be condemned. In any event, regardless of what a teacher may have heard about a student, either about his academic performance or his conduct, the teacher should not discourage the youngster or stand in the way of his improvement. The real point is that pupils have rights which the teacher who would be human must honor and respect. *Promote an attitude of mutual respect among your class members.* Teachers can go a long way in establishing such an atmosphere. Pupils in the schools are in their formative years and can be much influenced by the attitude of the teacher. For example, the teacher must not tolerate a pupil's ridicule of a classmate's sincere efforts to respond in class, no matter how inadequate the response may be. Instead, a teacher who is dedicated to the idea of mutual respect among class members will promote the attitude that perhaps teacher and fellow classmates might be helpful to the student who is struggling and in need of aid.

Another means by which the classroom teacher may help to build a tone of mutual respect among class members is through a genuine effort to help class isolates become acceptable members of the class group. Students will follow the lead of the teacher who makes an honest attempt to give isolated members a feeling of well-being in the group. Very frequently the teacher may move a great distance toward this end by discovering something, small or large, that the child can do well and by bringing this ability before the class for teacher and pupil encouragement and praise. The important matter is a classroom tone of consideration and acceptance.

Do not make your pupils suffer the sting of your personal problems. The teacher who expects to have a mentally healthy climate should bring to the classroom a sense of stability and mature adjustment. Pupils should not be made to suffer from sharp invectives, excessive shortness of patience, acrimonious replies, or unwarranted reprimands as a result of a teacher's personal problems. Indeed, everyone has problems from time to time, but being able to handle them in such a way that they do not overtax people with whom we must come in constant contact is a sign of healthy adjustment. This does not mean that the teacher should never give open vent to depressing feelings such as distress over a sudden tragedy to an immediate member of the family or friend, but the overall tenor of the teacher should be one that does not make the pupils suffer the sting of teacher problems.

CURBING UNDESIRABLE COMPETITION

Be conscious of the need to curb the type of competition that sets pupils sharply against each other in a harmful way. As a rule of thumb, disadvantaged pupils and youngsters from a more average background are less likely to suffer as many stings of competitiveness as their middle-class counterparts. This situation is not a difficult one to comprehend. Since the motivation for achieving is generally far less in the less advantaged homes than in the more advantaged ones, the pressures from competing are similarly less in less favored surroundings. However, motivation within the child to achieve is highly desirable, and it is an implantation of the desire to forge ahead that usually accounts for the success of young people, but where there is too much pressure on the child to achieve or where one youngster is placed sharply against another, the outcome can be unwholesome for the young people concerned. In order to make this point clear, let us cite an incident that involved a parent who was insatiably ambitious for his daughter.

The fourteen-year-old youngster had done exceedingly well at her junior high school. And now that this was the year for her to graduate, academically she could look forward to ranking either second or third in a graduating class of approximately three hundred ninth-graders. Sharon had done very well, not only in schoolwork proper, but in other areas as well. She had rendered a vast amount of service to the school. She'd written stories for the literary magazine and, in general, had been particularly helpful in making a contribution to the literary publication. And so it was that when Sharon's father came to check on his daughter's progress some months before her graduation, her teacher beamed with delight when she gave him the excellent report on his daughter. But to the teacher's astonishment, the father just sat there with a poker face expressing no amount of appreciation for his youngster's accomplishments. Then finally he asked about the status of one of Sharon's classmates, Elaine. "But is my daughter as good a student as Elaine?" he asked. The teacher knew that the salutatorian of the class would be either Elaine or Sharon, both of whom were excellent students and outstanding contributors to the programs of the school, but she was much too professional to discuss the affairs of another pupil with a non-family member. On Commencement Day, Elaine was the salutatorian and won a few more awards than Sharon. Figuratively speaking, Sharon's father swelled as big as any frog you've ever seen. He was angry with all the teachers and in fact with the entire school, so much so that Sharon tried to explain to some of the teachers: "My father may not be so understanding, but my mother is. Besides, there's still high school."

How pathetic it is when a child has to apologize for a parent who puts undue competitive pressure on his young one.

It becomes the obligation of teachers who observe the victims of undue competitiveness to do what they can to minimize and help eliminate the source of the youngsters' difficulty, even when this means apprising the parents of the extent to which their child is being adversely affected by the unwholesome rivalry or when this means encouraging any professional help that might be needed.

It is recognized that we are members of a competitive world, but there are types of competition that are less brutal than that which sets one youngster sharply against another in a detrimental way. It would be helpful for both parent and teacher to remember that perhaps the most healthy type of competition for our young people is the kind that encourages the youngster to compete with himself, to strive to improve or outdo what he has previously done, to endeavor to make the most of his own potential while de-emphasizing the capabilities someone else may have. However, when two youngsters elect to compete of their own accord, the results are not likely to be disastrous, for in this instance the youths have already made the determination to accept the outcome, whatever it may be. Teachers are further reminded that group games which involve competition are generally wholesome. Since, in this instance, it is an entire team that wins or loses, no individual pupil needs to feel himself unduly under pressure.

As already indicated, in classes where the pupils as a whole have not been highly motivated through the homes, it will certainly be the responsibility of teachers to try to stimulate these youths to achieve to optimum extent, but teachers will usually find that pupils with the backgrounds we are now describing are more likely to take in their stride the accomplishments of their peers. More specifically, they are generally far less worried about individuals who surpass them in achievement than are youngsters from homes where the parents have prodded them into trying to excel or compete favorably with superior achievers. Consequently it is particularly within this latter group that the teacher must be concerned about relieving pressures when the atmosphere becomes too competitive.

At times it may be necessary that the teacher de-emphasize grades. In addition, he may need to take special care to keep the grades of individual class members a private matter, in order to help curb unhealthy competition. In fact, the grade each student makes is a private affair whether or not the group is a highly motivated one, and this privacy should be honored. If various pupils choose to display their own grades, this is quite a different matter. And it might well be pointed out that when it becomes important to divulge the level of work done by the class as a whole the grades made may easily be read without associating name with the grade received.

We need to motivate or stimulate youth to make good of their potentials, but as we do so we must guard against setting one individual against another in ways that my be detrimental to their emotional well-being. Wherever the effect of competition is becoming unhealthy, it is the obligation of teachers and parents to curtail it.

GRANTING RECOGNITION, REWARDS, AND PRAISE

Even the blustering youth with a chip on his shoulder likes to be recognized, though he may convey the idea that nothing matters to him. There seems to be a natural propensity for recognition. Yet academically speaking, by far the majority of the students are not top achievers. It stands to reason, then, that classroom teachers will need to use a variety of means of satisfying pupil need for the recognition that plays such a dynamic role in building within the person a worthy self-image. May a pupil, for instance, who is a poor student in most of his subjects be recognized for his noteworthy work in one subject area? May a student who, for the most part, has a poor grasp of a particular subject receive recognition for a special phase of that subject in which he has some proficiency? Is it possible that an average or below-average youngster who has a special talent in art, dancing, music, sports, or in some other area might be called upon at pertinent times to give of his special talent or knowledge for the enrichment of a social studies class, English class, or some other class? It should be of significance to teachers that frequently when a youngster is recognized for any one aspect of achievement, the satisfaction that he experiences is a source of encouragement in his total school efforts.

Remember that the granting of rewards can enhance your pupils' sense of well-being. It goes without saying that the greater the sense of worth a pupil feels, the less likely he is to give trouble in behavior. The kinds of rewards that may be granted are diverse. There are the regular types of prizes for various kinds of achievement, displays of students' work that bring about a great amount of student pride and satisfaction, commendation cards for special services rendered, as well as many other types of compensation. But an important reminder to the teacher is that in addition to rewards given to the brighter pupils, an adequate proportion of rewards should be given to average and below-average students for achievement and for such accomplishments as unusual effort and outstanding improvement or growth. In short, it is to be remembered that average and below-average pupils, who are often largely overlooked when rewards are bestowed, can be much encouraged by the recognition that comes from such remunerations. There follow accounts of two systems of rewards that were productive. The first system had its setting in an elementary school.

Recently, the author was in the company of an elementary school principal who was escorting a few guests around his school. He indeed had something he could proudly display. Practically all the classrooms from first grade to sixth—the classrooms of average, bright, and slow children—were most appealingly decked with colorful and attractive displays. A representative portion of the displays, of course, consisted of student work and commendation cards. As the principal traveled from room to room he asked various students questions about the work they had on display and requested others to explain how some of the class commendation cards had been won. Faces glowed in obvious satisfaction as the pupils received added recognition for the rewards that had already been granted them. There was ample evidence that worthwhile learning was taking place. It was a background conducive to constructive classwork and demeanor.

The second system of rewards was implemented in a junior high school. It was a highly effective venture associated with a "Readers-Leaders" program.

All students who had read at least six books during the school term marched onto the auditorium stage and were presented "Reader" buttons. Pupils who had read twelve books were given "Leader" buttons. The poor readers were permitted to consider several short stories, several essays, or several other shorter pieces of work to be the equivalent of a book. It was a delight to see how chests expanded with pride as youngsters strutted onto the stage to receive their buttons. A great many students had become readers as a result of the "Readers-Leaders" program. One young fellow, who was thought by all to be far below average, liked the idea of being called a "Reader" so much that after receiving his first reward, he was rarely seen without a book under his arm. And, strangely enough, he could actually give a respectable account of his books. The rewards served a worthwhile purpose in that junior high school.

Generous praise has been known to improve both the quality of classwork and the level of classroom behavior. Some pupils, however, are in considerably greater need of praise than others. Getting to know your customers is one of the safest guides to the amount of praise needed by individual class members.

To praise a child, however, does not mean to praise insincerely. Rather, it means picking out some factor, however small, for which you may offer the child sincere praise and encouragement. At times, this may mean praise for notable accomplishment; at other times, praise for meager advancement; and at still other times, praise merely for sincere effort. The important matter is to offer your pupils the type of support that will encourage advancement.

KEEPING STUDENTS ALERT

Students who are kept alive, alert, and a part of the group are kept under the type of control that provides very little time for adverse behavior. There are important steps the teacher might take to help promote the desired type of teacher–class togetherness or communication.

Maintain eye contact with your students. Eye contact is directly related to effective communication and to bringing the pupils within your grasp. Look at your various class members as you conduct the lesson, not at the ceiling, floor, and outside surroundings. This not only keeps them alert and under control, but also lets each student know, personally, that he is an important part of the class.

As a general rule, move about when you teach; and when advantageous, circulate among your students. You will at times find it helpful to move about freely across the front of the room as you conduct your lesson. At other times, you will find it advantageous to move among your students or up and down portions of the outside or inner aisles. Free, relaxed movement can prevent you from giving the appearance of a tense, stilted mentor and in addition can aid considerably in keeping your students interested, lively, and well behaved. It is possible that as you circulate among your students you will be able to bring some potential troublemaker to attention merely with a firm look or light touch from the hand, without distracting the attention of the entire class. Still an added advantage of the teacher's circulating among the students is the greater assurance of proper voice projection. Teachers with weak or soft voices may be helped by moving closer to the students. The more appropriate the communication, the greater chance there is of keeping your students well within your grasp.

Standing while you teach is generally more advantageous than sitting. There are times, however, when a teacher will wish to sit in a circle with group discussants or in a reading circle. These are two of the types of exceptions that are certainly to be encouraged. As a general rule, however, the teacher who stands can do a better job keeping a class alive, interested, and reasonably controlled than can the teacher who conducts class from behind the teacher's desk. And particularly does the beginning teacher who tries to be a "sitter" run the dangerous risk of losing the type of control of the class that may generally be realized when the teacher is enthusiastically moving among the students in such manner as to keep the pupils alert and on their toes.

BEING CONCERNED FOR ALL STUDENTS

As part of your philosophy, accept the position that to you all students are of equal concern. Some teachers like bright classes and express their aversion for borderline and slow pupils. Other teachers prefer average and slow pupils, not out of real concern for them, but out of a mistaken belief that no class preparation is required to work with them. And, alas, it must be said that there are some teachers who refuse expression of due concern, regardless of the types of students with whom they work. Yet it is amazing how quickly and accurately students get the message when they are grudgingly tolerated. But, on a happier note, there are the dedicated teachers who genuinely give of themselves to all of the various types of students—average, slow, and bright. The hope of education lies in individual teacher acceptance of the philosophy "All students count and are owed my best efforts and consideration." It is always to be remembered that warm pupil response and wholesome student demeanor come largely in accordance with the degree of positivity the teacher brings to the students.

6

COGNITIVE ANTIDOTES FOR BEHAVIOR PROBLEMS

We have seen managerial and afffective tenets at work as antidotes for problems in discipline. In this chapter our stress is on cognitive aspects, on the pupils' acquiring knowledge in such meaningful ways as will engage their interest, cooperation, and desire to learn. In brief, the emphasis is on the teacher's presenting knowledge in ways that will prevent or minimize numerous behavior problems, from the outset; and the positive, constructive tenets advocated for offsetting the difficulties are cognitive in nature.

SELLING YOUR SUBJECT

In a nation like ours where children up to a designated age must attend school under the provisions of a compulsory education law, it is inevitable that youngsters reveal varying degrees of internal motivation. With respect to incentive to learn, some young people are highly motivated because of the stimuli received from home; other pupils receive only moderate encouragement from the home environment; and still other young ones seem to be sent to school merely in compliance with the compulsory edict, there being little or no inducement from the home to make the children want to achieve. And so it becomes the responsibility of the sincere teacher to try, wherever possible and as often as possible, to raise the level of motivation, or the desire to learn, particularly within individuals of the latter two groups.

Letting youngsters know what a subject can do for them is one means of helping to motivate them. Many young people need this type of knowledge in order to exert the kind of effort needed to grasp diverse phases of a subject. In regard to certain aspects of work taught in some classrooms, some very vocal youngsters have been known to make such observations as "What good is that?" Other students have been observed to sit impassively in their seats almost with the attitude "Your job, teacher; teach me if you can" while they await the arrival of the day when they will be old enough to end their school days.

In connection with the idea of selling, one trainer of teachers asks the prospective teachers of her class what has seemed to them to be a rather spontaneous question: "Can each of you sell the value of your particular subject area, or part of it?" Then with keen interest the instructor awaits the reaction of her teachers-to-be to a question which she has indeed considered at great length. Usually it has been obvious from the silence that has followed that this question had not previously occurred to the majority of the teacher candidates. But in most of the instructor's training courses there have been some trainees who after brief reflection have been ready to volunteer a response. One speech major, for example, was sure she could sell the value of her subject area and gave the following spontaneous explanation of how she would do so.

At the beginning of the term I would ask my high school students what they thought a course in speech could do for them. I would expect to get from them certain implied answers, such as: (1) Improved pronunciation and clarity in expressing oneself will help one in interviews and in getting desirable jobs. (2) Better speech habits will help one to be respected and further one's chance of being accepted by more desirable types of friends. (3) Being able to express oneself with greater clarity will help one do a higher level of work in all school subjects. (4) The person who can clearly express himself orally has a greater chance of writing clearly; and, generally, the clearer speakers and writers achieve the greater amount of success in life. The four anticipated answers are not all of the implied answers I would expect to get. If the students omitted key goals, I would phrase questions that would help them to see functional goals that had not been mentioned. Then, too, in various individual lessons I would incorporate questions and activities of applicability that would allow the students to see how they were being helped toward the goals that the class and I had drawn up. For example, as one form of activity lesson I could have my students report on their investigation of the speech patterns of some people who have achieved in various areas that would be of interest to the members of the class.

Certainly each teacher should be able to sell the importance of his own area of concentration. Periodic discussions of the value of various phases of an area will also aid in the sale of what the teacher has to offer. And, without doubt, including in the teaching procedures various ways the subject matter may be concretely used to the students' advantage is a dynamic means of bringing to the children's awareness the value of a particular area.

EXPRESSING ENTHUSIASM

Show as much enthusiasm as you can for your area or subject matter. Usually, the salesman who expresses very little enthusiasm over his own merchandise cannot hope to be highly prosperous in making sales. Neither can an indifferent, drab teacher engender very much concern for the contents of his subject; yet the teacher who shows zeal for his work enhances his chance of arousing interest among the students. Why should pupils buy something which the teacher himself is not particularly concerned about selling?

BEING WELL PREPARED

The teacher who prepares his presentations thoroughly with worthwhile daily and long-range aims in view goes a long way toward gaining the respect and confidence of class members. It cannot be denied that being consistently well prepared makes inroads upon one's time and energy, but the favorable response that such preparedness engenders in your young pupils is well worth the required expenditure of time and effort. As a general rule, if you, as a teacher, have your pupils at heart so that you prepare unstintingly and appropriately for them, you may establish excellent rapport, and they will put forth special effort to give you the cooperation you desire. In fact, any really successful teacher of experience has learned that preparing well and teaching well are dominant ingredients in this whole matter of establishing and maintaining good discipline in the classroom. A youngster who is drawn into the worthwhileness of real learning situations hasn't the time to be a constant troublemaker. Good teaching is an antidote for many disciplinary problems.

STIMULATING INTEREST

Strive to make your lessons interesting. It can be readily understood, of course, that the more fascinating the lessons, the more willing pupils are to become involved in what is taking place in the classroom. And the more engagingly involved the pupils are, the less chance there is for disciplinary problems to creep in. There are some very specific guidelines that make for interesting lessons, some of which are listed below.
Make every possible effort to select teaching material that is suitable for your particular class. Remember that attractive, readable print is palatable. And, very important, your materials should be geared to the reading level

of your class. The obvious statement "To interest students, you must reach them" is fully meaningful. Oftentimes, the defiant, belligerent pupil is reacting negatively to materials imposed upon him with which he is unprepared to cope. It is most frustrating to students to require them to use, as basic study materials, printed matter that is too advanced for them.

When advantageous, use examples that are familiar to students to explain abstract concepts or concepts that are difficult. This form of application that builds new knowledge on old information has a potent way of enlivening the class and captivating interest. Let us look at one such effective lesson that a speech teacher taught to quite an average tenth-grade class.

The teacher stated the aim of the lesson: "What qualities do we look for in a good public speaker?" The pupils were asked to name speakers they knew and to give reasons why they should be considered good, bad, or moderately good. Among the speakers the pupils chose to be subjected to critical judgment were the mayor of the pupils' particular city, the governor of their state, and the principal of their school. In fact, all of the personalities the youngsters chose were outstanding figures they had witnessed on television programs or at special gatherings in the community. As the pros and cons of the speakers were discussed, the good qualities of public speaking that were derived were listed on the chalkboard. The teacher injected questions, when necessary, to help clarify any additional good qualities that should not have been omitted. Student role playing was used from time to time and added much to the lesson. Some students, for example, showed how it would look if a speaker never glanced at his audience; others demonstrated poor posture. Finally, the list of good qualities were categorized under such headings as "Delivery," "Posture," "Poise," and "Eye Contact," for the pupils would need the guidelines when they prepared their own speeches to be delivered before the class.

This lesson, which built new concepts from familiar examples, was a very live one that captured a great amount of interest on the part of the students.

Make frequent use of audiovisual aids. Slower classes need many of these aids, to make abstract ideas concrete; and the brighter students must not be barred from these enriching materials simply because as alert pupils they are more adept at handling abstract subject matter. One very discerning teacher enthusiastically described the visual aid he used to teach a portion of a mathematics lesson.

The class was comprised of a group of sixth-graders. The teacher was teaching the concepts of intersecting, parallel, and skew lines. To help his students understand the concepts involving the relationships between two lines, the teacher used two classroom pointers to represent two lines. Two students were asked to go to the front of the room and to hold one of the pointers in a stationary position. The teacher then moved the second pointer in various positions around the stationary pointer showing the class what intersecting, parallel, and skew lines are. After that demonstration the class members were readily able to define intersecting lines as two lines that meet at a point; parallel lines as two lines in the same plane, that never meet; and skew lines as two lines in different planes, that never meet.

The teacher was convinced that the use of the pointers, in addition to other visual aids employed during the course of the lesson, kept the pupils highly interested and helped them to learn material in a meaningful way.

And indeed, it would be unthinkable, for instance, to anticipate putting real zeal, attraction, and interest into lower-elementary teaching without the use of the chalkboard, coloring, flash cards, and various audiovisual aids that help in such a major way to bring the lessons alive. Certainly audiovisual aids, aptly chosen, are of inestimable importance in teaching. *As one of your visual aids, the chalkboard can be used to clarify or illustrate a variety of subject matter.* The chalkboard is always readily available, and the use of this aid is of tremendous importance in gaining and holding attention and interest, in breaking the monotony in procedure, and in helping pupils get a firm grasp on much of the material taught. The power of the chalkboard should never be underestimated.

Vary your procedure. Variation can make for interest. Besides, varied methods are desirable because the attention span of students is relatively short; and particularly is this true in the slower classes and in the lower grades. Variation in procedure, of course, has reference to preventing the same activity from continuing over such a long period of time that boredom or a lack of interest sets in, for when class procedure reaches this state, inattentiveness and a propensity for misbehavior are likely to be the result. A number of activities can make for variety in what is taking place in the classroom: audiovisual aids, student reports, student summaries, questions asked or answered, role playing, buzz sessions, and games may all, at times, be used to break the monotony or to prevent the same activity from continuing too long without a change of pace. It should be stressed, however, that some continuous activities can succeed in holding pupil interest longer than others. Teachers must therefore use discretion in determining when the pupils' receptiveness to an activity has reached a point of saturation so that there is need for change.

When using the question–answer method, keep the class alert with your question–answer technique. Assuming that your content has been appropriately chosen, the question–answer approach you use will in large measure determine the extent of involvement in your class. The greater the real involvement, the greater the scholastic attainment should be and fewer the chances of unwholesome conduct. Appropriate content and skillful question–answer technique can make for live, rewarding class sessions.

GEARING PACE AND SUBJECT MATTER TO THE CLASS

Pace your teaching appropriately for each of your classes. It is better to progress somewhat too slowly than to proceed too rapidly, for work which moves too fast for the majority of your students often causes class members to become bewildered, to lose interest, and to become behavior problems. It is most frustrating to young people to be continually faced with classwork which they do not reasonably comprehend. It should not be surprising that in these circumstances students become obstinate or rebellious.

It is good policy to ask your students questions that will adequately determine the degree to which they are grasping what is being taught. Do not hesitate to welcome honest answers regarding your pace or the extent to which you are reaching your pupils.

Gear your subject matter to the level of the class to be taught. In an attempt to reach the group at large, teachers generally aspire to reaching the average audience, the majority of the students that make up the class. This practice, however, sometimes leaves the above- and below-average pupils on the outside, for even in the supposedly homogeneous class, there are variations in pupil ability. Frequently, then, the teacher may be called upon to provide further work for the brighter members of the class and individual attention and help for the slower ones. The additional work for brighter pupils may on occasions involve enrichment activities or extra tasks, and more may be expected of these youngsters in terms of assignments, and in general. The slower pupils usually need more individual attention and assistance from the teacher than do the majority of the children. In some classes the brighter youngsters, too, are willing to help with the slower members of the class. But if the teacher is convinced that a bright or slow pupil is so far above or below the level of a class or group as to warrant a different placement, it will be to the advantage of the class and child concerned for the teacher to make provisions for the change. The greater the possibility of actually reaching the group, the greater are the chances for meaningful learning and good teacher-pupil relationships.

PROVIDING CONSTRUCTIVE ACTIVITIES

Keep your students constructively busy. The emphasis here is on keeping the pupils engaged in worthwhile endeavors. Students should not be given busywork. Unfortunately, there are too many teachers whose game it is to foster fruitless activity. An account of one such teacher is noted here.

During lunch hour, Mr. X was sitting in his classroom with several of his colleagues. Realizing that the lunch period was fast coming to a close, Mr. X grabbed one of his own science reference books while saying to his co-workers: "Now let me see—what am I going to give my kids to copy today? I want to give them enough to keep them busy most of the period, but yet I don't want to give them too much. If I overburden them, they'll surely scream." Mr. X made his decision on what he would have his tenth-grade students copy, and scribbled the material onto the board. When the below-average science students entered the room, some of them yelled to their teacher, "We have to copy that, Mr. X?"—whereupon Mr. X assured them that the copying session had surely begun. After some preliminary wandering about the classroom, the youngsters, who had not the slightest idea of the meaning of the material they were about to copy, did manage to begin the copying, but, figuratively, in enough din to lift the roof completely from its posts.

Work that students are required to do should be the type that will be of very clear value to them, not what may be termed busywork or time fillers. Constructively busy students have very little time to be authors of the kind of disorder that eventually leads to problems in discipline. To keep students engaged in worthwhile and interesting work will, of course, demand much in the way of teacher time, preparation, and creativity, but this expenditure of time and effort on the part of the teacher will ultimately be well worth the investment.

7

LESSON PLANNING AND PRESENTATION
AS THEY RELATE TO DISCIPLINE

It cannot be overemphasized that classwork which is carefully prepared and presented so as to promote interest, challenge, and meaningfulness invites the type of pupil involvement that averts and reduces considerably problems in discipline. There are, of course, teachers who prepare diligently for their work and do a splendid job. But far too many of our teachers fall short of making schoolwork the productive delight it should be. Among this group are some who fail to be on their toes because of a lack of know-how, many out of a lack of real concern. Even very competent teachers who have taught a grade or subject for many years need to determine how they can bring to the classroom more freshness and greater effectiveness. The teacher who scratches his head on the way to school quizzing himself on what he will teach that day, without real thought given to preparation, is begging for trouble.

Lesson plans were never meant to harass the teacher. Like a map that points the way to some predetermined destination, plans should be conceived of as guides to purposeful classroom endeavor. A plan is offered as insurance against aimless wandering that wastes the pupils' time and succeeds in frustrating the youngsters. Our concern in this chapter is the type of planning that provides for fruitful learning and diminished propensity for misbehavior.

DAILY LESSON PLANNING

Let us first concentrate on the elements of the daily lesson plan.

FORMAT

Certainly it would be presumptuous of me to offer the lesson plan format that follows as the only acceptable one; nor has there been any intent
to do so. Yet it would seem fair to point out that a great majority of full-
length plans are comprised of most of the categories indicated in the outline, or at least of equivalent categories. Some plans carry more divisions,
some less. In any event, the following format with its eight categories is
quite a substantial outline upon which to build a detailed plan.

LESSON PLAN FORMAT

Topic
Aim(s)
Motivation
Development
Illustrative Materials
Summary
Application
Assignment

Among other categories that are sometimes included in a plan are Related Activities, Practice Exercises, Enriching Activities, and Evaluation.
Actually, however, a summary may be a form of evaluation. With respect
to synonymous terminology, the aim is sometimes referred to as the objective or goal; the motivation as the orientation or launching; the development
as procedure, classroom activities, or content plus methods; and illustrative
materials as audiovisual aids. What we are more concerned with at present,
however, is the fact that careful attention to each of the categories of the
format is directly related to competent teaching and concurrently to averting problems in discipline.

TOPIC

The topic is a designation of the material to be taught. Often topics for
a class are indicated in the course of study or syllabus. Perhaps a home
economics course of study for one of the grades will stipulate that "Labels
on Foods" and "The Function of Vitamins" be among the topics to be
studied. One social studies class may have among its topics for emphasis
"Benjamin Franklin as a Politician"; another class, "The Organization of
the United Nations."

AIM

An aim of a lesson is whatever it is the teacher wishes the pupils to derive from the lesson at hand. It is an indication of the purpose the teacher hopes to achieve. A clear-cut aim is a check against a wandering, purposeless lesson that has no place special to go. An aim is the teacher's map. Without it, what should be a unified lesson may turn out to be a fragmenting in many directions. The teacher who doesn't know where he is going is causing untold confusion for himself and his pupils. This sort of wavering or chaos promotes disrespect and inattention that lead to problems in discipline.

An aim for a lesson is achieved through an appropriate slanting of the topic to be treated. The aim is derived when the topic is studied to determine what point of view will govern the consideration of the topic. It is of course the teacher's responsibility to try to shape the aim into a narrow enough point of view to be treated within a specified time. The aims "To determine Franklin's place as an inventor" and "Which vitamins are most essential for a fifteen-year old?" might well be derived from the topics "Benjamin Franklin" and "Vitamins." Of course, the arrival at appropriate aims requires considered thought.

The conscientious teacher will recheck his aim after the lesson has been completed to determine to what extent it has been achieved. This procedure is important in verifying the clarity of a plan. It is a means of evaluating the lesson that should be encouraged. Naturally, of course, the degree to which the presentation reaches its audience will constitute a major facet in the evaluation.

The question of when a teacher may justifiably lay aside the aim of the lesson to pursue a topic interjected by the pupils is frequently an issue in the minds of beginning teachers. There is no clear-cut answer. By and large, teachers must use their own discretion in judging instances when the interposed subject is of such moment as to warrant its replacing the development of the teacher's aim. Generally speaking, if the teacher's aims have been carefully studied in the light of class needs and the lessons have been carefully worked out, the times when the plan should be sidetracked are few and far between. Teachers are reminded that it is frequently the game of youngsters to try to waste time by getting the teacher off the subject. They are aware of what they are doing and are pretty well able to spot teachers who are easily vulnerable to their game. As a rule, when a teacher allows himself to be led off the track for considerable blocks of time, he should be thoroughly convinced of the real justification of his move; if he is not, he should tactfully lead the lesson back to the aim. The suggestion offered does not, of course, mean that lesson plans should place pupils in a straitjacket. On the contrary, plans should allow enough leeway for youngsters to express themselves freely and interestingly within the framework of the plan. The point is that teachers must guard against being needlessly led astray.

MOTIVATION

The motivation of a lesson is whatever is said or done to get the pupils interested in doing the work at hand. It is a means of exciting the students or of stimulating their interest so that they will want to share in the lesson. A good motivation is not a waste of time or a mere decoration tacked on to the lesson. A worthwhile motivation that takes the lesson off the ground and starts it rolling will get the pupils set to enter gainfully into the activities that have been planned. It will put the pupils in the state of mind to work, and it will establish a frame of reference for the lesson. A promotion of involvement is the terrain of motivation. The child who becomes considerably involved is in a position to learn and has little time to engage in misbehavior.

There are many motivations that have a great deal of merit. Let us consider first the two-pronged question, a particularly strong motivating device. On the one hand, the question asked is a personalized one, for it touches upon the pupils' experiences, store of knowledge, interests, thoughts, opinions, or feelings; on the other hand, the same question is in some major way related to the content comprising the lesson to be taught. A discussion of the story "Cemetery Path," which concerns a weak protagonist who is dared to cross a cemetery on a winter's night, may be motivated by a two-pronged question: "Describe a dare you once accepted. Why did you accept the dare?" Here the motivating inquiry delves into the pupils' experience with dares and at the same time leads right into the heart of the story or into the content to be explored.

A number of other motivational techniques may be used to get the lesson going. Among them are an anecdote, role playing, a problem to be solved, a quotation, proverb, demonstration, newspaper or magazine clipping, an audiovisual aid, and a picture. Though a picture, such as a drawing or painting, is a form of visual aid, it has been singly pointed up because pictures may serve as such a powerful motivating factor. Youngsters love to look at them. Appropriate and attractive ones can play a forceful role in getting the lesson off to a vigorous start. In general, though, the content of the lesson, the class to be taught, and the degree of teacher ingenuity will dictate the motivating device that is to be used for a given lesson.

Certainly motivation is not needed for each daily lesson. Groups of youngsters who receive substantial long-range motivation from home and, in general, the brighter groups are pretty much self-motivated and can often fare well without an introductory stimulating device. Yet these favored pupils need not be too frequently barred from the pleasures and enlightenment good motivations may provide. As a rule, youngsters who are less well motivated on a long-term basis and, in general, the less able groups can frequently profit greatly from motivational techniques.

Two additional occasions should be mentioned as times when the motivation might well be omitted. Sometimes the content of the lesson is inherently of such keen interest that an attempt to impose an introductory incentive would be superfluous. And, when a unit of learning is going well, there may be an enormous amount of built-in motivation. This sustained interest in the total project may make unnecessary the motivation of each daily lesson used to develop the unit. As a final remark, it is worth noting, however, that though there are occasions upon which the motivation of a lesson might well be omitted, a great many classes may frequently stand to gain from motivational techniques that have been skillfully planned.

DEVELOPMENT

Much like the body of a letter, the development is the main part of a lesson plan. This category is the plan's reason for being. It should provide for content and methods that challenge, excite, or interestingly inform, or that do a combination of these things. Classwork that nets unstinted involvement is a key to learning and improved behavior.

There are diverse types of classroom methods which, in whole or in part, may make up the body of a plan. Among them are the question-answer method, discussion, lecture, role playing, problem solving, demonstration, reporting, chalkboard activity, and games. Frequently, these and other techniques are used in combination, and the question-answer and discussion approaches are such mainstays for each grade and subject area that they are considered fully in Chapter 8.

By and large, teachers should be wary of just plain lecturing over long periods of time. The attention span of the average youngster is relatively short, and a continuous droning on and on without a different activity to change the pace is more likely than not to invite the boredom and inattentiveness that lead to behavior problems. There are, of course, distinct times when no method other than the lecture may achieve the desired results, and in these instances the lecture method should be used, but with caution and certainly not for an entire period.

Role playing is basically a form of dramatization which does not make use of a script. The role player performs on the basis of what he has read, or he acts on the basis of the knowledge or experience he has gathered through class discussions, observations, or interactions with others in or outside the classroom. The drama of role playing, then, is unlike the formal play, which has a full script, a structured plot, and cut-and-dried action. Role playing, instead, places the participant in the unique position of creating his own action, for the role player has only the broad outline of plot and role relationships but is charged with the responsibility of getting inside the character roles and of acting out a story spontaneously.

The technique of role playing provides a particularly useful means of gaining insight into varied subject matter, and it offers a helpful avenue for dealing with classroom problems as well. In such subjects as literature and social studies, role playing may assist the youngster in gaining insight into characters, personages, current events, and diverse movements. Following an introduction to the plot and characters in a short story, play, or novel, pupils may, for instance, be asked to role-play sections of the literary selection; and encouraging the students to identify with the characters and incidents through these creative dramatizations should foster increased understanding of and deeper insight into incidents, characters, and actions. Similarly, role playing may be employed to offer pupils an opportunity to act out historical or contemporary events in such a way as to dramatize the feelings and conflicts of the actual participants.

Role playing may likewise be utilized to teach interpersonal or human relations skills in the classroom. Basically, the actor steps out of his own role and assumes the role of some other person, either a real person or a fictitious one. In this assumed role, the performer has the opportunity to gain an understanding of the thoughts and feelings of others or a chance to come into an awareness about himself in relation to other people. The method of playing roles which we are considering may help young people examine with care diverse ways of meeting social and personal conflict and assist them in assessing the advantages and disadvantages of the various possible moves. Role playing is therefore a means of helping youngsters investigate actions, behavior, and, in fact, our social life in general.

The teacher is charged with the responsibility of seeing to it that the problem situation to be role-played is clearly described to class members. Teacher X, for instance, might wish class members to role-play the welcoming of minority students into the class. In this case she might well describe the problem situation in the following manner.

Next week, our second week in school this term, three hundred black students will be bussed to our school as a step toward integration. Three of the black pupils will be members of this sixth-grade class. What are some major steps you, as class members, might take toward welcoming the students to the class?

Prior to the actual role playing, the teacher might further help by briefing the actors on their roles, by explaining to each of them the part he will play; but the instructor will help as well by briefing the audience on its role. The audience or class observers, like the actors, should understand necessary background information and should be clearly aware of the educational goals of the improvisation. Briefing sheets for each participant may often serve a useful purpose. The audience, as well as the actors, should be given something special to do, either as a single unit or as two or more groups. Class members may be asked to observe one or more of the participants, to serve as critics with respect to the quality of the peer performance, to suggest how certain roles may be performed differently or more competently, or to comment in some other helpful manner. And finally, after the role playing has been completed, there should be feedback on the degree to which the actors stayed within the roles they were portraying and, in general, the degree to which the dramatization achieved its goals. The class as a whole should join the teacher in the evaluation.

Problem solving can be a powerful method of teaching that challenges pupils with interest and excitement, provided that the problem to be solved is appropriate for the class and students are led to follow through on the basic steps of the procedure. The method encourages critical thinking and indeed is the essence of a thought-provoking process.

The problem-solving method is an inductive approach, for selected information is carefully examined and from it a generalized principle is drawn. If, for example, the members of a class were asked to use this approach in arriving at their own definition of a compound sentence, the youngsters would carefully examine a collection of such sentences. On the basis of this concentrated study they would form a hypothesis of what a compound sentence might be. If the hypothesized definition should prove to be sound when tested against a sufficient number of compound sentences, the hypothesis would be accepted, and the generalized principle or definition arrived at would be declared. Should the hypothesized definition be proved inadequate, however, because an accurate description of compound sentences did not evolve through an application of the proposed definition, new hypotheses would need to be formulated and tested until a workable hypothesized definition could be found.

Requiring young people to delve into data and arrive at their own conclusions, yet results that may be substantiated, is a healthy technique, and a strong one. It can be the essence of involvement. The method should be used unstintingly. This does not mean, however, that the deductive approach is to be ignored, for sometimes it is necessary first to state the generalized principle and then to work toward an understanding of the principle through an assortment of examples. The problem-solving approach may be used to advantage in all subject areas and at each grade level. Basically, the substance of the method is presented in the steps that follow.

BASIC STEPS IN PROBLEM SOLVING

1. Recognition of the problem to be solved.
2. Gathering data that have a bearing on the problem.
3. Careful examination of the data with a view to solving the problem.
4. Formulation of a hypothesis.
5. Testing the hypothesis.
6. Acceptance of the hypothesis if it proves to be workable; rejection of the hypothesis if it is unsatisfactory and a repetition of the problem-solving steps until a satisfactory solution is reached.

Demonstrations, student reporting, board work, games, and other activities that could be mentioned may make for both lively and fruitful activity. Additionally they may all be used to promote variety in technique, when a change in pace is needed.

ILLUSTRATIVE MATERIALS

In the context of lesson planning and presentation, illustrative materials refer primarily to various kinds of audiovisual aids. It is to be expected that some aids are more helpful than others. Some of the more useful ones for the teacher have been listed below.

> Blackboard
> Overhead projector
> Pictorials (cutouts from magazines, postcards, photo-
> graphs, watercolors, sketches, etchings)
> Pictorial reproductions in perspective (maps, globes,
> graphs, charts, tables)
> Recordings (with record player and tape recorder used
> as items of equipment)
> Films
> Filmstrips (also referred to as slide films or pictorials)
> Three-dimensional reproductions of reality: (1) a model,
> such as a life-size reproduction of the human heart in
> plastic form; (2) a small-scale model, such as a minia-
> ture reproduction of a typical Elizabethan theater; and
> (3) a replica, such as a life-size reproduction of Abraham
> Lincoln's bed made from comparable or simulated
> material

The idea that a picture may be worth many words has relevancy here. Audiovisual aids help to make verbal presentation more understandable. In brief, they assist in clarifying abstractions. Hence a liberal use of the aids often becomes an absolute necessity in the case of slower pupils or greatly disadvantaged ones, for, in general, they handle abstract ideas far less skill-fully than do more advantaged youth. The aids can help tremendously, as well, in getting the attention of children who receive little or no long-term motivation from home. Audiovisual aids, however, should be made available to pupils of all levels, both disadvantaged and privileged. Certainly the more able children should not be bored or deprived of the illustrative goodies when it would clearly be to their advantage to have them. Audiovisual aids can add strength to learning through a multisensory approach. In addition, they can make for a welcomed variety in procedure.

Because the chalkboard that is so common may sometimes be taken for granted, teachers are reminded that it is a powerful illustrative device. Its potential for promoting forceful teaching should not be overlooked. The teacher who writes an unfamiliar word on the chalkboard, for instance, helps youngsters visualize the word. The teacher who when introducing the story "The Lady or the Tiger?" sketches on the board the type of arena alluded to in the story helps to capture the interest and attention of his audience. The chalkboard may be particularly helpful in providing adequate space for recording developmental outlines, making lists, clarifying words, drawing sketches, recording assignments, and giving instructions. Many are the uses of the classroom board. Indeed, the effectiveness of some subject areas like mathematics and languages would be utterly lost without the chalkboard. Without doubt, it serves as a focal point for attention and learning.

Illustrative materials, as a category, may be placed at any point in the lesson plan. An audiovisual aid may be used as the motivation. It may be used at several places in the body of the plan or, for that matter, could comprise the major part of the development. Or illustrative material could be used for the summary. Above all, audiovisual aids should be as copiously used as is feasible.

SUMMARY

A summary that appropriately grows out of the lesson to be taught is a sign of careful preparation. Young people should be left with the sense of completeness that a suitable conclusion conveys.

Varied types of summaries may be legitimately used. Among other things, the nature of the lesson will determine the kind of closure to be utilized. At times a running summary of the work covered may be needed. This is indicated when the lesson has consisted of difficult or basic material that is fundamental for future work. At other times just one question, the answer to which would imply a grasp of the important points of the lesson, will be sufficient. Often this kind of single-question summary may be centered around the aim of the lesson, since knowledge about this key query would symbolize an understanding of the main ideas. Sometimes summarizing has occurred all along, or perhaps there has even been a listing of major points on the chalkboard as the lesson proceeded. In such cases, a formal summary may not necessarily be needed, but rather just a smooth rounding off of the lesson. As one approach to this type of conclusion, it is possible that the teacher may wish to round off the lesson merely with a pertinent comment, statement, or very brief activity. And finally, a summary may indeed be a form of application. In this instance, pupils would be asked to apply the knowledge gained from the lesson to other pertinent situations. The illustrations cited, of course, are only a few of the varied summaries that may be used.

On the matter of who should do the summarizing, either the teacher or the students or both may be responsible for the conclusion. It is of course a healthy sign that the lesson has gone well if the pupils can formulate an effective summary. In a very real sense, summarizing a lesson appropriately is one means of evaluating its effectiveness.

APPLICATION

In almost all worthwhile lessons, one or more concepts or principles are the focusing points for learning. Application, then, is a process of applying the principle learned in the lesson to a further situation. Actually, it is a form of practicing in relevant situations what has previously been studied. Thus, youngsters who have been learning how to use a dictionary key to pronunciation subsequently may be asked to look up a given number of words, to mark them off with diacritical markings, and to stand ready to pronounce the words correctly in accordance with the pronunciation symbols. After concentrated study of the concepts involved, a class working on percents might be given additional examples or problems which require the youngsters to demonstrate the extent to which they can perform acceptably the arithmetical principles studied. Class members who have concentrated on the role of the United Nations in bringing about international peace could justifiably be asked to determine what role they think the United Nations should play in attempting to bring about peace between two groups currently engaged in conflict. The child who is learning the principles of counting may be requested to indicate his understanding of what he has studied by counting certain objects which he owns. And finally, youngsters who have been working on the distinction between fragments and what society accepts as complete sentences may be asked to improve some of their own writing by eliminating all of their sentence fragments.

At times, application falls into a distinct category, but it may be used jointly with a summary. Actually, application may itself become a homework assignment, or it may be provided for in subsequent lessons. It is important that it be used as often as needed.

ASSIGNMENT

It is of special importance that an assignment be meaningful. It should not be busywork, but rather serve in some way to augment the work of the classroom. Making pupils responsible for senseless exercises can easily decrease respect for school and what it stands for. An assignment may be legitimately made to reinforce content already covered, pave a way for new material to be introduced, or serve as an activity for enriching the background.

Work that is assigned should be unmistakably clear. Ambiguous requirements can be both frustrating and discouraging to youngsters. The teacher may need to call on a representative number of students to verify an understanding of what is being assigned. In addition, the teacher should make the pupils feel free to ask for any further clarifications needed. At times it is good practice for the teacher to have pupils begin the assignment far enough before the termination of the class for him to be able to supervise the beginning of the assignment, giving pupils help wherever it is needed.

Teachers should have the option of making assignments in accordance with the needs of the particular class. Some youngsters may be in need of a long-range assignment such as reading a book and preparing for a special presentation. Another group may need assignments two or three times a week; still another class, as the need arises. There are classes for which it is largely a waste of time to make assignments, because pupils are so poorly motivated they can't be relied upon to bring in either their assigned work or their textbooks; in fact, it would be better if textbooks were left in the classroom if they are the books from which basic learning is to take place. Teachers are called upon really to teach and to teach hard in all classes, but in the extremely poorly motivated classes that we have described, it must be candidly recognized that the learning which takes place will come almost solely as a result of the teacher's hard work in class and not as a result of his relying on assignments that are rarely submitted and books that are seldom brought to class. It is to be emphasized, nonetheless, that assignments may be beneficial for many a class if they are meaningful and clearly made.

FURTHER INVOLVEMENT

As often as is necessary, material in the lesson plan should be made to relate as closely as possible to the interests, observations, and life experiences of the pupils. This means relating content taught to the types of families and personages the youngsters know, to the places these young people go, to the objects with which they are familiar, or to the TV shows they watch. It is a means of capitalizing on what the youths see, hear, feel, or in some other way experience. This kind of affinity brought to the classroom can make for a powerful mode of teaching. The use of situations close to students, as frequently as feasible, promotes the sort of live involvement that makes learning more pleasurable and pupils less vulnerable to malbehavior. Slower pupils and those less motivated on a long-term basis need as a source of encouragement this kind of linking together of school and life. But certainly the more able students should not be barred from these experiences when it would be clearly to their advantage to have them.

BETTER TOO MUCH THAN TOO LITTLE

It is better that a teacher have a little too much in the lesson plan for the day than not enough. This practice would obviate his reacting as one beginning teacher who, finishing her lesson every bit of ten minutes early, sat on the edge of one of the pupils' desks, with her feet dangling, as she discussed with her students any irrelevancies the youngsters were kind enough to pose. The young teacher was at a complete loss as to what she could do with the excess time.

If a teacher frequently completes lessons ahead of time, perhaps he should check to determine whether pupil understandings have been clear and applications sufficient. It is of course not possible to know precisely how much time a given lesson will consume. Some questions or activities may require more time for mastery than was anticipated. Others may take considerably less time. As the teacher comes to know his audience better, however, he will gain greater proficiency in determining approximately how much the class can cover within a given period of time.

Teachers should at all times have in readiness something constructive that may be done in extra time. The conscientious teacher of experience will, of course, have many possible activities at his disposal. Inexperienced teachers would do well to prepare a somewhat fuller plan than is needed, in order to be able to handle competently the exigencies of excess time.

In fact, the young teacher might well include in his plan some extra but pertinent material that may be used if time demands it but excluded if time is running short. As the concerned teacher gains experience, however, he will discover that excess time may frequently be advantageously used for answering further relevant questions pupils may have about the lesson, for making the lesson applicable to further situations in life, or for drilling pupils on an important skill that is pertinent to the work of the class though not immediately relevant to the particular lesson that has been taught. The element of time need not be an issue for panic. It is not a herculean task to handle it efficiently.

NEED FOR FLEXIBILITY

Though adequate preparation is prerequisite to successful teaching, teachers must not allow themselves to become slaves to their lesson plans. Pupils should not feel that the teacher is so bound to his plan that there isn't time for clarifications or for following up some essential aspect of the lesson more fully. A teacher must watch pupil reactions and see that understandings are clear. He should make students feel free to express themselves legitimately and to seek added information and explan   previously indicated, however, teachers must be discerning an   u against being led astray by those whose game it is to get the teacher off on tangents.

In connection with daily planning, and with unit planning as well, pupils should be allowed to offer what contributions they can appropriately make, without of course wasting each other's time. This procedure can provide a welcome change of pace and is encouraging and stimulating for the students. Illustrative of this type of student contribution is pupil opportunity to help make a choice of the selection to be read by the entire class or of the project the group would like to tackle. Aside from the contributions of a class as a whole, there is also the matter of individual pupil choices that may be highlighted. Individual pupils might at times be permitted to make their own separate selections for further reading, for an enrichment activity, or for an assignment. The teacher should provide for this type of flexibility wherever it is suitable for the class and the work to be covered.

TYPES OF LESSONS

Using a variety of presentations adds spice to the lessons. The teacher who resorts to the same lesson pattern day after day is inviting the kind of boredom and indifference that lead to problems in discipline. Besides, at a given time, different classes may need diverse sorts of lessons. The listing

that follows is not meant to be exhaustive, but rather illustrative of the
many types of lessons a teacher can use.

Question-Answer	Lecture Combined with Other
Discussion	Procedures
Question-Answer and Discussion	Committee Activity
Demonstration	Student Reporting
Workshop Period	Panel
Problem Solving	Games
Role Playing	Workbook
Drill	Visiting Speaker
Supervised Study	Field Trip
Audiovisual Aids	Debate

Review

The lessons cited may of course be used effectively singly or in combination. The point is that with so much variation available, there can be little
excuse for a large amount of sameness in presentation on the part of the
conscientious teacher. For example, if class members were asked to concen-
trat   uties of the mayor of their city, at least a dozen types of
lessons wou   appropriate for developing such a project. Some of the
types of lessons listed have been discussed elsewhere in this volume, but
brief remarks may well be made regarding other lessons on the list.

Drill exercises can be profitable and should be used when needed to
reinforce basic skills that should be practiced. A desirable procedure for
content that is the subject for drill is that the material first be used in context, then drilled, and finally returned to its natural context. Thus, if the
writing of complete sentences rather than fragments were the topic of concern, it would be appropriate first to consider fragments in samples of the
children's own writing, then to proceed to drill exercises that make a distinction between fragments and complete sentences, and finally to return the
concentration on avoiding fragments to its natural context in writing. It is
not drill for drill's sake that should be the important focus, but instead,
drill for the purpose of the improvement that may finally be effected in
context. In general, variety may be achieved in drills through such alternate
means as chalkboard, seatwork, and homework exercises.

Committee work provides wholesome variation when there have been
a number of lessons directed by the teacher. Though the various committees
are to a large extent encouraged to work independently, the following committee responsibilities rest squarely on the shoulders of the teacher:

1. To make certain that viable procedures are planned.

2. To be sure that guidelines proposed for committee activity are clear to all concerned.
3. To be certain that group members are supplied with suitable resource material.
4. To be sure that committee reports which are to be made to the class at large are acceptable or, whenever possible, superior.
5. To set guidelines for pupil interaction.
6. To see to it that constructive work does not break down.

Steering committees with proficiency is not an easy task. Until groups of pupils have learned to work together harmoniously, there may be a good deal of friction among the students. With some pupils always wanting to be the leaders, some wishing neither to lead nor follow, and still others plainly indifferent, it is understandable why confusion may exist. Usually pupils must be taught to work cooperatively and harmoniously in committees and to respect what each one has to offer. Often it will be to the advantage of the teacher first to think through the committee groupings that are likely to prove most effective and then to make committee assignments himself. Actually, for the most part, the teacher will be wise to reserve the sponsoring of committee work until he feels secure in his ability to handle the discipline of the class. In the hands of the teacher who has not established adequate rapport with class members, a classroom of committees could result in turmoil.

A special type of committee that should be mentioned is the small-group buzz session. The procedure, which may be used in connection with various types of lessons, consists of the impromptu grouping of pupils to work on a question or problem. The class is divided into small groups of about three to ten students to deliberate simultaneously on the same or different issues. The time limit set for the exploratory discussion or action of the groups is about six minutes. After this time has expired, the groups in some way report to the entire class. There are a number of forms the reporting may take. One possibility is to allot each group a designated time limit for a representative to make a report for the group. The teacher, however, should feel free to work out other means for having the small groups report their findings to the class at large. The buzz session approach may play an important role in increasing class participation, promoting liveliness, and achieving variety in classroom procedure.

The panel offers another type of variation that may bring life to an issue or project that is to be the topic of concern of the class. The three or more members who sit on the panel have, like a reporting committee, previously met, determined how the work should be divided among them, and made preparations for sharing their ideas with the class. One of the members serves as chairman and initiates the discussion, invites response from his colleagues, summarizes the points discussed, and, in general, steers the project. The panel should invite the group as a whole to participate in the discussion. More interest is generated when all class members feel free to play a part.

The visiting speaker and the field trip are procedures which require the teacher to make prior investigation and preparation. In the case of the former, the teacher should make certain that the speaker is of suitable caliber. Speaker and teacher should come to terms on the kind of speech from which the class may derive benefit. Finally, the teacher should give the pupils background information regarding the speaker and the purpose of his visit and should apprise the students of the kind of response expected from them. With respect to the field trip, it would be helpful for the instructor to be familiar with the place to be visited or the performance to be attended. Before the event takes place, pupils should be given careful instructions on what to expect or look for, if the excursion is to make a meaningful impact. In the case of both the speaker and the trip, some form of appraisal after the activities will reveal the significance of the procedures.

8

HANDLING YOUTH THROUGH QUESTIONING

"To question well is to teach well." There is an abundance of merit in this saying. From the first grade through the twelfth, questioning plays a significant role in classroom procedure. It is used as a part of practically every type of lesson. It then stands to reason that, to a great extent, teaching will succeed or fail in proportion to the manner in which questions are handled. We have already identified real involvement as a keynote to learning and to better teacher–pupil relationships. Our task is to incorporate questioning into teaching as an engaging activity. Pupils must be kept alive and alert as the querying proceeds. They should be made to feel an actual part of the questioning process through the skillful maneuvers of the teacher. This chapter offers the teacher important guidelines for handling youth effectively through the questioning procedure.

Initially, the two major questioning techniques that are our concern should be delineated. They are the question–answer and discussion techniques.

Many lessons that make use of questioning require response through the question–answer approach. This technique is used to help pupils probe into issues and meanings and to help them develop logical concepts and understanding. For the most part, the questions and answers are given in rapid succession, and the kinds of questions are both factual and thought-provoking. When printed materials are being used, factual questions may be thought of as "black and white" questions, since the answers to them may be found on the printed page, in the words of the text. On the other hand, the thought-provoking questions are primarily concerned with reasoning. The answers to them may not be found in the specific words of the print, but instead may be inferred or derived from indirect hints found in the text. There are, of course, times when the questioning will not be geared to the printed page in the hands of the students: the factual questions will be concerned with some reality outside the print while the thought-provoking questions will require the pupils to reason, with sensitivity, about some physical observation or to probe deeply into inner thoughts and feelings.

With respect to the discussion technique, questions that are phrased for a genuine discussion require extended answers. Examples of topics that give rise to discussion are "Why We Need to Do Homework Assignments," "Narcotics: Causes and Effects," "Should Our Nation Continue Its Involvement in the X War?," "Are We Spending Enough or Too Much Money on Space Exploration?" A careful consideration of these topics will clearly indicate that discussion calls for a tossing about of the topic among the discussants, a meeting of minds, and the expressing of varying points of view. Unlike the generally rapid succession of questions and answers characteristic of the question-answer technique, a true discussion requires extended give-and-take on the single issue at hand, as the participants consider, investigate, or examine the various sides of the question, topic, or problem. The prolonged study of the topic will admit of a conclusion in the form of a solution, of a consensus, or of areas of agreement and disagreement that have been logically sustained, or possibly of a combination of these factors.

THE QUESTION-ANSWER METHOD

Effective use of the question-answer method involves many factors of which teachers should be aware if the method is to have its desired dynamic function.

ASKING FACTUAL AND THOUGHT-PROVOKING QUESTIONS

In most lessons where the question-answer method is appropriate for a given piece of work, two types of questions are in order. Very frequently, it will be advantageous to ask a series of factual questions to insure basic understanding before moving into the reasoning queries, while at other times it will serve a more useful purpose to mix the two kinds of questions throughout the lesson. The less bright students will, in general, require the support of more factual questions than the brighter pupils in order to be prepared to cope with the thought questions. With consistent effort on the part of the teacher, average and above-average classes may be led to handle a considerable number of the thought-provoking questions that challenge pupils to keen observation and thought, and to resulting growth. But even the members of slower classes should gradually be led to answer a greater number of such provocative inquiries.

PHRASING QUESTIONS

To produce desirable responses, phrase your questions clearly and precisely. It is important to keep the questions short in order to promote clarity. A majority of students have difficulty trying to grasp the meaning of long, involved questions. Similarly, the vocabulary level of questions must not be too difficult for the class at hand, if clarity is to be achieved.

Before including your questions in your plan, you will find it helpful to pretest each question to assure yourself that you are asking your pupils exactly what you intend to ask them and to determine whether or not the phraseology of each question will bring you the type of answer you expect. "What about the song 'We Shall Overcome'?" and "Tell what you know about Jackie Robinson," for example, are much too broad and vague, and could cause your students to offer a wide variety of answers before the answers you want or expect are uncovered. However, more specific questions like "Why did 'We Shall Overcome' become popular among black people?" and "How did Jackie Robinson become famous?" would seem to indicate that you know precisely what you wish to get from your students.

A great many educators look with favor upon questions that begin with such terms as the ones that follow: *what* (What sentence gives the main idea of the first paragraph?); *when* (When was the Declaration of Independence adopted by the American colonies?); *who* (Who were the muckrakers as identified by President Roosevelt?); *name* (Name a noun that remains the same for both the singular and plural forms.); *how* (How does the excretion of waste matter contribute to the health of an individual?); *why* (Why should a person have the right to a fair trial if arrested?); *to what extent* or *to what degree* (To what extent has Ross made Ivan seem like a real person?); *under what condition* or *under what circumstances* (Under what condition would you consider accepting a dare?); *compare* (Compare the process of electing our governor with that of selecting our mayor.); *contrast* (Contrast present-day means of traveling by water with those of the seventeenth century.); *describe* (Describe the usual effect of heat on solids.); *agree* or *disagree* (Agree or disagree with Alice's explanation of why telephone wires sag in the summer.); *summarize* (Summarize the major points made for and against an increase in appropriations for welfare families.).

The first four terms—*what, when, who,* and *name*—are, of course, very frequently used to introduce fact questions. The other terms listed often introduce questions that give rise to critical thinking, to the forming of ideas, concepts, interrelationships, and insights. Although other terminology may be legitimately and effectively used to begin a question, certainly questions carefully phrased from the point of view of the terms we've cited tend to take on qualities of preciseness and clarity that make for forceful questioning.

LIMITING YES–NO QUESTIONS

It is usually a goal to have pupils extend themselves beyond the mere "yes" or "no" stage, into probing, analytical answers. And although the teacher may use expectant eyes or a follow-up question to make pupils fully aware that they are to continue discussing a yes–no question such as "Is he a strong leader?" until the "yes" or "no" has been amply sustained, you will find it to your advantage not to overload your plan with questions that require you to signal continued response.

ASKING POLARIZED AND HYPOTHETICAL QUESTIONS

Don't forget the dynamic appeal of polarized and hypothetical questions, as special types of questioning. The teacher who capitalizes on the opportunity to poll the class on pertinent issues that lend to a division of opinion and encourages the pupils to sustain their varying points of view with logical reasoning can promote both live and fruitful response. The polarized question is particularly applicable to class material that is controversial or problematic.

The hypothetical question, too, promotes live, worthwhile response. When this method is used, each person is drawn into the assumed or hypothetical situation individually. In short, the effect is a question posed to each individual student. This makes the question highly personal and therefore of great appeal or interest. The personalized hypothetical question frequently takes such forms as: "Suppose you had . . . what would you . . .?" "Suppose you had . . . how would (might) you . . . ?" "Assume that you . . . how would you . . . ?" or "Pretend that you are . . . how will you . . .?" From the story of "Cemetery Path," for instance, in which a timid little man was challenged to cross a cemetery at night, one hypothetical question could be: "Suppose you had accepted a challenge to cross a cemetery at night; how might you have acted at the moment of your departure?" Still other types of personalized or hypothetical questions are these: "If you were asked to read a poem before the class, what selection would you choose?" "Danny has received instructions to return home by 12:00 P. M. To his surprise, he has learned that the prom will last until 1:00. What should Danny do?"

DISTRIBUTING QUESTIONS AND SELECTING RESPONDENTS

Direct questions both to volunteers and to nonvolunteers. This procedure impresses upon class members the idea that the lesson is for the benefit of all. It is the responsibility of the teacher to try to make each member active in the class group and to help to encourage him to acquire knowledge, to think, and to express himself in ways that lead to growth and to increasing maturity. Besides, after students have gained enough interest or confidence to respond, they generally derive a sense of satisfaction and well-being from their attainment.

Match question to pupil when this procedure is advantageous. Get to know your students well so that at opportune times you may ask some of the slower or more reluctant students questions you are sure they can handle with some measure of success. The matching of question to pupil is often an effective means of encouraging the less able student. It helps to give him a sense of belonging, of being able to make his contribution to the group.

Do not use a set pattern for selecting respondents. Calling on pupils to answer questions on the basis of a seating chart or alphabetical listing, for example, furnishes an obvious clue as to when a student will be questioned. Such a set pattern may encourage students to be inattentive until it is near time for them to respond. Again, to a vast degree, trouble in the classroom is avoided to the extent that pupils are kept alert or constructively engaged.

As a general rule, ask the question first, and then designate the person who is to respond. This procedure will encourage the pupils to listen, since they will not know who will be chosen to answer the query. It is possible, however, that occasionally it will suit your special pupose to call the name of the student before asking the question. One instance would be the teacher's desire to retrieve a pupil from his daydreams, or any other inattentiveness, by first calling on the youngster to get his attention and then by following the alertness signal with a question.

After asking a question, give the class members as a whole adequate time to think before you call on someone to respond. This practice not only allows your pupils time to give your question due consideration but also provides you the opportunity to have a representative number of volunteers —perhaps five or six—from which to choose a respondent, assuming, of course, that the question is one that will give rise to a representative number of answers. This method is particularly encouraging to students who require a longer time to formulate their answers than do the fast thinkers. In short, the procedure prevents less able students from becoming disheartened and consequently indifferent about the activities of the classroom.

ASKING SINGLE QUESTIONS

As a general rule, refrain from asking "heaping" questions. To avoid confusion and possible discouragement on the part of students, it is usually better that the teacher ask a single question and pause for an answer rather than ask "heaping" questions, or a series of queries, before pausing for a response. These multiple questions actually are equivalent questions posed by the teacher, possibly out of fear of not getting a ready response through a single question, out of an effort to improve the original question, or possibly out of the sheer habit of asking a series of queries in lieu of a single, precise question. Whatever the cause, the teacher who, in a breath, asks such heaping questions as *What was the purpose of the meeting? What did the townspeople expect to come out of the meeting? Why had the meeting been called?* with the expectation of receiving a single reply is likely to make clear thinking a difficult task for some of the youngsters of the class.

AVOIDING REPETITION

Try, if possible, to avoid repeating questions. Liberal repetition of questions that have been asked may cause some students to become careless listeners through their reliance on hearing the question the second or third time around. Whether you unconsciously repeat questions directed to students, whether you repeat because you dread the silence that occurs as the students consider an answer, or whether you have become a habitual repeater for no reasonable excuse, through conscientious attack on the problem, you should be able to overcome the practice of constantly repeating. When asking a question, you should project your voice adequately and speak distinctly in a conscious effort to have your pupils hear and understand what has been asked.

By the same token, you are to be discouraged from a constant repeating of students' answers. Whether the repetition of replies given by students is the result of nervousness, of habit, or of a zealous desire to see that all student answers get direct confirmation from the teacher, you must not let the sequence of question-student reply-teacher's repetition of student reply become ingrained as a class pattern. A too constant repeating of student replies is monotonous, boring, and unnecessary. Some answers are forceful enough to stand on their own with a mere sign of recognition from the teacher. At times, a teacher's requiring a student to repeat an acceptable answer so that a pupil seated a distance away may hear will be an adequate device both to make certain that all class members have heard the response and to make sure that a particularly important answer is emphasized. As another means of making emphatic a response that should be stressed, the teacher may call on a second pupil to give in his own words the answer already given by a fellow student; or perhaps the teacher may have the original respondent repeat his answer, as a means of receiving praise for his outstanding reply.

PROMOTING INTERACTION

Very frequently when a student asks you a question, you should refrain from answering it until the pupil's classmates have had a chance to offer a reply. This helps reduce teacher domination of the lesson. It is, of course, obvious that generally it would be a waste of time to turn over to the class questions they have no way of answering; yet many questions originally directed to you may be answered quite satisfactorily by members of the class.

Consciously promote interaction among your students by asking some pupils to comment on the answers of classmates. For instance, request a class member to indicate in what ways he agrees or disagrees with the answer of his classmate. This type of crossfire response helps not only to keep your class alive but also to convey the idea that it is everyone's class. In addition, interaction helps to reduce teacher domination.

Pursue promising leads offered by your pupils. Often you may use the response of a student as a cue to ask further enlightening questions or as a cue to introduce additional clarifications that you had not anticipated including as part of your plan. When this procedure is clearly needed, do not overlook the strength of building on important student contributions.

GIVING FEEDBACK

For the most part, students like to know where they stand on answers they have given. And indeed they have a right to the security of knowing. If the particular question at hand is subject to a right or wrong answer, the pupil should be given feedback on whether or not he has answered correctly. Correctness may be indicated by a variety of comments and signals. For example, a teacher may remark "Correct," "Correct, Ronnie," "Yes," or "Very good"; or he may give a nod or smile of approval, or even a look of acceptance. At times, the teacher may elect to show that an answer is correct by proceeding to a follow-up question in a manner that is within itself indicative of the fact that the original question has been answered acceptably For instance, if a pupil should answer the question "What is the difference between these two groups of words?" by answering "The first group is a fragment, the second a complete sentence," the teacher might well ask the follow-up question "How can the first group of words be made into a complete sentence?" in such a way as will indicate that the answer to the original question has been acceptable.

If an answer given by a pupil is wrong, the members of the class should be made aware of the error. Allowing incorrect answers to float around uncorrected may confuse the pupils or undermine their sense of security regarding what they may or may not safely believe or accept. To correct a wrong answer, a teacher may give the original respondent another attempt to try his hand with the question; or he may break down the question that was posed into a series of relatively easy queries with a view to the respondent's resubmitting a response; or he may ask a different pupil to respond to the inquiry. Further still, the teacher may at times correct an answer by questioning the class regarding the partially or completely incorrect response. The following examples illustrate this process of correcting errors: (1) How might we revise Danny's answer so it will be acceptable? (2) What was left out of Marc's answer? Explain. (3) With what part of Sharon's answer do you disagree? Why? (4) Which answer is most satisfactory? Why? (5) What points have we studied today that contradict Karen's reply? (6) Why may we not accept Peter's answer as being accurate?

There are times, of course, when a question has no single answer; that is, more than one answer could rightfully be accepted. In this instance, it is wise that the class come to realize that the answer is a matter of choice. Individual class members should be allowed to determine what they think is the best answer, but they should be encouraged to sustain their choice with reason or adequate support, for this type of sustaining promotes growth and improvement on the part of the students.

In the course of giving your pupils proper feedback, it is important to give them sufficient praise for their efforts and contributions. Some students will need considerably more praise than others. Very often pupils from deprived homes need a great amount of praise because of the lack of proper guidance from home, lack of suitable and sustained motivation, and general lack of security. However, it must not be forgotten that there are certainly some children from the supposedly better homes who, for a variety of reasons, may likewise be in need of praise. Perhaps the safest guide to the students who need an abundance of praise as an incentive to be more responsive in the classroom is getting to know your audience.

Such expressions as "Very good" and "A very good try," or simply a nod of appreciation for effort, may often be needed as signs of encouragement. To praise a child, however, does not mean the acceptance of a wrong or partially wrong answer as a correct response. If the child has struggled diligently to answer a question but the answer is entirely wrong, there is nothing unethical about saying, for example: "A very good effort"; or "Thank you for your nice effort on this question, but let's see if we can look a little more closely at the question"; or "I feel sure you will eventually be able to understand the answer." If the response is partially correct, there is nothing amiss in saying, for instance, "Very good for the first part of the question, but let's see if we can work further with the second part." The important matter is to open, and keep open, the avenues of communication, to create an atmosphere of freedom and encouragement for an honest attempt, to promote a climate where no child's sincere effort is belittled either by the teacher or by fellow students. Proper praise and the encouragement that is associated with such praise may play an important role in promoting class-wide response and interest.

There are of course times when work is of such intense interest that motivation to respond is extremely high without the teacher's use of praise, even in the classroom where praise would normally be needed. And some classes, on their own, may be so highly motivated that no special praise is needed except perhaps in the case of a few individual pupils who may need the reassurance. As teacher, you will want to give praise or withhold it according to the needs of your particular class.

Often a teacher is so pleased to have class members respond favorably to the specific content of the course that there is some reluctance to correct errors speakers make in grammar or expression, for fear of thwarting the interest expressed in the subject matter proper. And yet some feeling of ambivalence may exist, for a sincere teacher feels that it is every teacher's duty to help pupils speak or express themselves more effectively. How to correct the pupil's errors and at the same time maintain optimum student interest in the subject matter can be a real problem for the teacher. Unfortunately, there is no cut-and-dried answer. You will need to face the problem with discretion. The better you get to know your pupils, the more likely you are to handle them with tact. For instance, some students who make an error such as "The . . . had began . . . ." may be corrected just with a passing comment from the teacher. After the speaker has completed what he wishes to say, the teacher may indicate the correct form by quickly saying "had begun" or "You mean 'had begun.'" But the important matter is to correct the error with a tone of appreciation for the pupil's contribution to the lesson proper, so that the youngster won't be discouraged from expressing himself in the future. You might find, however, in the case of a group of shy, reluctant speakers who are being daily encouraged to loosen up and express themselves, that you would be wise to overlook such errors as "had began" during the course of the lesson and get at the necessary remediation through appropriate corrective lessons for the entire class if the errors are widespread or through individual help if the problem of concern is for individual class members. The primary issue is to determine the best means of correcting the errors of the pupils involved while leaving the avenues open for live, enthusiastic response.

MAINTAINING A PRODUCTIVE CLIMATE

Try to handle excess enthusiasm with insight. The sincere teacher is generally pleased with students' expressions of enthusiasm over answering questions. This is as it should be. However, if the noise in your classroom rises to a high level with such action as the blurting out of answers, waving of hands out of desire to answer the questions, and yelling, it becomes your responsibility as teacher to check the disorder. Often it is sufficient to let the class members know that you are highly appreciative to them for their response or interest but that it is impossible for the work of the class to proceed advantageously in the presence of certain types of action, which you may wish to designate specifically. If after there has been ample caution the noise continues at a level that prevents the question-answer procedure from being productive, further steps should be taken, such as requiring the students to write the answers which they wish to give orally or having them engage in some other promising remedial measure that will check their boisterous behavior.

Set a classroom tone that encourages your pupils to be responsive. It is your duty as a teacher to set a classroom tone in which your pupils will feel free to express themselves without being ridiculed by you or by fellow classmates. Respect and encourage the sincere effort of all your pupils, and insist that members of your class do likewise. Instead of tolerating a fellow classmate's laughter at John's inadequate answer to a question, for instance, emphasize the attitude "How may we as teacher and fellow classmates help John to answer the question?" An atmosphere where a pupil feels free to disclose his honest efforts because of teacher-classmate support and consideration is a climate that is favorable for educational growth.

THE DISCUSSION METHOD

A genuine discussion emphasizes the interchange of ideas and opinions among the students of the class. The questions and answers tossed about among the pupils relate to a major topic or problem that has been selected for clarification or solution. In this type of lesson, the class members are in the forefront while the teacher acts as a moderator or pilot. The pure discussion is far less teacher-centered than the regular question-answer format. In the latter method, where the lesson is usually closely directed by the teacher, the communication, to a great extent, flows from the teacher to a student and back to the teacher, to a second student and back to the teacher, to a third student and back to the teacher, and so on. But in the true discussion, the flow of communication is circular. The teacher would introduce the topic to the group, and then the conversation would move from a first student, to a second, to a third, to a fourth, and so on, until the teacher felt called upon to do some piloting. After the direction from the teacher, the process of interchange would again flow from pupil to pupil.

Seats arranged in a semicircle make a desirable setup for a true discussion. When this arrangement is impossible, however, the teacher might have the students face the class as they speak, to impress upon them that the direction of the discussion is to each other rather than to the teacher.

CHOOSING TOPICS

Topics should be ones that make for fruitful discussion. They should be live and hold interest for the pupils who will be participants. They should promote growth rather than empty conversation. Clarification should be possible as the discussion of the issue takes place. The topic should not be narrow, but rather controversial or subject to examination from varying points of view.

PILOTING THE DISCUSSION

Although the genuine discussion is student-centered, the teacher has a special role to play. The teacher may, in fact, never relinquish the responsibility for the outcome of a lesson. In discussions, the teacher acts as a pilot who (1) introduces the topic for discussion; (2) when necessary, clarifies issues, backtracks, and, in general, sees that the discussion progresses toward a conclusion of the problem; (3) serves as a resource person when information is needed; (4) brings a discussion back to the topic through a pertinent question or comment; (5) brings into the conversation isolates who wish to be heard; and (6) summarizes what has been accomplished in the discussion by synthesizing for the discussants the conclusions or solutions that have been reached or by pointing up areas of agreement and disagreement.

ASSESSING READINESS

The teacher must use discretion in determining what classes may profit from a true discussion. Students in the elementary grades and in junior high school would generally not be expected to carry on a discussion as skillfully as some of the more mature high school groups. And similarly, less bright students would not be expected to move profitably into the discussion technique nearly so fast as brighter groups. Yet, the student-centered technique, with its emphasis on dynamic student involvement and interaction, is a democratic method and one that engenders a great amount of pupil interest and growth, when it operates effectively. To ask a class of shy, reluctant pupils who are having difficulty expressing themselves in an ordinary lesson to take part in a genuine discussion, however, would be to ask them to walk before they can crawl. A teacher will have to settle for moving classes into true discussion on the basis of their readiness to profit from the technique.

MODIFYING DISCUSSIONS

In actual practice, the discussion technique has a very wide range. Up to this point we have been describing the genuine or true discussion where the interaction or give-and-take among students flows freely with very little prompting from the teacher. But in practice, what is labeled discussion ranges from the genuine discussion to the discussion that is directed as closely by the teacher as any regular teacher–directed lesson. For instance, very frequently a teacher uses discussion as a developmental lesson to present a concept or idea; the discussion is both carefully planned and carefully directed; and the teacher–planned questions move step by step toward the teacher's goals.

9

WAYS OF DEALING WITH DISCIPLINARY PROBLEMS

Recently, at quite an elegant middle-class junior high school in the suburb of one of our large cities, a young teacher was fast being driven out of her classroom by a potentially cooperative group of seventh-graders. Within the course of forty-five minutes, she would threaten class members close to a half dozen times with what she was going to do if the class wouldn't quiet down enough to be taught. The teasing, giggling, and pushing one another off the seats that took place continuously precluded the teacher's executing her carefully prepared plan. The youngsters were challenging the teacher to put her actions where her mouth was. Fortunately, the teacher was able to receive from her supervisor, and to put into practice, instructions for handling her class. Otherwise, the youngsters could have permanently gotten out of hand.

In a similar type of school, in a practically all-white middle- and upper-middle-class neighborhood, an eighth-grade class was studying the play *Medea*. Although this selection is generally reserved for more advanced grades, those eighth-graders in that suburban vicinity were philosophizing about their reading, in terminology that virtually equaled themselves in size. The trouble with those bright youngsters was that they would neither respectfully listen to each other nor allow themselves to be brought under reasonable control by their teacher. Too many class members were carried away with their own rhetoric and ability. To be sure, the class ran circles around their teacher, who eventually had to be assigned to a less bright but, for her, a more manageable class.

Middle- and upper-middle-class students often present different problems in discipline from those of their less advantaged counterparts, as the two cases above have indicated. It is to be recognized, nonetheless, that all classes of pupils are subject to misbehavior. Some middle-class students are difficult to manage because they have been spoiled by administrators or teachers who have led the youngsters to regard themselves as extra special and deserving of having their every desire or whim satisfied. Further, some overprotective middle-class parents stand ever ready to oppose a staff member in his well-intentioned effort to handle their children properly. Frequently the indulgence of these parents, who seem to think their young ones can do no wrong, causes the offspring to become progressively more involved in unbecoming behavior. These, of course, are only some of the behavior problems of the middle-class school populace; certainly there are others. The point being stressed is that although less advantaged children will generally be expected to pose the greater number of disciplinary problems, it must be acknowledged that all children, regardless of ethnic or cultural background, will at times misbehave. Teachers must therefore be prepared to cope with wayward behavior whenever and wherever it arises.

Despite a classroom program filled with positive, constructive measures that leave limited opportunity for disciplinary problems to creep in, problems of one sort or another are sure to arise among all types of children. In this chapter, then, we explore approaches to handling problems in discipline that do occur in the classroom.

All teachers must come to realize that in the final analysis classroom discipline will be the responsibility of the individual teacher. Administrators may, and certainly should, assist with the more difficult problems, but still the remedy remains with the teacher. It has happened more than once that when a teacher weak in matters of discipline summoned the aid of an administrator, the class members sat like angels in the administrator's presence, only to resume raising the roof after his departure. Generally, a teacher's frequent summoning of assistance causes both pupils and administration to lose faith in the teacher's ability to handle the class. Teachers should make an exhaustive effort to manage their own classrooms; and yet in such an all-out attempt, the teacher must not be hesitant about making referrals when it is clear that his best efforts are not sufficient to handle a given case.

ESTABLISHING CLASSROOM DISCIPLINE

There are sound procedures the teacher can use to establish the kind of discipline needed in the classroom. Those basic practices follow.

SETTING THE STAGE

It is of inestimable relevancy to let the children know at the beginning of the term how the classroom will be run. This procedure precludes their being torn between what will and will not be acceptable behavior. It allows the youngsters to know specifically what is expected of them.

A crucial concern is that the youngsters thoroughly understand the content of each rule and further that they know precisely why each regulation is necessary. In short, it is desirable that the children give their tacit approval of each regulation as being requisite and fair. Youngsters are far more willing to abide by rules or regulations when they have had some part in formulating them and when they deem them to be just. Additionally, peer group togetherness or sanction of what will be done is in itself a particularly strong bulwark against unacceptable behavior. Certainly peer group approval is not to be scoffed at, for peers have a way of bringing pressure to bear against fellow members who are prone to violate what the group has sanctioned.

The setting up of regulations at the beginning of the term should also include certain consequences or types of punishment that are to be imposed on class members for breaking certain rules. Here again, the pupils, under the supervision of the teacher, might play as active a part as is advisable for the class involved. Matching consequences with misbehavior is relatively easy for some cases, but there are times when a predetermined response to misconduct cannot be made. In the process of citing a course of action regarding proper attention to the group and to the individual, Sheviakov and Redl (1956) cite an illustrative case which may make our point clear: A young girl is living under highly undesirable home circumstances. Under the strain, the child bursts out in a temper tantrum in the schoolroom, uses wild language, and hurls insults at the teacher. Ordinarily, the action would have evoked a consequence such as notification to the principal, severe reprimand, ostracism, or some special type of punishment. But, aware of the difficulties the youngster is experiencing, the teacher does not react to the insults but merely waits until the tantrum is over. She then goes over to the child and gives her every sign of unperturbed affection. This is just the support the child needs. If the teacher had reacted otherwise, the youngster would have experienced a terrible blow. The teacher, of course, later indicates to the class that she had real reason to react to the incident as she did even though she didn't approve of the child's behavior; for the teacher is quite aware that she may not handle every other tantrum case in the same manner (Sheviakov and Redl).

When rules are being set up, then, the class must be brought to an awareness that because of the nature or complexity of some problems, predetermined regulations for handling them may not be made, and only the teacher is in position to make an appropriate decision regarding a course of action to be taken. Examples of consequences which require sole teacher decision might well be cited for the benefit of the group. Children, it must be remembered, can be rather sophisticated in certain matters; they soon get the message when teachers are striving to be human and fair in connection with the cases they must handle.

In the initial stage of setting up regulations, care must be taken not to introduce so many rules that the list becomes formidable and discouraging to the pupils. It is best to introduce a reasonable number of basic rules and to rely on adding additional ones as the situation demands.

TEACHING THE CHILD HOW TO BEHAVE

Disciplining the child adequately to a very great extent entails teaching the child how to behave properly. It has been well established that underprivileged children need to be exposed to a considerable amount of teaching on specifically how to conduct themselves, because they have missed much of this type of training in the home. And though middle-class children will need substantially less guidance in the department of discipline, they will, nonetheless, need some training. In fact, all children will need instruction in this area. The fact that the youngsters are growing and reaching toward maturity means that they must be taught. Learning to control oneself in a manner acceptable to our society is a distinct product of teaching.

The teacher should provide for teaching disciplinary matters in accordance with the nature of the misbehavior exhibited by class members. In some classes, teaching may well be interspersed between the teaching of regular subject matter, as the malbehavior is performed; in other classes, special sessions on discipline will be needed as well.

CLASS SESSIONS ON DISCIPLINE

At the beginning of the term when behavioral rules are formulated, the teacher might inform the class of the possibility of having special sessions on discipline. The way would then be paved for having sessions with groups that indicate the need for this systematic approach to achieving better disciplinary control. The amount of time needed or the length of each session would, of course, depend upon the needs of the class.

In the sessions, discussions and demonstrations on how to behave could be aligned with a variety of specific situations. There could be discussions of areas in which a single child or a number of children are experiencing difficulty and, in particular, discussions of means of solving or coping with the problem behaviors. There could be a postulation of hypothetical cases, with children and teacher determining how the protagonist might best behave under the given circumstances. Such cases should, of course, be in line with types of behavior problems characteristic of the group."Social modeling," which is discussed later in this chapter, is a technique advanced by proponents of behavioral modification that is highly appropriate in the types of sessions under discussion. The models who would demonstrate for the class acceptable forms of behavior could be chosen from such sources as films, video tapes, and reading material. In general, teachers will be able to think of a variety of other ways in which teaching sessions on discipline might be productive.

CONSULTING THE PUPIL'S RECORDS

A scrutiny of pupil records as a means of minimizing or avoiding disciplinary problems has already been discussed. Here let us consider the exploration of records as an aid to handling behavior problems that have already occurred. Usually, added information regarding the child will help the teacher cope with the problem a great deal more astutely. There are varied records from which helpful information may be amassed. But perhaps two of the most beneficial records in offering the kinds of information most needed are the cumulative folder, which we have already examined, and the anecdotal record, which we will later consider. Teachers must be quick to use these and other sources whenever the knowledge derived from them is needed to deal acceptably with a given problem.

CONFERENCES: A BASIC TECHNIQUE

Private conferences with students and with parents are two of the foremost ways of dealing with problems in discipline that a teacher has. Both types of conferences may be used to cope with a wide spectrum of problems. Teachers should not fail to make optimum use of them.

STUDENT–TEACHER CONFERENCE

Benefits of the private student–teacher conference are quite specific. The meeting takes the pupil from the presence of fellow classmates so that he no longer needs to be on the defensive for fear of how his classmates will react to his dilemma. It helps teachers get to know and understand the student better. It affords the teacher an opportunity to establish greater rapport with the pupil through the youngster's awareness of the teacher's interest in and attention to his problem. The conference is a means by which teachers can get at the source of the pupil's problem. It is an approach which provides a chance to give the child help in planning a more effective course of action for himself.

The conference should be a heart-to-heart talk between teacher and pupil. Students are more prone to be self-conscious and to refuse to open up freely when others are present. The following list of reminders to teachers should, in fact, help to make the pupil-teacher conference purposeful and rewarding.

1. Relax the student—for example, by asking him to sit and by displaying a calm voice and manner. To show anger or a great amount of anxiety puts the pupil on the defensive and mars your chances of dealing with him as effectively as you might otherwise be able to do. If the student is angry or emotionally upset, give him an opportunity to cool off before proceeding with the conference. A meeting between pupil and teacher is not likely to be successful when there are excessive emotional overtones.

2. State the purpose of the conference early enough to provide ample time for helping the pupil work through his problem.

3. Point out specific examples of the misbehavior so the student will thoroughly understand why his action is considered improper conduct.

4. Mention some of the pupil's positive qualities along with the negative ones to prevent him from feeling that you are being maliciously critical.

5. Allow the pupil an opportunity to talk; let him tell his side.

6. Display a positive tone. Assume the position "How might I be helpful to you in improving your behavior?"

7. Work with the student on a plan for correcting his error, if correction is in order; or help him plan for improvement in whatever area of misbehavior is in question. Help the youngster to reason and to understand why each suggestion offered for improvement or for working through his problem is a valid one. If, for instance, the suggestion has been made that he change his seat, make certain he understands precisely why this step is to be taken.

8. Let the youngster know that you sincerely stand in readiness to help him with the implementation of his plans for improvement.

9. Without using a threatening tone, indicate to the pupil further steps that would be necessary if the undesirable behavior should continue.

10. Let him know, either by words or action or both, that no grudge is being held against him, so that he may feel there is chance for improvement.

11. Near the end of the conference, review the child's status in some manner; but be sure to end on a positive note. A negative termination would be discouraging.

12. Toward the end of the conference, determine whether or not the pupil has any further remark to make or question to ask.

13. In cases in which an additional conference is needed, make arrangements for it.
14. At the conclusion of the conference, you should be able to detect the child's feeling that the meeting has been helpful.

PARENT-TEACHER CONFERENCE

The schools cannot overemphasize the wholesome influence of having the interest and cooperation of the parent as teachers work with the child. Parent concern over what goes on in the school life of the youngster is in turn reflected in the attitude and response of the pupil. It gives the youth the feeling that he is cared about, a powerful sustaining factor for the child.

As we have pointed out, typical middle-class parents will usually apprise themselves of what is going on in the schools and take the initiative to see that conditions are reasonably congruent with their high goals for their children. Having been conditioned to striving for elevated sights, middle-class children are not likely to present as many disciplinary problems as disadvantaged groups who have not had this inspiration or high goals toward which to strive but rather have been entrapped by frustrating environs. Hence, it is largely among the parents of the disadvantaged that there needs to be considerable encouragement for forming firm relationships with the schools. Adequate communication between the school and the home is one of the gravest problems education as an institution faces. How may viable parent-teacher or home-school relationships be promoted? This is the big question to which schools at large need to address themselves. And certainly parents who are remiss in establishing substantial ties with the schools must learn to exercise concern and initiative in forming their rightful connections with the places of learning.

It should be stressed that it is the continuing parent-teacher relationship that should be a major point of concern, not sporadic parent interest when the son or daughter has misbehaved. The truth of the matter is that there would be far fewer disciplinary problems in the first place if parent-school ties were strong where they are presently weak.

As pressing as the problem of strengthening parent-school ties is, however, the topic for the moment is how the teacher may conduct an effective conference with the parent when a son or daughter has misbehaved and the parent has come for a conference about it with the teacher. Incidentally, it might be observed that frequently only one parent, usually the mother, reports to the conference; it is, of course, preferred that both parents attend. In the list that follows are important reminders to the teacher for conducting with success the parent-teacher conference.

1. Relax the parents by using a calm voice rather than an angry or highly emotional tone. A wholesome climate is needed for a fruitful conference.
2. If the parents are angry or upset, allow them a chance to ventilate their feelings. If, for instance, the parents display anger over having been sent for or over what their child has told them regarding the request that they appear at the conference, allow them to blow off steam; let them cool off without your trying to retaliate. If handled with tact, parents, for the most part, change from an unfavorable to a favorable attitude.
3. When the road is clear to proceed with the conference, describe clearly the child's misconduct that has necessitated the parents' reporting to school.
4. Give specific evidence or illustration of the type of behavior that has been unacceptable. To do so is to confirm the reality of the problem.
5. Mention some of the child's positive behavior along with your description of the misbehavior. This procedure will indicate to the parents that you are not maliciously critical.
6. Give the parents an account of what you have done to attempt to cope with the problem behavior.
7. Have at your disposal up-to-date records which indicate the level of schoolwork the child has been doing, in the event this information should become relevant to the conference. The records might consist of such items as record book (including grades and attendance record), tests taken, and papers.
8. Assume the attitude—and convey it to the parents—that the child's welfare, improvement, or progress is your primary concern.
9. Convey the point of view "What may 'we' (as teacher and parent combined) do to help your child improve his behavior?"
10. Invite the parents to help suggest how the desired correction or improvement in behavior might be achieved, that is, how you and the parents might work together for their child's progress.
11. Be a good listener; allow the parents to talk sufficiently. You will be able to learn a great deal about the child's background and the operation of the home that will help you deal with the child more advantageously.
12. At times, when you want to help the parents consider a particular possibility, ask a pertinent question that will steer their thinking in the desired direction.
13. Be sure the conference is terminated on a positive note but with resolution regarding a course of action to be taken in connection with the son or daughter.

14. Without using a threatening tone of voice, indicate to the parents further steps that would be necessary if the undesirable behavior should continue.
15. Decide with the parents how you might best keep them apprised of the child's subsequent behavior. This procedure will point up to the parents how important it is that they work toward helping to reshape their child's behavior.

GENERAL TECHNIQUES FOR HANDLING PROBLEMS

In coping with disciplinary problems, it is generally expected that the teacher will resort to the more mild procedures before proceeding to the more severe techniques. This means, for instance, that a simple appeal to a pupil to stop talking while the class is concentrating on an important point would precede calling in the parents to discuss the child's talking. Only when it became obvious that milder techniques have been ineffective would the parents be summoned. It scarcely needs saying that when an exceptional case arises, as when one child threatens another with weapons, the teacher will immediately resort to a severe technique such as requesting help from a specialist or administrator rather than attempting to work, generally, from the mild to the more severe techniques.

It is of inestimable importance, too, that the teacher resort to long-range treatment of the problem child whenever it becomes evident that lengthy attention is needed. Let us again consider the child who talks while essential subject matter is being explored. Should the first appeal stop the talking, no further action would be necessary. But if the child should fail to respond favorably to the appeal and indeed to increasingly more severe techniques used by the teacher but rather should insist upon disruptive talking during the most momentous points of the lesson each day, it would become evident that long-range or remedial treatment would be needed to deal with the pupil appropriately. In this case, for example, the long-range procedure might well necessitate such measures as the teacher's consulting the pupil's records to try to uncover clues that might be helpful in working with the child; having a private conference with him to pick up additional clues and to try to reason with him; using one of the more drastic techniques such as psychological isolation or behavioral modification, both of which are discussed later in this chapter; and possibly consulting the parents to get further background information and parental cooperation for working with the pupil to greater advantage. If none of these techniques should work, a referral to specialized psychoeducational personnel would be warranted. The teacher must at all times remember to resort to long-range or remedial procedures whenever they are needed.

The remainder of this section is devoted to a discussion of certain general techniques that may be used to combat disciplinary problems. For the most part, the procedures may be applied to a wide spectrum of problem behaviors.

STANDING NEAR THE OFFENDER

Some minor disturbances may be nipped in the bud simply by the teacher's operating from a stand within the vicinity of the misbehaving pupil. The teacher may deliver a few words of caution to the disturber, shake his head to signify that the child should not engage in the unseemly conduct, place a hand on the pupil's shoulder to indicate that the teacher is observing a behavior that must cease, or simply look at the disturber in a way that says discontinue the unbecoming act. In many instances, this technique may be used to put an end to minor disturbances with relatively little annoyance, if any, to the class as a whole.

THE APPEAL

We have already seen the appeal at work. It is a simple request for the restoration of order when there has been a disturbance. It is perhaps most frequently used when the teacher feels that a mild reminder to the pupil or group should be sufficient to restore acceptable behavior. When, however, the appeal goes unheeded, a more drastic measure becomes necessary.

FREQUENT QUESTIONING

Questioning is a technique that may be used to put an end to problem behavior that occurs during the time a lesson is in progress. A barrage of questions pertaining to the lesson is posed for the misbehaving child. The frequent questioning is a cue to the culprit that he must bring himself back in line with fellow students if he does not wish to be overtaxed with questions. The message to the pupil, in short, is that he is impeding the progress of the lesson and this interference must cease or he will pay dearly for hampering his and fellow classmates' chances to learn. Ostensibly the procedure is a reminder to the culprit that he can ill afford to jeopardize his and others' opportunity to learn through his own misconduct. The approach can be used to terminate such behaviors as constant talking or inattentiveness while a lesson is in progress.

THE REPRIMAND

The reprimand may frequently be used to restore a misbehaving pupil to order. The teacher is cautioned, however, that such censure is less effective with some children than with others. After having been reprimanded, some youngsters will settle down and behave themselves. In these instances, reproof is highly beneficial. But there are pupils who after having been censured go into a shell from which it is difficult to retrieve them. Often these are children who are inclined to be withdrawn and to whom a public reprimand should not generally be administered. Usually it would be best to talk privately to these kinds of students regarding their conduct. There is still another type of youngster whose game it is to invite the reprimand in order to try to get the attention and approval of his classmates. To reprove him publicly would be to give him just what he wants and to encourage him to engage in further misbehavior. In this instance, too, it would generally be better to deal with the youngster through a private conference. If his attention-getting antics should continue, however, it would perhaps be possible to handle him successfully through a more severe measure, such as one of the isolation techniques that are discussed in this chapter, but certainly through a long-range plan to uncover endeavors that would allow him to get the attention of the group in a favorable manner.

The reprimand may be used to terminate a variety of adverse behaviors such as talking too much or too loudly, not paying attention, getting out of one's seat, deliberately disobeying instructions, and engaging in many other deviating acts. But the teacher must make judicious decisions regarding the children who will benefit from the procedure.

CHANGING THE PUPIL'S SEAT

Changing the seats of youngsters who get into trouble when they are seated near each other is a means of eliminating a great variety of problems. Here again, there are cautions the teacher will do well to observe. Some troublemakers whose seats are being changed will fare better near the front of the classroom or in a position where their behavior may be under the teacher's close surveillance. There are other candidates for a change of seats who would welcome the chance to sit near the front or in another conspicuous position, so that they might have the opportunity to perform their antics for all to see. These pupils would fare better in the rear of the room or in another inconspicuous location, but away from fellow troublemakers.

The teacher may frequently find it helpful to offer a youngster the chance to reclaim his original seat, after good behavior over a designated period of time. This practice of giving the pupil a goal toward which to strive precludes discouragement. And last, in the case of a problem youngster who would possibly make a scene over having to change his seat, the teacher would be wise to make arrangements for the change in a private conference. In privacy, the teacher would have the opportunity to reason with the pupil and to help him understand why it had become necessary that he change his seat in order to improve his behavior.

A TEST TO QUIET THE CLASS

A boisterous, unruly class that refuses to be quiet enough for the teaching to be done may generally be successfully quieted through a series of tests administered by the teacher, provided the class comprises members who are reasonably concerned about their academic achievement. The procedure would consist of giving the class a test each time there was too much commotion to carry on a successful lesson. In short, what was to have been an oral session becomes a test for which pupils are graded. A test to quiet the class is indeed a negative rather than a positive approach, and certainly one the teacher would rather not use; but it gets results and is far better than allowing the class to waste time or to run the risk of having their needs unmet.

A class reasonably concerned about what happens to them school-wise will readily understand the rationale behind this technique; and class members will begin to quiet each other, first because the majority don't relish taking the tests in lieu of the oral work, and second because they are basically concerned members. The approach, however, would not be suitable for highly disadvantaged classes or for classes exceptionally difficult to handle. In the first instance, the threat would be too discouraging to the pupils; in the second, the students would comprise those who, for the most part, place relatively little value on tests and grades per se. And finally, it might be remembered that this technique is generally more suitable for youngsters in the last few elementary grades and above rather than for children in the lower grades.

REGULAR SCHOOL-HOUR DETENTION

Some schools are fortunate enough to have a detention room in operation during regular school hours. These rooms, frequently manned by teachers from the faculty, can be a godsend when the teacher needs to be relieved of a hot case, a case which involves a problem child whom the teacher needs to get out of the classroom immediately to prevent the favorable classroom climate from deteriorating. But teachers must not pile pupils into the detention room for every little rumpus. In so doing they would mar the forcefulness of this type of service and overburden the detention personnel with many cases that should rightfully have been cared for by the classroom teacher.

The teacher should send a note to the detention personnel explaining clearly the nature of the misbehavior of the pupil who is being sent to the detention room, for youngsters are quick to imply that the teacher sent them out of the room for no reason at all. The note, of course, should be forwarded by another student, not by the child who has misbehaved—or else note and culprit might never reach their destination. And finally, as early as possible after the detention period, the teacher must remember to deal with the youngster further, in whatever manner the case demands.

AFTER-SCHOOL DETENTION

Whether requiring a misbehaving pupil to remain a period after school brings desired results is a controversial issue. Some teachers claim to have achieved outstanding results from the practice; others feel the improvement to be virtually nil. If the technique is to be used, there are cautions that should be heeded. In some detention rooms where students report as a result of misbehavior, the pupils have been allowed to run wild, talking loudly, running over the room, poking each other, and engaging in diverse horseplay; and certainly in these rooms no attention has been given to the pupils in a remedial way. In general, a detention room should be orderly and quiet, except that the person in charge might help the youngsters by talking with them about ways of achieving more satisfactory behavior. Some educators, however, prefer to have the students remain absolutely quiet and study throughout the detention period. One thing is certain: unless after-school detention is administered with special care, its effects will not be rewarding.

Of prime importance, too, is that teachers and administrators come to an agreement regarding the type of misconduct for which a teacher is at liberty to have a pupil serve detention. This understanding can preclude teachers' having pupils remain after school for mere trivialities. It might be added, however, that after-school detention is perhaps most suitable for the last few elementary grades and above. A final consideration is that it may be necessary to arrange to have the youngsters serve their detention period the day following the misconduct so that some students can make necessary plans for traveling adjustments, for missing after-school activities, for delaying participation in some other activity that is affected because of the detention period that must be served.

SUSPENSION FROM CLASS

Usually schools have adopted special policies on suspending pupils, and it becomes requisite that teachers go through special channels before being able to execute a suspension. Some schools will allow teachers to have some of the more troublesome students suspended until parents come to have a conference with the teacher regarding the misdeeds. This arrangement makes compulsory the desirable practice of having the parent come in to confer with the teacher about the conduct of the child. In general, teachers should familiarize themselves with the procedures required by the school.

SPECIAL TECHNIQUES FOR HANDLING PROBLEMS

There are some very special techniques for handling behavior problems, procedures particularly helpful for coping with some of the more difficult cases in discipline. Three of those techniques are discussed in this section. Specifically, they are (1) psychological isolation, (2) soliciting the assistance of the class, and (3) behavioral modification techniques, also referred to as learning theory.

PSYCHOLOGICAL ISOLATION

As the term suggests, "psychological isolation" involves the teacher's completely isolating the misbehaving pupil from teacher attention as if the student were not present in the room. It is a psychological means of dissociating the pupil from both teacher and fellow classmates until the perpetrator is willing to bring himself back in line with other members of the class. Young people want to be a part of the group; hence this approach can be highly effective in causing them to reshape their behavior into a socially acceptable fashion.

In the case of smaller children, the isolation may be physical as well as psychological. Having the small child sit apart from classmates when he has misbehaved is a powerful message to the youngster that he may not always have his way but instead must make his actions compatible with rather than obnoxious to the group, if he is to get along well. It should be mentioned that although some authorities consider physical isolation appropriate only for small children, there are those who approve of the technique for somewhat older students as well.

It is highly desirable that the teacher using psychological isolation have the cooperation of the class. In the initial planning session devoted to the formulation of rules for the class or in the regular class sessions on discipline, or in both, the teacher may wish to explain thoroughly to the class members the principles behind the technique, making certain that the students understand the need for the procedure in connection with making the classroom a fruitful place for the group and for the individual members. The teacher might wish to explain to the pupils that he is not in the classroom to fight them either physically or verbally but rather to use the best means available to help them take judicious advantage of their opportunities. In imposing psychological isolation, the attitude of the teacher should not be hostile, but firm and basically the posture that the psychological isolation is used for the good of the youngsters of the classroom. With the students' understanding of the procedure as a just one that has their progress and welfare at heart, the teacher would expect to enlist the type of pupil cooperation that would bolster the effectiveness of the technique.

In all fairness it should be mentioned that psychological isolation as a technique for dealing with problem children is a controversial one. There are those who oppose its use; yet among its proponents are those who loudly claim that psychological isolation has been proved to work in a great many cases. It is assumed, of course, that teachers who utilize the method will guard against its use in extreme cases when its application would prove detrimental to the pupil involved. For instance, a teacher would be unkind to subject a youngster to psychological isolation if the teacher has reason to know that the impudent victim is so emotionally burdened with home crises that he is in need of the teacher's attention and support despite his wayward actions. As previously indicated, pupils of the class should be able to come to the realization that the teacher will take care of problems that require a variation from usual procedures in a fair and competent manner.

SOLICITING THE ASSISTANCE OF THE CLASS

The technique "soliciting the assistance of the class" to help bring a pupil in difficulty back in line is a cooperative teacher–peer approach. In accordance with this procedure, when the problem child is out of the room the teacher explains to the class members that X, the problem child, needs their help and the teacher's in order to get back on the right track. The teacher lets the class members know that he would be appreciative of their aid, and invites the class to offer suggestions of how the assistance might best be achieved. Because favorable peer cooperation is a forceful procedure, this technique may be used to handle difficult cases such as rude impudence, defiance, the tendency to fight a lot, and many other of the more difficult problems.

A great amount of care must be exerted in the use of the technique, however, to avoid conveying the impression that the procedure is encouragement to class members to work negatively against a fellow classmate. Instead it must be clearly understood that the approach is a supervised effort on the pupils' part to help each other in a continuing program toward acceptable self-control. Here again, it is essential that either in the initial rules-planning sessions or in regular sessions on discipline, or in both, the teacher see to it that the pupils thoroughly understand the principles underlying the technique and that they consider the approach just and a sincere attempt to promote growth and development on the part of the pupils at large. Perhaps it should again be stressed that the teacher who would use the assistance of the class as a technique for coping with certain difficult behaviors should without doubt have good rapport with the class as well as the assurance that the class understands the genuine intent of the teacher in having peers come to the aid of pupils who need it. Otherwise it would perhaps be better that the teacher refrain from using the procedure altogether, lest he be charged with encouraging class members to degrade and pass unfair judgment on their peers who are experiencing problems in discipline.

BEHAVIORAL MODIFICATION

Within recent years, "behavioral modification" has gained increasing attention as an approach for dealing with behavioral problem children. There is, among the proponents of this method, some individual interpretation of certain assumptions associated with the approach. But the position taken on behavioral modification in this book is expressly based on the principles advanced by Robert H. Woody in *Behavioral Problem Children in the Schools* (1969).

As applied to the schools, "behavioral modification" is concerned with modifying the behavior of problem children—youngsters who cannot or will not conform to the socially acceptable norms of behavior, but rather are inclined to thwart the learning process both for themselves and for their classmates. The behavioral approach is a means of coping with the pupils' behavioral difficulties. The assumption is that the unacceptable behavior was learned; the way to correction, then, is the elimination of adverse, learned behavior through a conditioning or learning process that stresses the acquiring of acceptable behavior to replace the maladaptive conduct. Behavioral modification is therefore a conditioning or learning technique. It is based on learning or conditioning theory. It is a process that concentrates on the actual behaviors as a means to the extinction of unadaptive behavior. "Behavior therapy" or "conditioning therapy" is the method through which behavioral modification seeks to achieve its goal.

Let us turn our attention to the learning theory or conditioning aspects of behavioral modification. We might well consider "A System of General Behavioral Modification Techniques" (which follows), a system that may be advantageously used by classroom teachers for the implementation of behavioral modification in the schools. The reinforcement techniques presented can, of course, be used by psychologically trained personnel, for example, counselors and psychologists, with considerably more depth than is true with teachers. And further still, there are reinforcing procedures that have been omitted because they are advocated for use only by highly trained personnel. As previously implied, the intent here is to present a system of behavioral modification techniques that can, for the most part, be used by classroom teachers to cope with problem behaviors in the schools.

POSITIVE REINFORCEMENT

Object Reward—a concrete reward given to the child, to reinforce acceptable or appropriate behavior. Exemplary rewards: toy, candy, coin, or token that can be redeemed for a privilege or gift.

Recognition Reward—verbal or social recognition bestowed on the child, to reinforce acceptable or appropriate behavior. Exemplary rewards: a kind word of praise or encouragement, literally a pat on the shoulder, a smile.

Reciprocal Inhibition—the use of a non-anxiety-provoking situation in the presence of an anxiety-provoking stimulus for the purpose of lowering the power of the anxiety-provoking stimulant and finally for the purpose of actually eliminating the anxiety-ridden condition.

Desensitization—a technique used in conjunction with reciprocal inhibition for the purpose of systematically desensitizing the child to the unacceptable stimulus. A method by which the non-anxiety-provoking situation is made to inhibit or block the anxiety-provoking stimulant, through gradual but progressive steps. Three types of inhibitory responses used in desensitization techniques: (1) affection, (2) feeding, and (3) social reassurance.

Social Modeling and Shaping Behaviors—exposure of the child to the desirable behavior of a person who may serve as a social model to help shape the child's behaviors. The imitating of acceptable behaviors to be achieved, through such means as viewing films or video tapes, observing live demonstrations, and reading about specific behaviors of others. Problem behavior to be shaped into nonproblem behavior. The problem individual to be exposed to a hierarchy of acceptable behaviors—that is, the child to be exposed to behaviors progressively more different and more desirable than the child's own problem behavior.

Positive Reinforcement Combined with Punishment—positive reinforcement such as object or recognition reward granted to the behavior problem child for acceptable behavior; withdrawal or withholding of positive reward when unacceptable behavior is evidenced—the withdrawal of reward conceived of by the child as being punishment.

Robert Woody has reported on illustrative cases that clearly reveal how various principles of behavioral modification may be put to use. Let us consider some of those cases, which may well generate ideas on ways in which the behavioral modification approach may be used to modify problem behaviors in the classroom.

Object reward for a brain-injured child. An auditory stimulus such as a buzzer or bell was paired with candy and pennies. A ten-year-old hyperactive, brain-injured boy was equipped with earphones that could be activated by means of a radio device. When the youngster wiggled too much in his chair, left his seat, or in some other manner misbehaved in the classroom, he received no reward. But when he sat still in his chair for a reasonable period of time and in other ways demonstrated acceptable behavior, the radio device transmitted the auditory stimulus to indicate that the youngster had earned a reward for appropriate behavior (Woody). The illustration demonstrates the strength of the object reward even in conditioning a brain-damaged child to better behavior. In all fairness, it should be mentioned, however, that some classroom teachers take exception to presenting children with object rewards such as candy or money, upon the youngsters' demonstration of acceptable behavior. These critics tend to feel that offering these tangible rewards savors of paying children to behave. Most of these same teachers, however, do not object to words of praise for improved behavior. In fact, the verbal or social recognition types of rewards, as opposed to the object ones, have found approval among a number of authorities and classroom teachers. Nonetheless, there has been more than meager claim of success in the use of the tangible rewards to condition very poorly adjusted classes to approved behavior.

Social recognition reward, to control aggressive behavior. Means were sought to control aggressive responses of twenty-seven three- and four-year-old nursery school boys. To effect the desired results, the teacher systematically ignored all aggressive reactions, offering social recognition only to nonaggressive responses. Physical, verbal, and overall aggressive acts were successfully modified after a relatively short period of conditioning (Woody). It is quite possible to use a combination of object and social recognition rewards in the process of conditioning a child to acceptable behavior; nevertheless, some educators have emphasized the idea that the object rewards are generally more acceptable to small children than to the older youths, while the latter show more appreciation for verbal rewards in the form of praise.

Social recognition reward to modify the behavior of a withdrawn child. A kindergarten pupil was a nontalker. His teacher used attention and approval to condition him to interact. These, of course, are classified as social reinforcement. Verbal and nonverbal communication factors were reinforced. After a year of no talking at school, within a span of four weeks the child began to talk (Woody).

Reciprocal inhibition, to desensitize a youngster to fear of a rabbit. Peter was in much fear of the rabbit. In order that the fear might be eliminated, however, the youngster was fed while the rabbit was in the room. Gradually the rabbit was brought closer and closer to the child, as he ate, until Peter was finally desensitized to the fear (Woody). The feeding was a non-anxiety-provoking situation used in the presence of an anxiety-provoking stimulus (fear of the rabbit). Systematic desensitization to fear of the rabbit was achieved through the child's gradual, but progressive exposure to the rabbit during the pleasurable act of eating. In addition to "feeding," two other inhibitory responses, "affection" and "social reassurance," may be advantageously used for desensitization to anxiety-based problems. And particularly do "affection" and "social reassurance" from the teacher have encouraging implications for counteracting anxiety-rooted conditions in behavioral problem children.

Social modeling and influencing peer identification. There were eighty-four boys with mean ages of five years and eleven months. Each youngster was randomly assigned to one of the following four subgroups for film viewing: (1) film model rewarded for deviation in play procedures, (2) no consequence to the film model for deviation, (3) film model punished for deviation, (4) no film shown. Youngsters assigned to Groups 1 and 2, where there was either a reward or no consequence for deviation, were found to deviate readily in their own play sessions in a manner similar to the deviation by the peer film model. But the children from Groups 3 and 4, where there was punishment for deviation or no film at all, were observed to deviate very little from their former patterns of play. The study clearly points up how influential peer models may be in shaping the behavior of fellow youngsters. It is significant to note that the children are not likely to pattern their behavior after the actor who is punished for his actions, particularly if there is a film model who is rewarded for acceptable behavior (Woody).

Social modeling may be used alone to shape behavior or it may be used jointly with other behavioral modification techniques; but it has vast implications for the improvement of behavior whether the influencing of behavior takes place via films, video tapes, demonstrations, reading, or other means. It is recognized, too, that a highly essential factor is that the teacher take particular care in selecting the types of behavior models that are worthy of emulation. It should perhaps also be mentioned here that social modeling may be especially helpful in improving the behavior of the pupil who acts out to get attention. Such a youngster might be placed in a group of well-behaved members. The well-mannered children could both bring peer pressure to bear on the misbehaving youngster and serve as a social model after whom he could pattern his behavior. Above all, it must be remembered that the possibilities of social modeling for shaping behavior are legion (Woody).

Positive reinforcement combined with punishment to eliminate compulsive stealing. A ten-year-old youngster living in a home for mildly disturbed children was given to compulsive stealing. The use of scolding and disapproval as a form of punishment had only strengthened the unacceptable behavior. Thus it became necessary to withdraw social acceptance whenever the boy stole. In this instance, the acceptance or positive stimulus that was withheld only when stealing occurred was the boy's companionship with a favorite cook. Within a span of three and a half months the stealing was eliminated (Woody).

Positive reinforcement combined with punishment to eliminate temper tantrums. A boy of three and a half years was subject to having temper tantrums. The initial conditioning treatment (punishment) consisted of isolating the boy in a room when a tantrum occurred. Isolation lasted until the end of the tantrum. During the isolation period the child was not permitted to have social contact, since such social recognition would have reinforced the tantrum even if the recognition had been an admonishment. At bedtime the boy was cuddled and the door to his room was left open (positive reinforcement, that is, affection—social recognition). But if a tantrum occurred, the door was immediately closed, and the youngster was left alone until the tantrum ceased (withdrawal of positive reinforcement—punishment). The temper tantrums were eliminated. The conditioning procedure first took place in a hospital but was later transferred to the child's parents and into the home (Woody). The basic principles used in this case, however, are highly recommended for handling many of the temper tantrums in the classroom.

In inaugurating principles of behavioral modification in the schools, the teacher should regard several essential factors. Rules that are scheduled for administering positive reinforcement or punishment must be kept if the behavioral techniques are to be effective. After the child has made considerable gains, however, so that his performance of acceptable acts substantially outdistances the performance of unacceptable ones because he knows he will be rewarded for favorable behavior, the teacher may delay the reward or possibly bestow rewards every second time of preferred performance, then one out of three times, and so on. Eventually, acceptable performance will persist without reinforcement. It should be remembered, nevertheless, that the process of conditioning (unlearning of unacceptable behavior) should last long enough for the unadaptive habits or behavior to be permanently unlearned. The introduction of learning theory into the classroom may at first appear to be chaotic, but there must be the faith that with consistency and sincere attention to behavioral principles the approach will become increasingly effective.

Some nonprofessional aides and parents have been trained to assist with the reinforcement procedures of behavioral modification. In connection with the parents, with whom the child must live, it is particularly helpful for them to understand the basic procedures of learning theory and to be able to assist with its implementation. On a cautionary note, the teacher must not be reluctant to consult with counselors, psychologists, and other specialists well versed in psychology when the assistance of these personnel is needed to strengthen or effect a behavioral modification program within the classroom.

SOME DO'S AND DON'TS

Of interest here are certain cautionary measures that are valid for those who work with the misbehaving child. Teachers will do well to take into ample consideration these reminders.

Try, if possible, not to make the offense personal. Frequently the results will be more effective if instead of cautioning the pupil that he is annoying you as a teacher you will indicate that the youngster's misbehavior is disturbing the class or interfering with the progress of the group. This approach, which is a far-reaching one in implication, tends to prevent any triumph the pupil might otherwise have over provoking the teacher; instead, it puts peer pressure on the misbehaving youth to bring his action in line with that of the class members as a whole. Emphasis on cooperating with the class is a potent tool for working advantageously with the misbehaving child.

Don't insist on punishing a student unless there is direct evidence that the suspect has committed the misdeed. If the teacher has reason to believe that the pupil has committed the offense yet the pupil stanchly proclaims his innocence, the teacher would be wise to forego any kind of punishment unless he can uncover convicting evidence. A pupil becomes antagonized over an unjust penalty, and so does the class as a whole.

Handle discipline cases as promptly as possible. A pupil is less likely to make the proper connection between punishment and misconduct when a great amount of time separates the two. Particularly does this situation hold true in the case of the more difficult students who are little inclined to give due regard to their misbehavior in the first place.

Make the punishment suit the behavior. The child who defaces the classroom wall can see fairness in being asked to wash down the wall, as opposed to being required to copy a randomly selected paragraph fifty times. Pupils sense justice in punishment that fits the act and, accordingly, are more likely to accept willingly the penalty imposed.

Don't always give attention to the least rumpus. We have previously established the idea that the teacher should be observant of and attentive to what is going on in the classroom and convey this alertness to the pupils. Yet despite this generally wise advice, there are certain extenuating circumstances under which the teacher must have foresight enough to overlook some little acts of misconduct. As one example, in a class where pupils have formerly been highly disruptive but have improved immeasurably, the perceptive teacher will overlook certain minor acts of misbehavior, the correction of which would at the time induce discouragement or look like nagging. It would not be practical to attempt here a definitive guide of situations in which it would behoove the teacher to overlook petty offenses. Teachers are called upon to exercise sound judgment in identifying such instances.

Be broad enough to change your procedure when it becomes obvious you have made a mistake. To do so is better than sticking to the wrong guns. If you have erred in your decision for handling the discipline of one or more individuals, giving a sensible explanation of the reasons for an altered course of action will bring far greater pupil respect than relentlessly sticking to a technique that is at fault. Similarly, the teacher's candid correction of mistakes he makes in subject matter generally induces greater student respect than the teacher's trying to cover up his errors. The important matter is to strive to make the mistakes few and far between.

Avoid constant yelling. Youngsters become immune to the voices of teachers who try to control the class through vibrant screams for every other act of misconduct, major or minor. Pupils soon write off these adults as naggers and refuse to hear their chatter. An occasional yell at one or more pupils, however, may produce effect.

Refrain from making sarcastic remarks. For the most part, sarcasm from the teacher triggers off the wrath of students, for it has the effect of disdain directed toward the pupils themselves rather than toward their acts. Youngsters are highly resentful of being shamed in the presence of their peers. They generally expect their teachers to be above such belittling tactics as sarcasm. What is more, when the teacher is sarcastic to one student, the sting of the ridicule frequently spreads throughout the class, for others visualize themselves as possible targets for the teacher in the future.

Do not make empty threats. The actions of a teacher must be well attuned to his words or youngsters will lose confidence in the unfulfilled pronouncement of what the teacher will do to those who misbehave. Associated with a loss of confidence is a loss of respect. The thoughtful teacher will take inventory of the avenues open to him and will keep his promises to students aligned with possibilities of fulfillment.

Don't force older youngsters to apologize for their misbehavior. Apology comes hard for the somewhat older pupil. To back down before his classmates and beg forgiveness is a humiliating experience for him. Rather than serve the purpose of making him desire to improve his behavior, the apology is more apt to release from the youngster bitter resentment toward the teacher for putting him in such an untoward predicament. If, however, out of his own free will, the pupil apologizes, this means that he has come to terms with himself and is willing to look at his behavior constructively. In this instance, the apology should be looked upon as a welcome symbol of the youth's desire to mend his ways. The situation, however, is quite different in the case of small children. For instance, a goodly number of teachers attest to being able to have two small combatants apologize for their offense to each other without bitter repercussions on the part of either of the youngsters. Rather, the procedure tends to help the little ones determine what is expected of them and build a worthwhile set of values.

Refuse to hold grudges against your pupils. The mature teacher will reprimand, punish, or do whatever is demanded, but afterward will hold no malice toward the students. The teacher's willingness to forgive has a salutary effect. It sets an example for pupils and bears out the point that corrective measures were focused on the undesirable acts and not on the students.

Remember your obligation not to turn a pupil out of your classroom with no indication of where he should go. It is understandable that at times an individual case can reach such proportions as to make the teacher desirous of being rid of the troublesome student involved, if only for a short time. Yet no matter how thin the teacher's patience has worn, the pupil who is ejected from the room should be sent to the proper administrator or personnel in charge of disciplinary cases or to the room of a fellow teacher. Youngsters who are allowed to roam the corridors banging on doors and calling into classrooms can cause headaches for other teachers. Perhaps it scarcely needs saying, as well, that the pupil who is permitted to wander about on the loose is subject to becoming involved in situations for which the regular teacher could be legally held responsible. It perhaps bears emphasizing here, too, that it may frequently be the case that two or more teachers may make reciprocal arrangements to keep each other's troublesome students for brief periods of emergency. When the youngster is removed from his familiar environment, away from his audience before which he is accustomed to performing, he is not likely to feel encouraged to continue his antics in the new environment.

Strive to be duly patient when the progress made by delinquent pupils is slow. Poor behavior patterns that are deeply rooted were built over a period of time and often require considerable time for undoing. Here, the familiar saying "Rome wasn't built in a day" is relevant to the task of the teacher.

Try to make the child feel that you like him even though you must condemn his unbecoming behavior. If you can simultaneously reprove the youngster and convey the idea that you like him and have his interest at heart you will have won much of the battle of establishing and maintaining good discipline. The youngster will have the needed assurance that you accept him, even though you don't condone his wayward actions. He receives impetus, therefore, for greater cooperation and improvement in his manner of behaving.

Don't blame yourself for not being able to handle every behavior problem that confronts you. While you will want to be able to handle the majority of the problems that arise in the classroom, the average teacher is not favorably situated or equipped to cope with all cases in discipline. Teachers must be willing to pass on to the proper administrator or personnel worker a case which needs the attention they as teachers are not able to give.

MAKING REFERRALS

In dealing with problem behavior, sincere teachers often ask the question "When should referrals be made?" Although the answer to this query cannot be definitive because of individual circumstances that surround various cases, it seems relatively safe to offer a generalized answer that should be helpful. It might first be said that when the teacher has exhausted all logical means at his disposal for dealing with a specific disciplinary case but the repertoire of ways has not produced desired results, the teacher is justified in seeking help elsewhere. And second, at whatever point it becomes apparent to the teacher that the case is one which is impossible for him to manage or that the child is suffering from an emotional disturbance which the teacher is not properly equipped to handle, a referral should immediately be made to the proper administrator or personnel within the school.

It is the responsibility of each teacher to become familiar with the procedure for making referrals in his school. In a number of schools, teachers are required to refer the problem child to a supervising chairman or assistant principal; the supervisor in turn is charged with the duty of making any necessary referral to the proper psychoeducational specialist, such as school counselor, school psychologist, or social worker. The avenues of recourse vary in different institutions for learning. Whatever the referral procedure may be, teachers should become acquainted with each required step in the process, and with the services offered by each personnel worker.

Where psychoeducational services are adequate, it is requisite that teachers take advantage of them; where they are inadequate, it is incumbent upon teachers to exert their influence toward helping to make them suitable. Ideally, schools should provide the services of such specialists as school counselors, school psychologists, social workers, nurses, physicians, and psychiatrists. It is the duty of these psychoeducational personnel to act as consultants to teachers and administrators and to provide means of coping with children who have deep-seated emotional disturbances and other serious behavioral problems. Teachers and administrators must not be reluctant to avail themselves of the benefit of these specialists. Additionally, schools are expected to provide the services of reading specialists and of speech and hearing therapists on whose knowledge teachers and administrators can capitalize for the benefit of youngsters who have needs in the areas indicated. Actually, in the final analysis, it is the responsibility of school administrators to make certain that teachers are apprised of all the special services that are available to the school and to seek to bring about a harmonious interprofessional relationship between teachers and special psychoeducational personnel.

In order that classroom teachers may detect with some degree of prognostic know-how behavioral problem cases that should be referred to psychoeducational specialists, they are urged to make optimum use of anecdotal records. These records are written notes which the teacher jots down, from time to time, regarding the reactions or behavior of a pupil. There is real value to be realized from anecdotal notes that are systematically kept. They help to provide a developmental picture of the progress, or lack of progress, made by the pupil, in matters of conduct. The anecdotes may assist the teacher in making a more objective judgment regarding the behavior of a student. Such appraisal may be used both by the teacher who has recorded the observed behavior and by fellow teachers with whom the recorder may wish to share pertinent information. The anecdotes may serve the teacher a very supportive role in teacher-pupil and parent-teacher conferences, and certainly the periodically recorded behavior of pupils should help the teacher decide, with reasonable assurance, when it is proper to make referrals.

Enough has already been said to make it clear that anecdotal notes must be meaningful if they are to be helpful. To record that Cheryl, a third-grade youngster, was emotional this morning would not be very enlightening. Instead, the specific behavior that constituted the emotional state would be needed. It should be noted, for instance, that Cheryl cried profusely when she was asked to stop talking and that she banged on the table then proceeded to suck her thumb when the teacher required her to take her place in the reading circle. The more precisely the notes depict the behavior of the student observed, the more assistance they may afford the teacher toward making valid judgments regarding the pupil.

10

SPECIFIC PROBLEMS AND HOW TO HANDLE THEM

One teacher of considerable experience insisted on addressing his ten-to sixteen-year-olds as "Mr." and "Miss." He reasoned that if he treated his potentially rowdy groups as grown-ups, his youngsters would strive toward conducting themselves as such. His claim to the degree of effectiveness of the venture was more than modest.

Among a group of prospective teachers who were being trained to teach in the inner city was one young man who perched himself upon his desk and unfolded his lesson to his class of youngsters with the verve of a competent teacher of many years. The students were fascinated; and although the supervisor had informed beginning teachers that they could effect better pupil control standing than sitting, she readily admitted that perhaps this man's unusual personality and command of communicative skills would allow him to become a "sitter" from the outset.

A female teacher of much experience confided in her co-workers her best aid to taming a wild, uninhibited class—keeping them in for an hour after school for each day of rowdy behavior. She insisted that the controversial issue of after-school reporting worked wonders for her.

The three examples above should cogently emphasize teacher individuality and the impossibility of offering definitive guidelines for handling problems in discipline. There are teachers who because of their discrete personalities are able to achieve excellent results through controversial means or through ways that are quite at odds with general practices. If the individualized techniques do the desired job, there is usually no reason why they should be condemned. The techniques offered for meeting the specific problems treated in this chapter are merely suggestive and are by no stretch of the imagination to be conceived of as sacrosanct. Teachers may wish to use the guidelines in whole or in part, or simply as a springboard for creating individualized means of meeting the types of problems presented.

AGGRESSIVENESS

Enterprising aggression is to be nurtured. In this instance, the aggressor has outlined goals for himself; he is simply alert and zealous in an effort to attain them. Basically, however, he does not injure others in the process of achieving his objectives. The outcome is the type of spiritedness that leads to progression.

But our concern here is the type of negative aggression that leads to a behavior problem. This brand of aggressiveness offends. The offensive youngster may be accustomed to attacking other pupils; that is, he may be given to provoking, pushing, or hurting (physically or through words). He may be a noisy or boastful youth or a good example of a show-off.

One kind of aggressor makes a concentrated effort to acquire what he wants regardless of what persons or things he must push out of his way (Mikesell and Hanson, 1952). A pupil with this makeup is frequently highly motivated and has often come from a middle-class background where intense competition with other youngsters is the practice. The teacher must refuse to let him push others aside. In private conference with him, he might make the student thoroughly aware of the nature and extent of his aggressive conduct and point out to him that others have rights which must be honored. It may also become necessary to seek the parents' cooperation in helping the pupil mend his ways.

The overindulged child is another type of pupil who may often become a behavior problem. At home he has been the center of attention and finds it very disconcerting when at school he must take a place merely on equal footing with classmates. To show his superiority or accustomed degree of importance, he may resort to such aggression as the use of physical force or slanderous words (Mikesell and Hanson). The teacher must not give in to this spoiled child; to do so would only augment the problem. Instead, the pupil must come to realize that he is, after all, merely one child among many others. Such techniques as the teacher-student conference, the conference with parents, sessions on how to behave, verbal or social recognition rewards for progress made, and social modeling should help to bring him to this realization.

Then there is the youngster who is desirous of attacking or hurting someone physically or psychologically because he feels he has been wronged by one or more persons. He is angry and wishes revenge. He assumes a hostile or destructive attitude because of the unwholesome background that surrounds his existence. Frequently, though certainly not always, the disadvantaged pupil falls into this category. There are, too, various types of children who have not had security, love, and understanding in the home. Occasionally such a child will aggressively seek to compensate for his lack by trying to take by force the benefits that he has missed in a socially approved way—love, friends, money or other material goods, and so on. This is his weapon for dealing with intolerable frustration (Mikesell and Hanson).

Still another aggressive type is the individual who desires to dominate or exercise excessive control over someone or something. This undue dominance makes him feel superior and helps him compensate for his felt deficits. It is an aggressive attempt to help him eliminate his inferiority. Usually this type of person seeks to dominate a weaker individual (Mikesell and Hanson). A pupil who attempts to behave in this manner must not be allowed to crush another pupil. In private conference, the aggressor might be made aware of precisely how he is reacting and should be informed of how obnoxious his behavior is to some classmates. The youngster could be seated next to pupils whom he can't control. Additionally, the teacher might help the youth by uncovering one of his noninjurious talents that may be brought before the group in a favorable light.

And finally, there is the type of individual who tries to elevate himself by belittling others. Behind the sarcastic remark is a desperate attempt to raise himself at the expense of others. Usually the one who ridicules has not advanced to the level of his victim (Mikesell and Hanson). Again, in private conference, the child's attention needs to be called to precisely how he is reacting. Sessions on the way to behave and on social modeling should be of great assistance. Social recognition rewards for improvement in the unacceptable behavior should bring valuable results. And certainly the teacher might try to reason with the pupil, indicating to him the advantages of developing some of his stronger points in preference to resorting to the ridicule of others. In general, private conferences with the students and, if needed, conferences with parents; solicitation of class assistance in dealing with the problem, when this procedure would be helpful; the use of verbal or social recognition rewards for improvement in behavior; and social modeling may be advantageously used to cope with the various forms of aggression we have mentioned.

THE CLASS SHOW-OFF

The class show-off is frequently to be found in the classroom. Often we synonymously refer to him as the class clown, smart aleck, or attention-getter. Actually, the show-offish behavior of such a youngster is a form of aggressiveness.

Essentially, the youngster looks upon his teacher as a parent substitute and wishes to be accepted and loved by him. Even children whose behavior seems to belie this desire want love and acceptance. If a teacher spurns the youngster's efforts—and sometimes crude attempts—at getting attention, it is probable that the child will react with even more despicable conduct (Jersild, 1960). The wise teacher will capitalize on the child's desire for approval by giving him the necessary warmth and love, through providing wholesome activities in which the attention-seeker may gain attention in a favorable manner.

Aside from craving acceptance by the teacher, a youngster desires also to gain the attention and approval of his peers. Status in his relationship to other children is very important to him. If his efforts to gain peer attention and approval are rebuffed or ridiculed, the child's reaction may range from grief and despair to utter rage (Jersild). In short, all children want to be significant and to gain status in the eyes of teachers and peers. The teacher who can help these youngsters achieve their objectives will have far fewer disciplinary problems (Blair, Jones, and Simpson, 1968).

In a treatment program for the class show-off, the teacher–pupil conference is crucial. In privacy, the teacher may make it clear to the youngster that clowning is neither expected nor necessary either for meriting teacher attention or for gaining approval from classmates. The teacher might point out what is being missed while the youngster engages in attention-getting tactics. But more important, the conference will give the teacher an opportunity to get to know the pupil better so that one of the youngster's stronger points may be singled out for emphasis. The teacher will help considerably by finding something constructive the pupil can do and encouraging him to do well in that area, in order that the youth may gain attention and praise in fruitful ways. School records and the parent-teacher conference are, of course, additional informative sources for helping to uncover the child's potential strong point, which can then be stressed.

Positive reinforcement combined with punishment (withdrawal of reward) also has strong implications for conditioning the show-off to acceptable conduct. The child would receive warmth and understanding and various types of verbal and social recognition during good behavior, but upon the appearance of show-offish antics, these rewards would be withheld. And finally, various types of social modeling are very much in order for helping to reshape the behavior of the class show-off.

THE STUDENT WITH A CHIP ON HIS SHOULDER

The pupil who carries a chip on his shoulder may often be difficult to get along with. Basically he is given to quarrelsome or argumentative behavior. He may be irritable, cantankerous, or fiery in relationship to both the teacher and fellow classmates. Often this type of person feels he has been wronged in one way or another or that his is an arduous road to trod. He is resentful and subject to being cross with those with whom he comes in contact. For the most part, the pupil is laden with feelings of inferiority. Many times, though certainly not always, such a youngster is from a depressed environment where he has suffered the sting of impoverishment and embitterment. Often, he may be a member of a minority ethnic group.

At times when the pupil with a chip on his shoulder is being difficult, by finding fault with everyone and with each situation, for instance, the teacher might help by calmly directing a question to him that will allow him to realize how unreasonable or unfounded his behavior is. Arguing with him, however, will not help, but rather may induce him to be even more quarrelsome. The teacher may further assist by seating the pupil near children with whom he can best get along.

In private conference, the teacher might talk to the youngster about his quarrelsome behavior and allow him an opportunity to talk and release some of his ill feelings. The youth may be helped to realize instances in which he is inflicting his feelings upon innocent parties who have not wronged him and to recognize evidence of how unpopular his cantankerous behavior is making him with fellow classmates. The conference offers the teacher an opportunity to get to know the youngster better and to discover further appropriate ways of dealing with him.

Arrangements may be made to have the pupil drain off some of his resentment in such wholesome activities as arts and crafts, music, physical activity, and creative writing. Some youngsters may be found to have pronounced ability in one or more of these areas.

Though individuals with a chip on the shoulder are anxious about their status, they may frequently try to cover up their feelings with a facade of indifference. The use of reciprocal inhibition, with ample affection and reassurance from the teacher, may help considerably in desensitizing such children to their negative feelings toward others and toward life.

THE WITHDRAWING STUDENT

Withdrawal is an avoidance response, a retreat from the realities of life. It is a mechanism designed to lessen the stress and strain of everyday living. Though it succeeds in reducing defeat and failure, it fails to solve problems logically and realistically. It is, of course, the overuse of withdrawal, the tendency toward permanent escape and toward escape grounded in fear, that becomes dangerous. When an individual becomes ill at ease among people, when he generally prefers to be alone, and when he begins to avoid contacts with people, he is becoming seriously maladjusted (Mikesell and Hanson). The quiet, withdrawn children are not at the time causing anyone else trouble, but they are experiencing difficulty themselves. They are unhappy, troubled children. They are, like time bombs, likely to explode at any time, for they are the children who could possibly breed the headline "Model Student Kills X." Hence these withdrawing children must be treated as discipline problems. The teacher's job in teaching discipline extends beyond the classroom; he must produce youngsters who can live both with themselves and with others (Hymes, 1955).

Just as aggression may be the result of an inferiority complex, so may withdrawal result from inferior feelings. There are, of course, varied reasons why people withdraw. Although not all persons with physical defects are sensitive, some of them are. Among the sensitive persons is the individual who withdraws from people in order not to be hurt by what they say or do. Many a person withdraws because of fear—fear of being snubbed, ridiculed; fear of being rejected by the group; fear of losing friends. The reaction of other people to an individual, then, is highly important; when this response to the person is not substantial, withdrawal is likely to be the result (Mikesell and Hanson).

Comparing children with superior siblings or playmates, if continued over a period of time, may make for hatred, resentment, hostility, and feelings of inferiority. In a course of time these negative feelings may cause the child to withdraw and to try to find security in a dream world that he can control (Mikesell and Hanson). Teachers must be particularly careful not to push pupils into competitiveness that is harmful.

Goals that are set too high for a youngster are likely to lead to frustration and to subsequent withdrawal (Mikesell and Hanson). Teachers must see to it that objectives for students are kept within reason.

Lack of independence or overprotection by the home, or being dominated by parents or an older sibling, may cause a person to withdraw (Mikesell and Hanson). In such instance, it may be necessary that a teacher seek the cooperation of parents in discontinuing these negative influences.

A history of constant failure may cause a person to withdraw into his own world of daydreams where he feels he may be safe (Mikesell and Hanson). A teacher is enjoined to provide for this type of youngster such doses of success as will bolster his confidence.

In general, pupils who withdraw must be helped to cope with their difficulties without running away. In private conference with the child, the teacher might try to show him in what way he is withdrawing, what he is missing by doing so, and how he may become more outgoing. But then, since the types of children under discussion are so given to reticence, usually a conference with parents is also warranted so that pertinent background information may be uncovered for the purpose of dealing more appropriately with the child.

There are other steps that might be of essence in dealing with the withdrawn child. It may be determined, for instance, that the pupil should sit near the teacher for moral support or perhaps near children with whom he gets along well. During recitation time, teachers might give the retiring youngster some questions or work with which he may be successful in order to foster in the child courage and a sense of success. In making group assignments, teachers will help the withdrawn pupil by assigning him to work with group members with whom he can work with at least a fair degree of success. And finally, the teacher might try to uncover an area in which the youngster stands out, and help the child develop it. This procedure will go a long way toward giving the withdrawing child self-confidence.

In the process of helping to draw out these withdrawn children, teachers may use positive reinforcement of the verbal and social recognition brand in abundance. These rewards would of course be given for the youth's specific efforts toward becoming wholesomely active.

And last, an endeavor to drain off the bottled-up feelings of those who are quiet or withdrawn would be well worth the effort. Much of the draining of feelings may be effected through such mediums as involve creative writing, music, clay modeling and woodwork, and other arts and crafts.

THE CONSTANT TALKER

In the case of the pupil who talks too much, it is suggested that the teacher investigate the reasons for the persistent talking. For instance, is the classwork too easy, offering insufficient challenge; or is the work too difficult, causing discouragement to set in? If either of these reasons seems to be an operant cause of the incessant talking, the teacher must seek to bring about an adjustment that will make classwork appropriate for the class at large and for individual members.

When dealing with the usual talker, the teacher may often use milder techniques before proceeding to the more drastic ones. Simply standing in the vicinity of the talker is one mild approach that may work with some youngsters. With others, it may be necessary actually to make a mild request for order. Should this technique prove ineffectual, perhaps the teacher might wish to resort to such a measure as frequent questioning of the student over the classwork to call to the pupil's attention the fact that he is not listening though he should be. Some students may well be brought to terms through a reprimand. If none of these measures seem workable, the teacher may, for instance, wish to move to the more severe approach of separating the youngster from pupils to whom he talks, through a change in seating.

In the case of continued talking on the part of the pupil, a private conference with him obviously becomes necessary. In a face-to-face meeting, the teacher will wish to try to reason with the youngster and show him that when he talks constantly he impedes his own progress and that of others as well. It will help to point out to the youth specific instances in which his talking has stood in the way of achievement. It is essential that the teacher be sufficiently firm with the confirmed talker, letting him know that such talking as retards himself and others will not be tolerated. If it is discovered that it is attention the youngster is seeking, effort needs to be exerted to show him that wholesome attention can be gotten when, instead of constantly talking, he does the level of classwork that merits admiration. The teacher may also wish to provide for him greater opportunity to participate in conversation related to his schoolwork. And finally, soliciting the aid of the class, psychological isolation, and positive reinforcement combined with punishment have implications for dealing effectively with the constant talker, should more drastic measures be needed.

THE RESTLESS STUDENT

"Some restless and annoying children may have hyperthyroidism which needs medical attention" (Blair, Jones, and Simpson); or there may be some other physical defects which prevent the pupil from acting as a normally adjusted student. In some instances, the youngster may not be getting ample rest. In the case of illness, it is of course apparent that referrals need to be made to the specialists who may provide for the medical services needed. If the pupil needs more rest, logic suggests a parent-teacher conference to determine what steps may be taken to provide the child with the rest needed.

The fidgety pupil can be annoying both to the teacher and to fellow classmates. With his restive behavior, he stands in the way of his own learning and that of others as well. It is imperative therefore that the teacher try to discover the reason for the pupil's problem. If the cause does not stem from physical reasons, there are other legitimate questions a teacher may ask: Is the classwork meeting the student's needs? Is work too difficult or too easy? Is there enough variety in class activities? Does the schedule provide for wholesome release of excess energy? If the answer to any one of these questions is in the negative, it could be a contributing factor to the disturbing behavior, and corrective measures would be in order.

A determination of the causes of restlessness can be promoted through such means as direct observation and student-teacher and parent-teacher conferences. Additionally, an investigation of the pupil's cumulative folder and consultation with other teachers who have taught the student may offer promising leads. A discovery of causes would of course warrant making any referrals that might be needed, to the proper personnel specialists.

TEMPER TANTRUM

The child who stages a tantrum is often a youngster who has been spoiled. The youth is desirous of having his way and will usually go to great length to try to get it.

Generally, the procedure is not to condone the behavior of the temper tantrum protagonist or to permit him to wield the control he seeks. Instead, one of the isolation methods is frequently used. Through this means, the victim is consistently denied social contact, approval, or attention for the duration of a tantrum, for any such recognition usually causes the youngster to perform with even more violent outbursts, in his effort to try to have his way. Even negative social contacts, such as admonitions, are refused the child, since as a rule he favors negative recognition to no attention at all.

We have seen the workings of "positive reinforcement combined with punishment" to eliminate temper tantrums. The child was given warm attention and approval while there was no tantrum; but immediately upon an outburst, the youngster was punished, the punishment consisting of isolation and a withdrawal of attention. As a result of this behavioral modification technique, the child's tantrums ceased.

One consideration, however, is in order. We observed previously a girl who received considerable teacher support, following the youngster's violent outburst. The support was a broad gesture of sympathetic understanding. To have dealt with the child through pure isolation, with no support from the teacher, would in this instance have been detrimental to that young girl who was experiencing intense stress because of highly unfavorable home conditions. This situation is a reminder to the teacher that although isolation or the withdrawal of attention for the duration of an outburst is a recommended procedure for handling tantrums, some children under unusual circumstances may be in need of some special type of teacher support. The temper tantrum protagonist who is suffering from intense stress, extreme emotional upset, or physical pain is an example of an instance that may warrant a degree of deviation from the usual pattern of treatment for temper tantrum victims.

CHEATING

Teachers may help to minimize cheating by gearing the lessons as closely as possible to the pupils' level. In this way, the students will feel more secure in their ability to handle the classwork and less need for cheating. The classroom teacher will likewise find it wise to refrain from pitting one pupil so sharply against another that youngsters resort to cheating as a means of keeping their grades in line with or higher than those of fellow classmates. Similarly, parents who are so overly demanding as to make their children feel the need to cheat in order to attain certain grades should be apprised of the ill effects they are having on their youngsters and should be discouraged from continuing to entrap their young ones in detrimental behavior. Finally, when a test is to be administered, teachers should make certain that directions and explanations are perfectly clear. This practice will reduce the pupil's felt need to look at the work of other students to see how other pupils are handling requirements.

During a rules-planning session, it would be considerably meaningful if the teacher would set up clear-cut regulations regarding cheating. Pupils would then be well aware of how they are expected to conduct themselves for the duration of a test, and those who disobeyed regulations could justifiably be made to suffer consequences. The following guidelines for teachers should be particularly helpful in minimizing and eliminating cheating during the time tests, quizzes, or examinations are in progress.

1. Before administering the test, make the surroundings less conducive to cheating by having each pupil remove books and papers from the top of his desk and from the floor around his seat.
2. Require that there be no communication among classmates for the duration of the test.
3. Have a pupil raise his hand when he has a question. The teacher might establish the habit either of going to the pupil who needs help or of having the pupil come to the teacher, in accordance with the regulation that will allow the teacher to keep all pupils under adequate surveillance while the student's question is being answered.
4. Do not permit pupils to look at a fellow student's paper. They should keep their eyes focused in front of them. Circulate among the pupils to see that this regulation is obeyed. Specifically instruct the students to keep their eyes on their own papers.
5. While the test is being administered, move about among the students constantly, to reduce the propensity for cheating.

When the rules regarding cheating have been firmly set and well understood, the teacher must not be reluctant to confiscate the paper of the pupil found cheating and to give the youngster a zero or refuse him credit for the phase of classwork in which the cheating was done. It is not fair to fellow classmates to permit some class members to cheat. Cheating makes it difficult for those who arrive at their grades fairly to compete with those who cheat to secure theirs. In short, cheaters produce low morale among students who aspire to honesty. Finally, when a pupil is requested to turn in original work such as his own synopsis of a book or some other original product, the teacher should make the requirement totally explicit, then refuse to consider copied work acceptable.

After an act of cheating has been committed, the teacher should usually meet with the pupil in a private conference. Here, if the youngster has extenuating circumstances to present, the teacher should hear them and react to the situation at hand with the best teacher judgment. In any event, the pupil in conference needs to be helped to understand why cheating is not an acceptable approach to acquiring knowledge and how cheating creates an unfair situation for fellow classmates. If the cheating continues, the teacher, of course, may wish to enlist the cooperation of the parents or of an administrator in putting an end to the maladaptive behavior. In summoning the parents or administrative official, the teacher would do well to produce concrete evidence of the youngster's having cheated.

THE BOISTEROUS CLASS

Youngsters don't cherish the idea of having to take a test. When the teacher lets it be known that a boisterous class will either quiet down so that the lesson may proceed orally or be given a test on the work that ordinarily would be covered in nonwritten form, various class members may frequently be heard trying to shoo each other quiet. Some utter such invectives to fellow members as "X, why don't you shut up" or "Hush, X, I don't want to take a test." Many times the pressure of class members on each other to be quiet is sufficient for the lesson to proceed, without the test. In the case of some classes, just the idea that at any time a test might be administered if there isn't sufficient quiet for work to proceed is adequate within itself to produce the desired class climate.

Tests that are given to tame the class should be graded. After all, the work that has been written is not busywork, but rather a means of emphasizing relevant material that the class would not exercise enough self-control to permit the teacher to cover in the usual manner.

Rather than the test, the teacher may wish to give class members a considerable amount of seatwork that might ordinarily be covered orally were the class orderly enough to permit the classwork to proceed normally. As with the test, pupils may be led to feel the responsibility of exercising better self-control if they are held accountable for their performance in the seatwork activity.

Certainly another aid to taming the rowdy group is reasoning with the children regarding the disturbance that prevents a favorable class milieu. Many students are sophisticated enough to accept the premise that the level of work that will help them advance may not be carried on in turmoil. Indeed one teacher has often reminded her rowdy pupils, at the height of the noise: "I suppose I'm trying to knock myself out for me." Because the teacher is competent and wishes to do the greatest possible amount for her pupils, she is able to get away with this remark, short of its being considered a note of sarcasm. Her statement is sufficient to make her youngsters take pause.

Changing the seats of the worst troublemakers will prove helpful. The teacher's standing in close proximity to the most poorly behaved youngsters until they quiet down likewise has notable merit.

When dealing with any type of class, teacher–pupil and parent–teacher conferences, in connection with the greatest disturbers, are definitely in order. In the case of the parent–teacher conferences, word gets around that parents are being called in. Not all parents offer the support needed with their children, but even the assistance or cooperation of some parents may be observably helpful.

BEING A SUBSTITUTE TEACHER

In all fairness, the substitute teacher who goes into a room to take over a class during the regular teacher's absence faces a task that is decidedly not easy. It is only natural for youngsters to want to fool around or take advantage of the substitute when the adult directly responsible for them is not present. In addition to the misbehavior of the less well controlled youngster, some pupils who are ordinarily well behaved show off unthinkably under the new setup. What is more, a portion of the parents of these usually well-ordered children would have to be forced into an acceptance that their young ones had misbehaved so poorly. Rather than consider the action of the pupils a personal affront, however, substitute teachers must busy themselves with appropriate procedures for offsetting this natural tendency of children to try to take advantage of the surrogate leader.

Some authorities suggest that teachers keep their regular lesson plans, or perhaps a few extra lessons, at a convenient spot in the classroom, where they may be available to the substitute teacher in the event of teacher absence. This ruling, however, is one that perhaps gets more lip service than actual practice. Many times, the plans are simply not at the disposal of the substitutes. But even when they are and the surrogate teachers utilize them, if important work is entailed a number of the conscientious regular teachers will feel the necessity of going over the material presented by the substitute to make certain the work has been covered satisfactorily or that certain portions of the lesson have been duly stressed. At other times, lesson plans provided by regular teachers may not be used by the substitute because the surrogate teacher has been asked to teach work completely out of his area of specialization. A science teacher, for instance, may have been asked to substitute in an English class; a social studies teacher, in a mathematics class; a physical education teacher, in the regular elementary classroom, and so on. Wise substitutes, then, will arm themselves with a supply of surefire lessons that are capable of keeping any classes so constructively employed that class members will not seek recourse to their favorite game of making life annoying or unlivable for the surrogate leader.

Almost all children of all grades and subject areas like an intriguing story that is adventurous, racy, mysterious, or imaginative. Aside from the children's listening to and enjoying the plot itself, their empathy with various characters and guided exploration into points of interest regarding the setting may help these youngsters become gainfully engaged, when the regular teacher has failed to leave a lesson plan, or when a plan that has been left is one the substitute cannot successfully implement. "The Most Dangerous Game" by Richard Connell, "Cemetery Path" by Leonard Ross, "The Lady or the Tiger" by Frank Stockton, and "The Bet" by Anton Chekhov are a few examples of the kinds of stories we have in mind. And what is more, these types of stories may be adapted for enjoyment and constructive communication in quite a number of the different school grades.

Games or puzzles designed to identify such persons in the news as movie stars, entertainers, and politicians may also be constructively used by a substitute teacher of any subject area. Additionally, students of various grade levels very much enjoy making as many words as they can out of a very large word. This is a constructive endeavor for which a prize of paper, pencils, or some other objects may be given for the child's successfully finding in the large word a designated number of smaller words. Spelling and vocabulary exercises, too, may be converted into a variety of interesting and constructive puzzles and games. Surrogate teachers will, of course, find it to their advantage to rexograph, or mimeograph, as much of the exercise or game material as is possible. The use of individual rexographed sheets tends to cut down on the children's excuses to roam over the room and engage in horseplay. The better fortified the substitute teacher is with surefire lessons or activities, the greater chance he stands of handling the youngsters, who, by nature, are inclined to test the endurance of the substitute. Finally, regular teachers of the school will likewise be wise to have in reserve a group of surefire lessons from which to draw when, by chance, emergencies require them, as permanent teachers, to cover classes of fellow workers.

CASE STUDIES IN DISCIPLINE

Though the special cases that comprise this chapter may be classed as hypothetical, they are based on true occurrences. In every instance, of course, the names used are fictitious. Each disciplinary case is followed by three proposed solutions. The recommended solutions given at the end of the chapter were arrived at by a group of selected teachers and administrators who carefully read the cases and chose their answers. You are invited to read the cases, and then compare your answers with those based on the teacher poll.

ELEVEN REPRESENTATIVE CASES

CASE 1

Student: Bernard Allen	Ethnic background: black
Age: 9	Grade: 4
I. Q.: 101	Reading achievement: grade level
Father's occupation: father's	3.0
whereabouts unknown	Mother's occupation: factory worker
Brothers: none	Sisters: two (ages 12 and 14)

Gail Lind is a new teacher in an elementary school. In fact, this is her very first experience as a teacher. She was assigned an unruly fourth-grade class, to say the least. There are thirty-three pupils in the group—seven Puerto Ricans, two whites, and twenty-four blacks. It seemed to Miss Lind that when she first walked into her classroom all hell broke loose. As she described it, the children were literally climbing the wall.

Fortunately, Miss Lind was foresightful enough to seek the guidance of Susan Lubelsky, an outstanding experienced teacher of the school. Taking her cue from her veteran coach, Miss Lind has worked diligently to get on top of her rowdy group. She sees to it that the work moves quickly; she provides extra pencils and paper for those who aren't motivated enough to be responsible for bringing their own working tools; she uses much rexographed work of high interest that requires a minimum amount of milling around; she uses numerous pictures and other visual aids in connection with her teaching; and she provides for her pupils periodic exercises to release pent-up emotions. In all fairness, the class is much improved in conduct since the beginning of the term, for at least some lessons may be carried on, even if not in the most desirable fashion. It would be a gross exaggeration, however, to imply that behavior is close to par, for even while there is keen interest in the work at hand, there is more noise than in a regular class.

Rather recently, Mrs. Lubelsky suggested to Miss Lind that she call in the parents of some of her worst behaved children. This procedure has helped too, although Miss Lind was cautioned that she should not expect miracles from the visitations.

Among the troublesome students, one of Miss Lind's great concerns is Bernard Allen, a nine-year-old black boy. He has difficulty keeping his mind focused on the lessons for more than an exceptionally brief period of time no matter how interesting they are. Many times Bernard appears to be totally aloof and wanders around the room aimlessly, it seems. At times he does a lot of banging on desks, and yet he seems to be a shy, erratic child. Upon a very recent request that Bernard's parents visit the school, his mother came in. She frankly admitted that Bernard is a problem in the home. "He's much harder to manage than my other children," she reported. "He's all right when he can find a piano to play, and he can play just about anything he hears."

Miss Lind thought Mrs. Allen's report worth pursuing. Yesterday, she took Bernard to Mr. DelValle, the music instructor of the school, to have Bernard play some of his piano selections. Everyone who heard him was completely stunned by his performance. It appears that whatever he has heard played he can reproduce amazingly well. He's apparently a child prodigy of the first order. The important question is how he should be handled.

A. Miss Lind should intercede for the parent by having Bernard placed in a class where it's possible to get a better quality of classwork done.

He is only one grade behind in reading achievement. With some individual assistance from the teacher and possibly from some of the very bright students who may be willing to tutor, Bernard should be able to keep up with somewhat brighter youngsters of the school. A better caliber of students would no doubt stand a greater chance of inspiring him to make the most of his special talent. In connection with this arrangement, as well, perhaps it might be possible to permit Bernard to substitute additional music periods for some of his minor studies in other areas. In any event, it is hoped that the music instructor will take Bernard under his wing for purposes of guidance, help, and inspiration. If the youngster's urge for music is satisfied, chances are that he will not only be more inclined to behave and become a better all-around student but will be more greatly motivated to make the most of his talent as well.

B. No exception should be made for Bernard. There are doubtless other gifted pupils in the class, maybe not as much so as Bernard, but gifted nonetheless. If exceptions are made for one, they should be made for others. Bernard should be kept in the class and encouraged to make the most of his studies, as a foundation upon which to develop his talents in the future. Similarly, he must be made to behave. Firm demands in discipline must be made of him, and with an expectant tone of voice and unswerving eyes the teacher should stand in close proximity to him until he complies. If at last he can't be managed, he should be sent to the appropriate administrator to be disciplined.

C. The combination of Bernard's giftedness in an area in which the teacher has no competence, his tendency toward aloofness and uncontrollable movements in the classroom, the teacher's inability to reach him with subject matter that appeals to the majority of the class members, and the mother's lack of know-how for meeting her child's best interests all make a referral to competent guidance personnel the sensible step to take. No time should be lost in referring the case. Miss Lind should investigate the procedures of the school for making such a referral.

CASE 2

Student: Peter Kane
Age: 12
I. Q.: 99
Father's occupation: lawyer
Brothers: one (age 16)
Sisters: one (age 11)

Ethnic background: white
Grade: 7
Reading achievement: grade level 8.1
Mother's occupation: administrative secretary

Peter Kane attends junior high school in his neighborhood. It is a vicinity which consists of a population that is primarily middle class and above. There are thirty-one pupils in Peter's class, three Puerto Ricans, one Oriental, two blacks, and twenty-five whites. Toward the latter part of February, Peter's mother came to school to speak to Mr. Norris, Peter's English teacher, about the amount of reading the class was doing. Mrs. Kane complained that her son was not given enough reading to do. Mr. Norris explained that since the beginning of the semester in February the class had been reading and analyzing short stories in class with a view to starting the study of a novel within a week. He explained further, "A prior study of the short story has really helped us build up criteria that'll allow the children to read the novel with greater skill and appreciation." Mr. Norris thought that Mrs. Kane had not only heard but understood.

But several weeks after the novel was assigned, Mrs. Kane wrote a letter to the principal of the school complaining that Peter's class was not being given enough compositions to write. Strangely enough, Mr. Norris had just assigned a composition in connection with the novel just before the principal summoned him to the office regarding Mrs. Kane's letter. Mr. Rodner, the principal, was somewhat upset that the letter had been written, but he listened intently to what Mr. Norris had to say.

Not only did Mr. Norris describe to the principal the written work he had just assigned, but he indicated that he had already determined that more and more compositions would be assigned as the reading of the book proceeded. Mr. Norris did mention, however, that with five English classes to teach a day, he felt it useless to assign more written work than he could properly grade.

Peter has not been a particularly cooperative child in the first place. And now in the midst of all the turmoil about how Mr. Norris should teach his class, Peter's conduct is growing increasingly worse. Mr. Norris frequently has to ask him to stop talking and pay attention. The caution, of course, is effective for only a very brief period of time. And increasingly Peter snarls disrespectfully at his teacher. Under the present circumstances, Mr. Norris is having his troubles with parent, child, and administration.

A. (1) Since Mrs. Kane has criticized Mr. Norris's handling of reading and composition work, more than likely she will complain about his method of teaching some other phase of English. Mr. Norris should therefore refer the entire case to the Guidance Department for the guidance personnel's considered judgment. (2) Should the guidance staff be unable to handle the problem, Peter Kane should be sent home to his parents until Mrs. Kane and her son are willing to cease being troublemakers.

B.   (1) It would be helpful if Mr. Norris would record anecdotal notes of Peter's behavior that might be used in conference with Peter's parents. (2) Mr. Norris might also review his long-range plans for reading and writing to make certain he has provided for the best possible balance between the two areas and to be sure he has worked out as effective a program as he can in reading and composition work. (3) He might then discuss his overall plans with his English supervisor, asking for any suggestions or comments the supervisor might have. If necessary, a conference with the principal might also be arranged for discussing these same long-range plans. (4) Mr. Norris should then schedule a meeting with both parents. (5) In the conference with Peter's mother and father, Mr. Norris would do well to explain to them also his long-term plans for the reading and writing that are to be done in Peter's class. The mother's understanding of the overall outline may serve the purpose of relieving her of some of her anxieties. (6) In the face-to-face meeting, Mr. Norris should also discuss with the parents Peter's general welfare and should try to learn as much as possible about the youngster in order to be able to work with him to greater advantage. With the anecdotal notes before him, Mr. Norris should talk with the Kanes about Peter's poor conduct and ask for their cooperation in helping to bring the misbehavior to an end. It would be wise, too, for Mr. Norris to suggest to the parents in a tactful but positive way that talking negatively about teachers in the presence of the child makes the youngster disrespectful and undermines the type of cooperative spirit that is essential for their child's progress. (7) Finally, if the parents should not cooperate in helping to bring about improvement in Peter's behavior, his case should be referred to the proper administrator of the school.

C.   (1) Mr. Norris should review his long-range plans for reading and writing to make certain he has provided for the best possible balance between the two areas and to be sure he has worked out as effective a program as he can in reading and composition work. (2) He should then ignore all future complaints about classwork, from anyone, unless, of course, the complaints are specifically directed to him.

CASE 3

Student: Amy Cromer	Ethnic background: white
Age: 7	Grade: 2
I. Q.: 118	Reading achievement: grade level
Father's occupation: grocer	2.8
Brothers: one (age 17)	Mother's occupation: housewife
Sisters: none	

Amy Cromer has been the source of real trouble since she has been in Patricia Mercer's second-grade class. The group consists of twenty-three whites and one black youngster, and it seems that Amy doesn't get along well with any of the children.

During the time between the end of one class activity and the beginning of another, Amy generally finds something to drag over the floor, a pointer, a chair, an eraser, or some other object that has attracted her attention. She goes through the motion of imaginary hauling even during the time she is in the reading circle or in a group where some other activity is taking place. Amy is given also to hiding a classmate's personal belongings, such as a hat, a composition book, or a pencil. And always the hidden object may be found in the same hiding place. When Mrs. Mercer speaks to Amy about any of her histrionics, she cries loudly, and sometimes screams. Because of her conduct, she is not very popular with the children of the class, and they tend not to want her on their side when captains are choosing their teams for games to be played.

But even worse than Amy's dragging of objects or hiding of personal property is her tendency to hit her classmates. She has to be watched closely because of this bad trait. Mrs. Mercer is accustomed to permitting her pupils to take brief periods of rest at designated intervals, and the youngsters are encouraged to relax by putting their heads on the table. On a particular afternoon, class members had been scheduled for a brief rest period. Mrs. Mercer had observed them all to be relaxing. To make optimum use of her spare time, she proceeded to put up colorful pictures in the room. Before she could complete this task, she heard one of the children let out a scream and begin to cry loudly. Amy had really done it this time. She'd hit a boy with one of her shoes. Luckily, the lick didn't land on the back of the youngster's head, but on his left shoulder instead. The pupils and teacher have suffered enough from Amy's bad habits. Something must be done.

A. First of all, Mrs. Mercer should investigate the condition of the child who was hit, to make certain he was not really hurt. Then she should send for the parents immediately. Through arrangements with the appropriate administrator, she should have Amy remain at home until the parents come in.

In conference with the father and mother, Mrs. Mercer should tell them all that has occurred regarding Amy's poor conduct. She should obtain as much information as possible concerning the causes of the child's action. Mrs. Mercer might very candidly request the parents to help her understand Amy's reactions, because of the seriousness of the youngster's behavior. All knowledge gathered should be used to the child's advantage. Mrs. Mercer would do well both to work out with the parents a plan for the improvement of Amy's conduct and to arrange for future direct communication with them regarding the progress of their child. Further still, she should encourage the parents to seek competent guidance or psychoeducational help for Amy, if this step seems to be warranted.

Finally, Mrs. Mercer should talk to the child herself about the youngster's behavior. She should try to have her understand that her fellow classmates won't like her if she hits them, hides their belongings, and in other ways offends them. Mrs. Mercer should inform Amy how she should conduct herself. Until the necessary progress is made, of course, Amy's actions must be watched closely to make certain the child doesn't injure any of her classmates.

B.   Mrs. Mercer should check up on the child who was hit, to make certain he was not really hurt. Then she should try to see to it that Amy is handled much more firmly, both in school and at home.

At school, Mrs. Mercer should explain to Amy that she as teacher won't put up with the type of behavior the child has been exhibiting. When Amy drags objects, or goes through the motion of doing so, Mrs. Mercer should stand close to her and demand that she put an end to such action; when she hides a classmate's belongings, she should be requested to get the property and return it and should be reprimanded for having moved it; when she attempts to hit someone, she should be restrained from doing so, and should be made to sit alone until she indicates willingness to be with the group without attempting to injure anyone.

Mrs. Mercer should further request a conference with the parents. She should apprise them of their daughter's conduct and indicate to them in a tactful way that the youngster has many attributes of a spoiled child. Mrs. Mercer should ask the father and mother to cooperate with her in working with their child by seeing to it that Amy is handled firmly at home as well. Until the necessary progress is made in Amy's behavior, however, her actions must be watched closely to make certain the child doesn't injure any of her classmates.

C.   In the first place, Mrs. Mercer should investigate the condition of the child who was hit, to make certain he was not really hurt. She should then send for the parents.

In conference with the father and mother, Mrs. Mercer should tell them all that has occurred regarding Amy's poor conduct. She should obtain as much information as possible concerning the cause of the child's actions. In fact, Mrs. Mercer might candidly ask the parents to help her understand Amy's reactions, because of the seriousness of the youngster's behavior. All knowledge gathered should be used to the child's advantage. Further still, Mrs. Mercer would do well both to work out with the parents a plan for the improvement of Amy's conduct and to arrange for future direct communication with them regarding the progress of their child.

Additionally, Mrs. Mercer should talk to Amy herself about her behavior. She should try to have her understand that her fellow classmates won't like her if she hits them, hides their belongings, and in other ways offends them. Mrs. Mercer should inform the youngster how she should conduct herself. Until the necessary progress is made, however, Amy's actions should be watched closely to make certain the child doesn't injure any of her classmates.

Perhaps Mrs. Mercer should ask some of the nicer children of the class who act more in accordance with their age than Amy, to include Amy on their team sometimes or to include her in their group when selections are being made, in order to help her have a greater sense of well-being and to help pave the way for her acceptance by the class as a whole. Mrs. Mercer might also seek to uncover one of Amy's strong points, or something she does well, in order to bring her before the group in a favorable light. Perhaps, for instance, Amy might be able to create imaginative stories or art work based on the objects she has previously enjoyed dragging. Finally, Mrs. Mercer might praise Amy lavishly, both in pleased expression and in words, when she makes a sincere effort to dispense with her previous unwholesome behavior.

CASE 4

Student: Jose M. Torres	Ethnic background: Puerto Rican
Age: 13	Grade: 6
I. Q.: 79	Reading achievement: grade level
Father's occupation: truck driver	3.6
Brothers: one (age 18)	Mother's occupation: restaurant
Sisters: one (age 14)	waitress

Jose Torres, Miguel A. Sanchez, and Lorenzo Thomas sit near each other in Mrs. Glenn's sixth-grade class, because of the alphabetical arrangement of the seating. There are, in all, thirty-four youngsters in the group, twelve Puerto Ricans, nineteen blacks, and three whites. Jose and Miguel are two Puerto Rican children, ages thirteen and twelve, and Lorenzo is a twelve-year-old black youngster. This morning, the three boys, like their class-mates, were busily engaged with their seatwork as Mrs. Glenn circulated about the room to check understanding and to be assured that the work was being done.

Shortly after the teacher returned to her desk, however, a commotion began to take place in the back of the room, among the three youngsters. Somehow the boys tuned out completely on the assignment and became preoccupied within their own threesome. Mrs. Glenn yelled to them from her desk to stop disrupting the class and to get back to work. For a brief while they complied, but then pretty soon the talking and giggling started again.

Mrs. Glenn requested that Jose and Lorenzo move to different seats in order to place an appropriate distance between the misbehaving youngsters. Lorenzo promptly obeyed by taking his new seat, but Jose just sat there twisting and turning in his original seat in open defiance of Mrs. Glenn's command. Furious over this rebuff, she rushed in Jose's direction with a determined look, which Jose, from all evidence, interpreted as an unrelent-ing intent to eject him from his seat. Just as she was about to reach the youngster, he sprang to his feet and fled from the room leaving in Miguel's possession an entire picture collection of nude women and men engaged in sex acts. By this time, all other class members had become spectators rather than pupils busy with what had promised to be an engaging seatwork activity.

A. Mrs. Glenn should immediately inform the administrator in charge of disciplinary matters of Jose's leaving the classroom without per-mission. She should confiscate the pictures in Miguel's possession and request that a conference be held with both Miguel and Lorenzo after class or at the earliest convenient time. The classwork should then proceed as planned. If Miguel has refused to give up the pictures, however, he should be informed that he may not be considered an active part of the class until he brings himself in line with proper student behavior by honoring the teacher's reasonable request. Mrs. Glenn's demand for the pictures should finally be adhered to even if the request must be met through the parents' or administrator's cooperation. With respect to Jose, if the administrator turns him over to Mrs. Glenn to be disciplined, there should be a conference with him also.

Though Miguel, Lorenzo, and Jose are fast approaching the age to be naturally curious about sex, in conference it should finally be made clear to them precisely why they should not have the obscene pictures in the classroom. Mrs. Glenn should make provisions for getting each child's parents into the school for a parent-teacher conference, and each youngster should understand why the teacher considers the disturbance over the pictures an offense serious enough for the parents to be summoned. Additionally, if Mrs. Glenn judges the trouble previously caused by Miguel and Lorenzo's sitting near each other to be too extensive, she should make arrangements during the conference for the change in seating of one of them; otherwise she may wish to caution the two boys that additional trouble from them will instigate a change in their seating arrangements. But because Jose flagrantly disobeyed instructions to take the seat he was instructed to take, upon his return to class he should be required to use the seat that was pointed out to him until he demonstrates his willingness to obey reasonable requests.

In conference with Jose, as well, Mrs. Glenn should have him examine his reason for refusing to move his seat and for running away. He should be made to realize how and why he did not face his problem squarely. If the school permits a child who has offended to be sent home until the parents come in to see about him, to have Jose sent home until his parents visit the school would be a good reminder to him that he must comply with legitimate teacher demands.

Mrs. Glenn's conference with Jose's parents, by the way, may lend additional clues to his obstinate nature and to his tendency to run away. Finally, Mrs. Glenn might have the boy's parents help suggest means by which Jose may effect desirable improvement in his future behavior. She should make clear to the parents, however, the actions that must be taken if Jose fails to make the necessary progress.

B. The problems created by the three youngsters are too serious and complicated to be handled by the teacher. First of all, the children's possession of the lewd pictures was a serious offense within itself. Then one youngster's open defiance of the teacher's request to change his seat was intensified by the child's running away. The three boy's entire case should be referred to the appropriate administrator of the school, for his considered action.

C. Mrs. Glenn should look out in the corridor for Jose. If he is in the hallway, she should reason with him on the matter of why he should return to class. If Jose may not be seen, however, Mrs. Glenn should immediately send one of her most reliable students for him.

She should confiscate the pictures in Miguel's possession and request that a conference be held with the three boys after class or at the earliest convenient time. The classwork should then proceed as planned. If Miguel has refused to give up the pictures, however, he should be informed that he may not be considered an active part of the class until he brings himself in line with proper student behavior by honoring the teacher's reasonable request. Mrs. Glenn's demand for the pictures should finally be adhered to even if the request must be met through the parents' or administrator's cooperation.

In conference, it should be made clear to Miguel, Lorenzo, and Jose precisely why they should not have the obscene pictures in the classroom. Mrs. Glenn should make provisions for getting each child's parents into the school for a parent-teacher conference, and each youngster should understand why the teacher considers the disturbance over the pictures an offense serious enough for the parents to be summoned. Additionally, if Mrs. Glenn judges the trouble previously caused by Miguel and Lorenzo's sitting near each other to be too extensive, she should make arrangements during the conference for the change in seating of one of the two; otherwise she may wish to caution the two boys that additional trouble from them will instigate a change in their seating arrangements. But because Jose flagrantly disobeyed instructions to take the seat he was instructed to take, upon his return to class he should be required to use the seat that was pointed out to him until he demonstrates his willingness to obey reasonable requests.

In conference with Jose, as well, Mrs. Glenn should have him examine his reason for refusing to move his seat and for running away. He should be made to realize how and why he did not face his problem squarely.

Mrs. Glenn's conference with Jose's parents, by the way, may lend additional helpful clues to his obstinate nature and to his tendency to run away. Finally, Mrs. Glenn might have the boy's parents help suggest means by which Jose may effect desirable improvement in his future behavior. She should make clear to the parents, however, the actions that must be taken if Jose fails to make the necessary progress.

CASE 5

Student: Kenneth Ellis
Age: 17
I. Q.: 81
Father's occupation: custodian
Brothers: none
Sisters: one (age 14)

Ethnic background: black
Grade: 12
Reading achievement: grade level
  8.5
Mother's occupation: domestic
  worker

Kenneth Ellis is a tall, hefty-looking black boy in Janet Carr's twelfth-grade social studies class. The class consists of eight Mexican-Americans, eighteen blacks, and seven whites. Mrs. Carr is visibly disturbed because Kenneth sleeps in her class practically every day, no matter how interesting the lesson. This practice is bad for the morale of the class. In addition, Mrs. Carr has felt insulted and let down, for she considers herself a "number one" teacher of all types of classes. Aside from the deflation of her ego, though, she has genuine concern for the boy. She has examined the situation closely and has determined Kenneth's ability to do the work to be on par with that of the majority of the members of the class.

Mrs. Carr has had private conferences with Kenneth and has spoken to him any number of times about the sleeping. He hasn't been impudent or haughty, but still the sleeping has persisted. When asked if anything at all hurts or bothers him, Kenneth's answer is always "No." When asked if he gets enough sleep at night, the answer is "Yes." And so it was that Mrs. Carr came to feel the youngster's continued sleeping a gross affront.

She invited both parents to school to confer with them regarding their son. The mother came in and appeared to be pleasant and cooperative. She expressed a determination to put an end to her son's sleeping in class, but there has been no marked change in him.

Finally, Mrs. Carr consulted Kenneth's teachers of the the previous semester, regarding his habits. To her surprise, she learned that Kenneth was not only sleeping in her class but had been sleeping in his other classes throughout the first semester.

A.   Anecdotal notes of Kenneth's reactions should be kept, to provide a running account of the youngster's general behavior and of the extent of his sleeping. Mrs. Carr could then help considerably by sending for the parents again, both of them. With the anecdotal record before her and the parents, Mrs. Carr should try to convince the father and mother of the importance to the boy and to them of taking the youngster to a highly recommended doctor for a thorough medical checkup. The teacher may be asked to help the parents choose a suitable doctor or else a procedure for choosing one. If a competent physician works in connection with the school, however, the mother and father may wish to have the school doctor examine the son and make a referral to the proper medical specialist if such step needs to be taken. If the referral to the medical personnel should prove to satisfy the youngster's needs, then his case can be amply met. If not, the boy should possibly be referred to competent guidance personnel for their considered judgment. In any event, Mrs. Carr should work determinedly to have Kenneth's case adequately resolved.

B. Mrs. Carr should have Kenneth stay in after school to make up for any large portions of the lessons he misses because of his sleeping habits. Then if there is actually anything he can do to stay awake and be more responsive, this procedure should cause him to do so.

C. Mrs. Carr should send Kenneth directly to the administrator who handles special problem cases in the school. Kenneth hasn't responded to the measures his teacher has used thus far, even though the class members as a whole are responsive. His is a case that should be referred to an administrator to be handled as the administration sees fit.

CASE 6

Student: Linda Keefe	Ethnic background: white
Age: 8	Grade: 3
I. Q.: 136	Reading achievement: grade level
Father's occupation: fireman	4.9
Brothers: two (ages 10 and 12)	Mother's occupation: housewife
Sisters: none	

Linda Keefe is a third-grade pupil in a class of twenty-eight children. The group contains two Orientals and twenty-six whites.

The youngest child and only girl in her family, Linda has been greatly spoiled. She has often tried to monopolize the class recitation or to outdo everyone else in responding. Ellen Kantrowitz, the teacher, has frequently had to curb Linda's aggressiveness by some tactful reminder: "Now we've heard from Linda twice already; let's hear what Mary has to say." In private, Mrs. Kantrowitz has tried to reason with Linda, too, by pointing out to her that though she as teacher is greatly appreciative to her for her interest and hard work, she does have twenty-seven other children in the classroom who also must be heard and seen. Linda has had some difficulty working in small groups, as well, and Mrs. Kantrowitz has had to help her in this area.

Now today Linda has again made trouble for herself. She was not chosen to be first contestant on her side, to participate in a "word" game, though she had desperately wanted to be first. Linda suddenly went into a temper tantrum, cried profusely, stretched herself out on the floor, and flung herself about in utter abandon. Though Mrs. Kantrowitz had known Linda to sulk when she couldn't have her own way, never before had she known the child's reactions to reach such proportions as they did today.

A. Mrs. Kantrowitz should ask the child who is to be first contestant on

Linda's side to let Linda be first for the day, with the promise that Mrs. Kantrowitz will meet with Linda in a private conference.

B. The teacher should send Linda to the personnel worker in charge of discipline, while other pupils continue working with a view to having the contest.

C. Mrs. Kantrowitz should make certain that Linda does no physical harm to herself or to the other children, but should completely ignore her for the duration of the tantrum, while giving praise to the other children for their interest in trying to implement the game.

CASE 7

Student: Carmen Hernandez   Ethnic background: Puerto Rican
Age: 15   Grade: 9
I. Q.: 101   Reading achievement: grade level
Father's occupation: machinist   8.9
Brothers: two (ages 12 and 18)   Mother's occupation: housewife
Sisters: two (ages 6 and 16)

There are fourteen pupils of Puerto Rican descent in Mrs. Wells's ninth-grade social studies class; eight black students, and seven whites. All during the school year, Mrs. Wells has observed that Carmen, a Puerto Rican girl with a slightly brownish cast in skin tone, is simply in a dither when by chance she comes in close contact with any of the black youngsters of the class. Indeed, on more than one occasion, she has been known to look at Mrs. Wells, a black instructor, with some disdain. The classroom seating was alphabetically arranged, but even with this setup Carmen chanced not to be sitting in close proximity to any black pupils.

Toward the last part of May, there was the usual picnic for the classes of prospective ninth-grade graduates. Mrs. Wells assigned specific seats to each of her pupils who rode one of the busses to the picnic grounds, in order to be able to check her group on and off the bus with the greatest facility. Carmen was given a seat next to Mildred, a dark-skinned black youngster. Discontent was written over Carmen's face for the full fifty-three miles, and when she arrived at the picnic area, she lost no time in joining the six students, Puerto Ricans and whites, with whom she prided herself in associating.

Then this morning the picture that was taken of Mrs. Wells's graduating class was sent around. There was so much eagerness to view it that many students at a time piled around the group photo to get a glimpse of themselves. When Carmen saw herself, she frowned and squirmed; and finally her inner thoughts so overpowered her that she blurted out, "Um—m, I look dark." Mildred, who was also looking at the group picture, quickly took up the issue with "And what's so bad about being dark?" With both disgust and embarrassment, and perhaps some concern about how much resentment she would arouse among the other blacks in the class, Carmen tried to cover up for the boner she'd pulled, by muttering, "Well, there's nothing *wrong* with being dark; I just said I *look* dark." At this pronouncement Mildred called her a dirty Spick, and there ensued a bitter exchange of words between the two girls. Obviously taken aback, Mrs. Wells just stood looking and mulling over what she should do.

A.   Since Carmen has already indicated her embarrassment and discomfort over the words she let slip, she is not likely to make this type of error again. It is better therefore that the teacher ignore the incident and consider it one that leveled itself off through the words the girls had with each other. Children forget their differences and make up easily. Delving into the racial conflict would only call undue attention to the matter of race, augmenting the bitterness between members of the two ethnic groups.

B.   There needs to be a private conference with Carmen as an effort toward uncovering reasons for her bearing such pronounced hostility toward black people and toward whatever is symbolic of blackness. The teacher should be frankly specific about instances in which she has observed the child to be prejudiced and try to cull from her the reasons for such bitter action. More than likely the conference will also reveal definite ways that would be logical in dealing with Carmen. In all probability, the private session will indicate, further, the need for a parent-teacher conference. The youngster's spontaneous outburst regarding the dark appearance of her picture is possibly only an outward sign of the inner turmoil she is experiencing over "color," a conflict which may be partially embedded in family history and in the interrelationships with family members. If this analysis bears any truth, certainly the parents need to be made aware of the extent to which the disturbance is tearing their daughter apart. If they cannot lend adequate support toward rectifying her behavior, then arrangements for Carmen's having sessions with the appropriate guidance personnel of the school would perhaps be warranted, no doubt with provisions made for a continuation of guidance services after Carmen enters senior high school.

Mildred, of course, may not be exempt from her part in the conflict. Even though she feels that Carmen's remark degraded the black race, Mildred must learn that she has no rightful authority to mete out retributions in the classroom. If a private conference with her cannot bring her to this realization, then reprimand, consultation with her parents, or, if necessary, referral to the appropriate administrator must be made.

C. The disdain which Carmen has shown both toward the black members of the class and toward the teacher is well out of the hands of a classroom teacher. The hostility demonstrated is indicative of the need for immediate referral to the appropriate administrator, who may in turn see fit to put the case into the hands of psychoeducational personnel. The more time lost in referring this problem behavior, the greater likelihood there is of permitting Carmen to become a social misfit.

Mildred, of course, may not be exempt from her part in the conflict. Even though she feels that Carmen's remark degraded the black race, Mildred must learn that she has no rightful authority to mete out retributions in the classroom. If a private conference with her cannot bring her to this realization, then reprimand, consultation with her parents, or, if necessary, referral to the appropriate administrator must be made.

CASE 8

Student: Eric Holmes	Ethnic background: black
Age: 12	Grade: 5
I. Q.: 83	Reading achievement: grade level
Father's occupation: father's	3.5
whereabouts unknown	Mother's occupation: housewife
Brothers: two (ages 3 and 10)	Sisters: six (ages 4, 5, 6, 7, 8, 10)

Eric Holmes, the oldest of his mother's nine children, is in a class of twenty-eight pupils, five blacks and twenty-three whites. Up until some weeks ago, Eric had been the instigator of enough trouble for all the class members combined. Speaking out constantly had been his common game. Often he was disruptive, annoying others who showed interest in their work. He was known to make explosive threats, inviting classmates to engage in fights with him. At times he was observed to kick class members and throw spitballs at various ones of them. His classwork, too, had usually been erratic, and he often accused his teacher of "picking on him." In fact, Eric had frequently been impudent and argumentative. He charged his teacher with making unfair judgments and constantly questioned her decisions and directions regarding the classwork. But in addition to all of the bullying and other misbehavior that created such a grave problem, a factor that had been greatly disturbing about Eric, a left-handed child, was that he turned his paper upside down in order to write. To read, he turned the reading matter upside down as well.

Though this was the first year Eric's teacher had taught in the school, she had found it particularly difficult to understand why something hadn't previously been done about Eric's problems. But Miss Hines, the teacher, did not sit idly by. She had not been in her classroom terribly long before she had acquired a store of background data on Eric. She'd consulted teachers in the school, members of Eric's family, and whatever records she'd found available. She had held private conferences with the youngster as well. The information she uncovered was appalling.

She learned that Eric lives with his maternal grandparents, as do some of the siblings. He and a few of the other older children bear the surname of the absent father, while the other children carry their mother's maiden name. Most of the siblings were, in fact, born out of wedlock. The mother drinks a good deal and seems to be irresponsible. Indeed, many of the fights and other infractions in which Eric had so readily engaged stemmed from his schoolmates' disparaging remarks about his mother's way of life. He of course visits his mother, but expresses ambivalence toward her. He seems confused and angry because he can't remain with her permanently, although he loves his grandparents.

Miss Hines practically had to nail the principal to the wall to get her to have Eric's emotional problems and his upside-down reading and writing looked into. Finally, about six weeks ago, the administrative head brought necessary pressure to bear on the grandparents to have them take the boy to a mental health center. After three or four weekly visits, Eric was administered pills which act as tranquilizers. The improvement in his conduct and writing has been phenomenal. Before he began taking the pills he was generally erratic, and so was his writing. As a matter of fact, his conduct had been literally unbearable. Even now, when for any reason Eric is off the pills and their calming effects, he reverts to aspects of his former poor behavior. Under medication, the tranquilizers, Eric's caliber of writing has greatly improved, but he still holds his printed material and paper upside down when he's reading or writing, the upside-down ailment having been diagnosed as a neurological condition that is actually a special type of eye problem. Miss Hines is immensely happy over the behavioral changes Eric has made; yet she questions the propriety of the control of his conduct through sedation. She wonders if she should initiate an investigation into the doctors' administering of drugs to Eric and into specifically what can be done in connection with his neurological ailment.

A. Miss Hines should relax and accept the fact that the doctors will cease administering the drug if they find it to be harmful to the youngster. She should be concerned, however, as to whether anything specific can be done in the way of the control or cure of his neurological condition.

B. The teacher would do well to investigate the administering of the drugs. The attempt to control disruptive behavior through sedation is unwarrantable. The actual source of Eric's original conduct and the treatment of the neurological condition should be the points of concern.

C. Miss Hines must realize that if the doctors are competent they are justified in using the pill as a tranquilizer to calm Eric down and control his conduct since without the sedation his behavior is literally unbearable; but the administering of the drug and the administering of therapeutic treatment should go hand in hand. Likewise, every effort should be made on the part of all concerned to improve and, wherever possible, amend undesirable situations that are the source of Eric's poor behavior. Where unwholesome conditions may not be changed, the youngster should be helped to face them with the greatest possible courage and facility. And certainly all efforts should be made to have Eric's neurological condition treated competently and fully.

CASE 9

Student: Lora Fenner	Ethnic background: white
Age: 13	Grade: 8
I. Q.: 98	Reading achievement: grade level
Father's occupation: construction	7.1
worker	Mother's occupation: housewife
Brothers: one (age 8)	Sisters: one (age 5)

Lora Fenner is now in Larry Boyle's homeroom class. This is Lora's first year to attend the junior high where she is presently enrolled, for her family has lived in the neighborhood only since June.

The class contains eighteen whites, five blacks, and three Orientals. Mr. Boyle himself teaches his homeroom pupils their science course.

Lora is the largest girl in her eighth-grade class. In fact, she is quite a large child for her age, and not very attractive in appearance. Her disposition, too, leaves much to be desired. Since the beginning of the term, she has had an acid tongue.

Just a short time ago, Mr. Boyle was writing some science notes on the chalkboard, and the children were copying them. The notes were to be used as preparatory study for a subsequent science experiment. The teacher had begun to write on the blackboard at the extreme left front, and of course would be moving to the right as the copying proceeded. Lora, who sits near the front in the last row on the right side of the room, complained that she couldn't read the notes. Mr. Boyle quickly retorted: "It seems to me if I were you I'd move where I could see; that seems to be the sensible thing to do." Lora became furious over this curt accusation and quickly rebuffed, "But you're not me, Mr. Boyle. I'm Lora Ellen Fenner." Then there ensued a heated exchange of words between teacher and pupil.

"It's obvious I'm not you, Lora, and I'm awfully glad I'm not."

"Well, I can write better than you, and you're the teacher."

"It's too bad you can't also read."

"You ought to write large enough. Who can read that little old writing?"

"I think I know my work quite well enough, as well as how to execute it."

"Your head's sure big enough."

From time to time, some of the spectators, the class members, cheered for Lora while some cheered for Mr. Boyle. But some sat totally aghast as the acid remarks ricocheted around the room.

A. Mr. Boyle should make a seat available to Lora where he is certain she can see the board well. He should make sure his writing is legible. Then he should cease arguing with the youngster immediately, ignoring her and all further statements she might make until she has put an end to her unwholesome behavior.

   Near the end of the period, Mr. Boyle should go over to Lora and quietly ask her to remain after class for a brief conference with him. In the face-to-face meeting, he should calmly reason with her about the way to make a complaint in a courteous manner. Apparently the youngster needs some instruction in this area. In addition, he should try to uncover what it is that disturbs the child to the extent that a reproach from the teacher can trigger off such violent reaction. To make the designated discovery a meaningful one, it may be necessary that Mr. Boyle also consult with the parents as early as possible. He should use all information gathered from all sources as a basis for working with Lora in a remedial way.

B. Mr. Boyle should make a seat available to Lora where he is certain she can see the board well. He should make sure his writing is legible. Then he should cease arguing with the youngster immediately, ignoring her and all further statements she might make until she has put an end to her unwholesome behavior.

Before the end of the period, Mr. Boyle should go over to Lora and quietly arrange for a private meeting with her. In conference with her, he should reason with the youngster about the way to make a complaint in a courteous manner. Apparently she needs some instruction in this area. He should further try to uncover what it is that disturbs the child to the extent that a reproach from the teacher can trigger off such violent reaction. To make the designated discovery a meaningful one, it may be necessary that Mr. Boyle also consult with the parents as early as possible. He should use all information gathered from all sources as a basis for working with Lora in a remedial way. In large measure, however, Mr. Boyle should accept blame for the explosive incident of the day.

C. Because of the heated encounter between Mr. Boyle and Lora, there is little help he will be able to give her from now on. She will simply have no respect for him. Mr. Boyle should therefore refer her case to the administration in charge of discipline, for appropriate handling.

CASE 10

Student: Dennis Jones	Ethnic background: black
Age: 16	Grade: 10
I. Q.: 90	Reading achievement: grade level
Father's occupation: policeman	8.4
Brothers: two (ages 14 and 19)	Mother's occupation: nurse
Sisters: one (age 12)	

Dennis Jones, a black youngster, is attending a high school torn with racial strife. This is the first school term blacks have been noticeably visible at the former practically all-white senior high, and a great many white parents have not yet accepted the idea that their sons and daughters must share their classrooms and teachers with black boys and girls. Some parents have met the situation with open resistance; some with passive hostility; some with impassive silence. Naturally, the overwhelming feeling of the adult population has taken its toll in the attitudes and reactions of the white youngsters themselves. Many black students, feeling themselves unwanted at the school, have grown sensitive; and on occasion some have reacted violently.

This morning in Dennis's mathematics class, comprised of six blacks and twenty whites, there was a direct repercussion of the racial conflict so evident in the vicinity. Class members were copying a few math problems that were to be worked out as a subsequent assignment. Usually during assignment time, pupils of the class talk freely and do their copying at the same time. As Dennis was writing his work, he was engaged in conversation with two of his black pals, Larry Morgan seated in front of him and Howard Bain seated to Dennis's right. Mr. Justin, the teacher, observed that Dennis was involved in heated discussion and realized he was quite upset; yet he said nothing, for he had not wanted to fan the flame. Mr. Justin recalled that since the beginning of the term Dennis had at times been a bit sulky and seemed to carry a chip on his shoulder; still, the youngster hadn't really given any trouble that could be pinpointed. But this morning, all of a sudden, Mr. Justin heard Dennis swearing. Then he heard him affirm, "Man, I'm not taking any more stuff off those white cats; I'm ready for them." Mr. Justin was sure that Dennis and his friends were speaking of a group of white students with whom they had had some differences. He moved in Dennis's direction, but as he did so, Dennis flipped open a knife with a blade every bit of five inches long, in order to demonstrate how ready he was. Mr. Justin was stunned. He knew he would have to figure out quickly but painstakingly the best move to make.

A.   Mr. Justin should approach Dennis calmly, requesting that the young-ster immediately turn over the knife to him. The boy, together with his friends, should be required to meet with Mr. Justin just after class. In conference, Dennis should be permitted to tell his side of the fracas. Similarly, Larry and Howard should have the opportunity to say whatever they might wish to add. The teacher should, of course, request the identity of the group of white boys about whom Dennis made his complaint.

   Mr. Justin would do well to indicate to Dennis that he understands how he must feel over what he considers maltreatment because of his being a member of the black race, and hopefully Mr. Justin can assure the black youngsters that he for one is determined to do his part in treating minority members justly. But Mr. Justin should point out to Dennis the many ill effects of seeking to retaliate by the use of dangerous weapons.

   Additionally, the entire incident should be reported to the appro-priate administrator for his reaction, for friction between black and white groups in a racially torn area is too explosive an issue to go unreported. Dennis and his friends should understand clearly why there must be a referral even though there has been a teacher–pupil conference.

   Incidentally, if Dennis had refused to relinquish the knife when asked to do so, or to attend the conference, or if either of the other boys had refused to stay for the conference after class, an immediate referral to the appropriate administrator would have been warranted.

B.   If Mr. Justin feels Dennis will relinquish the knife if requested to do so, he should ask the youngster to give up the weapon. Then Dennis and his friends should be sent immediately to the administrator in charge of disciplinary matters, and a note should be sent by a reliable student, indicating the gravity of the case. A threat with a dangerous weapon is too serious a matter to be postponed even for a short while. If, however, the teacher feels relatively certain that Dennis would fail to comply with a request for the knife, or if he asks the boy to give up the weapon and Dennis refuses, Mr. Justin should immediately send for the supervisor in charge of matters of discipline.

C.   Mr. Justin should ignore the whole incident until near the end of the period. Just before time for dismissal, he should go over to Dennis and request that he and the other two boys remain after class. After the fellow classmates leave, Mr. Justin should ask Dennis to give up the knife. Then a conference should follow.

In the face-to-face meeting, Dennis should be permitted to tell his side of the fracas. Similarly, Larry and Howard should have the opportunity to say whatever they might wish to add. The teacher should, of course, request the identity of the group of white boys about whom Dennis made his complaint.

Mr. Justin would do well to indicate to Dennis that he understands how he must feel over what he considers maltreatment because of his being a member of the black race, and hopefully Mr. Justin can assure the black youngsters that he for one is determined to do his part in treating minority members justly. But Mr. Justin should indicate to Dennis the ill effects of seeking to retaliate by the use of dangerous weapons.

Additionally, the entire incident should be reported to the appropriate administrator for his reaction, for friction between black and white groups in a racially torn area is too explosive an issue to go unreported. Dennis and his friends should understand clearly why there must be a referral even though there has been a teacher-pupil conference.

If Dennis had refused to relinquish the knife when asked to do so, or to attend the conference, or if either of the other boys had refused to stay for the conference after class, an immediate referral to the appropriate administrator would have been warranted.

CASE 11

Student: Ronald Zerman	Ethnic background: white
Age: 16	Grade: 11
I. Q.: 116	Reading achievement: grade level
Father's occupation: wealthy busi-	12+
nessman	Mother's occupation: housewife
Brothers: none	Sisters: none

Ronald Zerman lives with his parents in a wealthy and exclusive sub-urban area. He attends the all-white senior high school of his surrounding neighborhood. Because of his poor grades and general lack of academic interest, he was previously dismissed from a prominent preparatory school.

At his neighborhood senior high, Ronald has proved himself to be a regular nuisance in Mrs. Odell's American history class. At any time during the course of the lesson he is subject to blurting out some comment irrele-vant to the work at hand or to asserting himself loudly, dogmatically, and out of turn regarding some issue under discussion. In sum, he engages him-self by talking out in class, monopolizing the attention of fellow classmates and teacher. Particularly does he frequently busy himself directing some self-centered comment or question to his teacher.

Recently, when the topic of "Welfare Funds for the Poor" was being intelligently discussed by class members, Ronald stormed, "Me—I don't care about material things. Fifteen thousand's all I want to live on a year." In his haughty pronouncement was the ambivalent tone of regard for and rejection of money and of what it stands for. Frequently, too, Ronald is known to interrupt the teacher at the peak of her supervision of a lesson, to invite her to answer one of his personal and off-the-subject questions: whether she watched a particular game the previous night or viewed some special show. Many times he seems relentlessly determined to involve his teacher in his own personal concerns. Needless to say, his classwork has declined in proportion to his poor behavior, even though Ronald has the ability to do a representative level of work.

When Mrs. Odell requests that Ronald bring his conduct in line with that of his classmates, he either ignores her demand entirely or ceases his annoy-ing acts briefly only to resume them with his prior vigor. Mrs. Odell has had her fill of Ronald's conduct. More and more he is impeding his own progress and that of the class. She is well aware that something must be done.

A.   Mrs. Odell should instruct Ronald that his irrelevant and obnoxious blurting out in class must cease, at all costs. She should cite specific instances of the conduct in question. He is an intelligent boy. Mrs.

Odell must try to have him understand the rationale behind her plea that he is unduly interfering with his own progress and that of class members. In the meantime, she would help considerably by trying to cull from Ronald reasons why he seems to find it necessary to perform in the manner he does. Both indirect and direct questioning should help to shed light on the causes. All this advising and probing, of course, could best be done in private conference.

Should the face-to-face communication not put an end to Ronald's outbursts or should the meeting uncover poor adjustment problems on the part of the youngster, the teacher's conference with both parents would be needed. Prior to scheduling such a parent-teacher meeting, Mrs. Odell might pave the way for a fruitful conference with the Zermans by making careful anecdotal notes that could be used to present a representative picture of Ronald's behavior. If the parents should be unable to offer the help needed to correct the pupil's conduct, referral to guidance personnel would perhaps be warranted, and the anecdotal notes could again be used, this time to give the guidance administrators a developmental picture of Ronald's actions.

In any event, reports from Ronald in his area of interest, especially oral reports, would no doubt be helpful to challenge his potential and to provide for him some of the warmth and recognition he seeks.

B.   In the privacy of a conference, Mrs. Odell, among other things, might try to uncover some of Ronald's specific areas of interest. She could then restructure her lessons in such way as to permit the youngster to make some contributions to the classwork that are centered around his special concerns. To accord him this opportunity for favorable response as opposed to the unpopular distractions that have become a part of his classroom living would be to offer him a means of redeeming his poor behavior. In addition, Mrs. Odell might sometimes arrange to divide her class into working groups so that Ronald will have the opportunity of working and sharing his experience and knowledge with classmates.

Finally, during a time Ronald is not in the classroom, Mrs. Odell might ask the class members to help suggest ways of helping Ronald modify his conduct. The pupils' assistance in this matter would also remind them that they must not in any way condone improper behavior on Ronald's part, but rather offer a helping hand.

C.   During private conference with the youngster, Mrs. Odell should firmly caution Ronald that he is not to be guilty of further wayward outbursts in class. Should he not comply with her request, she might completely ignore future outbreaks, giving the social approval of smiles, pleased expressions, or favorable comments only when Ronald is not engaged in adverse behavior. After all, being an only child, Ronald might possibly have been greatly spoiled. If his negative conduct is continued, however, the services of the guidance personnel may be needed, and in making the referral Mrs. Odell would do well to have kept anecdotal records of Ronald's behavior that she may place at the disposal of the guidance staff.

RECOMMENDED SOLUTIONS BASED ON TEACHER POLL

CASE 1: BERNARD ALLEN   Solution: C

Comments: A case like Bernard's should be placed in the hands of competent guidance personnel. Hopefully, the principal would see to it that all necessary specialists inside and outside the school were utilized. If, for instance, such batteries of tests as I. Q., aptitude, achievement, and personality tests were to be administered and they could be adequately handled at school, well and good. But with respect to necessary guidance services and information from music specialists that could be gotten only outside the school system, the administration would be expected to strive to obtain them. From all evidence, access to Special Performing Arts Education would be a major need. A very careful study of the child's case would determine how the youngster could best be handled. It seems fair to assume that the child's behavior and interest in school would improve as his musical needs and interests were met.

CASE 2: PETER KANE   Solution: B

Comments: In the situation on which the Peter Kane case is based, it was revealed that Peter's sixteen-year-old brother was an exceptionally good student who was ambitious of becoming a lawyer. The mother was overanxious regarding the future of the younger boy, fearing that his plans and accomplishments would lag far behind those of her elder son. The father seemed to take the matter more in stride, but the mother was an overbearingly aggressive parent.

In Peter Kane's case, for the boy's sake it would be helpful if Mr. Norris would schedule another conference with the Kanes to suggest to them, tactfully, that constantly comparing Peter with their older son could cause

Peter to suffer from an inferiority complex that would lead to unhappiness and possibly maladjustment. Pitting Peter sharply against his brother could even serve as a block to Peter's producing merely satisfactory work.

CASE 3: AMY CROMER   Solution: C

Comments: In the actual situation on which the Amy case is based, there were likewise a number of years between the daughter and son. The parents as well as the brother spoiled the only little girl of the house terribly. Big brother frequently pulled her around in what used to be his little wagon. She simply loved these rides and projected this pleasure onto the objects in her school.

Similarly, Amy Cromer is spoiled, She has no friends in the class. Thus she relies much on the pleasure she has brought from home. She wants desperately to be a member of the group, however, but doesn't know how to be. As a result, she compounds her problem, for when she tries to fight her way into acceptance by hitting her classmates and hiding their property, she makes it even more difficult to achieve the relationship for which she strives. It will take the support of Mrs. Mercer, the parents, and pupils of the class to assist Amy in finding an acceptable place in the group.

CASE 4: JOSE M. TORRES   Solution: A

Comments: Mrs. Glenn will certainly be justified in notifying the proper administrator of Jose's leaving the room without permission. This step is an important safety precaution. Besides, Mrs. Glenn's reporting the incident will preclude her being legally held responsible should Jose become involved in some difficulty while out of the classroom.

It is, however, unfortunate that Mrs. Glenn did not move near the youngsters sooner to see what they were doing instead of yelling to them from the front of the room. It is possible that in close proximity to the boys a shake of the head and a quiet request for the pictures, as well as for the boys' return to their classwork, may have brought the desired results. Even if the youngsters had refused to relinquish their possession, however, a calm request that the boys remain after the dismissal of class would have allowed the assignment to proceed uninterrupted, since the other members of the class were diligently devoting their time and attention to the assigned seatwork. Indeed, a quiet settlement of the case would have been a desirable outcome, in view of the fact that the boys are not very far from the puberty stage, generally a period when youngsters are naturally curious about sex.

In fact, though the children could not be condoned for interrupting their study and that of their classmates through the commotion over the pictures, it is, nonetheless, to be recognized that a current trend in education encourages answering the children's questions about sex and satisfying their curiosity through regularly planned sex education programs in the schools.

CASE 5: KENNETH ELLIS   Solution: A

Comments: A case similar to Kenneth's actually occurred. When the parents were persuaded to take the youngster to a competent doctor, he was found to be suffering from a glandular condition that was in dire need of treatment.

CASE 6: LINDA KEEFE   Solution: C

Comments: In a case like Linda's, a conference with the parents should be held as early as possible. They should be made aware of all their child's actions that are indicative of a spoiled youngster, and the parents' cooperation should be sought in refraining from the use of further procedures that tend to spoil the child. The parents should be led to understand how difficult life can be made for their youngster if she is indulged and allowed to feel she must always have her way. They must come to realize what grave disappointment and frustration a spoiled child must certainly encounter when, alas, she must learn that her desires may not always be met.

CASE 7: CARMEN HERNANDEZ   Solution: B

Comments: In the incident on which this case was based, it was found that the fifteen-year-old daughter who had a loathing for blackness was like her mother and twelve-year-old brother in having a brownish cast in skin tone. The other children of the family were fair like the father and consequently could readily be identified as being white. The fifteen-year-old was quite sensitive about the color dichotomy within the family, from which source stemmed her aversion to dark people and even to the idea of associating with them, for fear of being mistaken for a black person.

The suggestions for handling the Carmen Hernandez case, as offered in solution B, are appropriate ones. It is unfortunate, however, that Mrs. Wells didn't isolate Carmen for treatment during the early part of the school term. No doubt a fair amount of help, at least, could have been instigated during

Carmen's junior high days had an early analysis of her case been made. Mrs. Wells could certainly have rearranged the classroom seating in order to mix Carmen in with some black class members in such way that she could at least have had an opportunity to get some understanding of, and hopefully some appreciation for, black people. Group work could to some extent have provided for a mixture of black, Puerto Rican, and white pupils. And certainly units which emphasize appreciation for the culture and contributions of blacks and other ethnic groups could have been appropriately worked into a social studies curriculum.

But the cooperation of the parents would certainly be needed in not showing prejudice among the children at home and in working toward building in Carmen a sense of self-worth. She, however, would need to be led to the reality of accepting the brownish tinge in her skin. Finally, if school and home couldn't effect necessary improvement in Carmen, then guidance or psychoeducational services would definitely be warranted.

CASE 8: ERIC HOLMES   Solution: C

Comments: To a very great extent, Eric is an angry child. This feeling is understandable. He is ambivalent toward his mother because he would like to love and be loved by her in a normal setting; yet, unlike a great many of his schoolmates, it has not been his experience to live with and have the love of a mother and father living together under one roof; nor has he had sustained attention or supervision from his mother. Obviously his love for his grandparents has helped to soften some of the pain he would otherwise feel, but certainly not enough to offset the lack of close care from one or both of his parents. The questionable situations in which his mother has constantly engaged and other shady aspects of her character have not made it easy for the boy, especially considering the fact that he is being derided by schoolmates because of the unfortunate family conditions over which he has no control.

In the classroom Eric expresses his anger in diverse ways, for instance through fights, through arguments with other students and the teacher, and through noncooperation. His ire tends to lead him to the kind of unfair sense of justice that causes him to blame his teacher for his ill feelings; as a result, he is easily ready to charge her with "picking on him." The hostility the youngster demonstrates is in no small measure a feeling of insecurity and a sense of dissatisfaction with the unwholesome situation that surrounds his life.

There are some things Miss Hines may well do in connection with Eric's case. She can build a classroom tone where no one is derided because of his unfortunate circumstances. Social modeling through such means as selected films and readings should be particularly beneficial in helping the pupils treat a classmate humanely. In addition, Miss Hines might seat Eric near fellow pupils with whom he is most congenial. But if the youngster is at the point of instigating a fight, he should be restrained from doing so. If he threatens a child, he should not be permitted to carry through on his bold invitation, even to the point of being detained until his intended opponent is well out of reach. In conference with Eric during times that he is calm, Miss Hines might find it helpful to try to reason with him, showing him that it is his anger that largely leads him to threaten, fight, argue, and falsely accuse others. In short, since the teacher knows so much about the youngster's condition, she is in a position to help the youth face his problems more realistically and to help ease him over his roughest roads.

We must not, however, make any mistake. With his emotional and physical disturbance, Eric needs competent professional help outside the domain of the classroom. To do the greatest good, the psychologist, psychiatrist, or mental health workers who attend the youngster would need to counsel other family members concerned, mother and grandparents as well. In the actual situation on which the Eric Holmes case is based, the mother was originally reluctant to admit that her son had a grave problem, either in terms of emotional upset or in terms of the neurological condition, possibly a reluctance that stemmed from her guilt feelings over her illicit relationships and failure to provide a worthwhile home environment for her oldest child and other young ones.

In connection with Eric and his predicament, it is inexcusable that the school allowed him to drift along so long without proper concern for him. Even if the youngster was being allowed to carry out his unusual waywardness, surely for a long time it was obvious that there needed to be an investigation into Eric's upside-down reading and writing, with a view to helping get done what should be done to meet his physical problem.

With respect to the administering of a sedative to a hyperactive child, though the issue is a controversial one, certainly some educators are going along with the practice so long as the medical use of the drug is accompanied by proper therapeutic treatment. Such drug use to make a child manageable should not, however, be considered a cure–all, and only the children who clearly need this kind of treatment should receive it. Finally, it should be re-emphasized that the basic cause of the child's problems should be given ample and competent attention.

CASE 9: LORA FENNER   Solution: B

Comments: Teachers must try to be discerning regarding the needs of an individual pupil. Many times they must imagine themselves in the place of the youngster. In the case of Lora, it is unfortunate that Mr. Boyle didn't weigh carefully the possibility of her being overly sensitive and burdened with feelings of worthlessness because of her large size and ungainly appearance. It is unfortunate, too, if Mr. Boyle was unaware of the fact that age thirteen is frequently thought of as one of the difficult ages. Certainly it is an age when a youngster is generally considered to be prone to moodiness, to an unusual amount of worry, to increased concern for self, and to a tendency to be critical of adults. It is indeed a time when the child needs considerable understanding. A knowledge on the part of Mr. Boyle of what to expect from children of the age levels he teaches, while not an infallible guide, could certainly help him to be familiar with trends of reaction to look for in his pupils. Such information, for instance, might have helped him avoid instigating unnecessarily action that would puncture Lora's vulnerable spots.

As a teacher, Mr. Boyle should, of course, come to realize that he himself had a sharp tongue and in a very real sense provoked the unwholesome incident. His comment "It seems to me if I were you I'd move where I could see; that seems to be the sensible thing to do" was a stinging remark. And second, Mr. Boyle wasn't a very gallant recipient of criticism. He would have fared much better if he had capitalized on Lora's complaint by readily seeing to it that all pupils could see the writing clearly, yet by refraining from making a negative comment, particularly since he must have known that at the least provocation he would be susceptible to Lora's impudent attack. If after his arranging for the class members' clear view of the board, Lora had felt disposed to unload her barrage of impudent comments, Mr. Boyle's ignoring her until she brought herself in line with the rest of the pupils would no doubt have been effective. She couldn't have found pleasure in a continuous wrangle all by herself. In any event, it does not pay the teacher to engage in verbal combat with his students. A pupil can certainly afford to take part in more low-brow harangues than can the teacher. The teacher who can conduct himself in a manner to avoid bitter pupil–teacher embattlement stands a much greater chance of gaining teacher respect. In short, teachers must in every way strive to avoid creating problems.

It would have been helpful for Mr. Boyle to have had class sessions in discipline. Then at some of the meetings he could have explained to the youngsters that he would do all he could to help them learn and make the most of themselves but would not stoop to fighting with them physically or verbally. Accordingly, he would have had no need to try to match Lora in argument in order to try to save face. Yet his change for the right direction, even after the mistake has been made, is likely to be looked upon with favor by Lora, for she is in need of an enormous amount of help. Actually, it is the teacher's responsibility to help build a class tone of acceptance for the individual class members. Lora particularly needs this extra assistance since she is a relatively new youngster in the neighborhood and school. Mr. Boyle would be likely to discover too that Lora is suffering from problems at home. In an actual case similar to that of the Fenner family, there was so much bickering both over the wife's dissatisfaction with her husband's frequent change of jobs and over her displeasure with her husband's "low" work, as she termed it, that the situation contributed considerably to the oldest child's highly explosive temperament.

As a final remark, it might be noted that Mr. Boyle would facilitate classroom discipline if, in the case of extensive class notes, he would have the work dittoed rather than have pupils copy from the board. The suggestion is made, however, with the realization that in the schools, unfortunately, it is not always possible to have classwork duplicated when the teacher so desires.

CASE 10: DENNIS JONES   Solution: B

Comments: Dennis should be handled firmly and decisively for displaying the knife threateningly and harboring the idea of inflicting harm on his schoolmates, and hopefully the administration will so handle him. But there is much that teachers and administrators may do to help promote better human relations in the type of school and community described. As one small gesture, for instance, teachers might help by arranging the seating so that the pupils of the various races must intermingle in a way that offers greater opportunity for the development of respect and understanding among members of diverse ethnic origins. The teacher's conscious distribution of ethnic groups when group assignments are made may likewise be used as a scheme for promoting greater understanding among pupils of different racial backgrounds. Often, too, units that point up the contributions of the various racial classes may be appropriately and gainfully studied.

With respect to the principal, he is a key figure to set the tone for a better relationship among racial groups, both in the school and in the community. In school assemblies, in staff meetings, and in parent–teacher meetings, for instance, the principal may, if he will, be a herald for greater respect and understanding among the races.

CASE 11: RONALD ZERMAN   Solution: A

Comments: In a case similar to Ronald's, pupil-teacher and parent-teacher conferences revealed that the son was suffering terribly from lack of parental care and attention. The father was so engrossed in his business that he had practically no time to spend with his son to satisfy the boy's craving for fatherly interest. The mother had ample time for her youngster but lacked sufficient firmness. As a consequence, the boy had gotten almost completely from under her control. It is no wonder the confused youth tried to take attention and love at school.

In connection with the occurrences on which the Ronald Zerman case was based, a plan was worked out, through a parent-teacher conference, that demanded the father to spend time with the boy, father and son alone, at least once a week. Suggestions were offered to help the mother both to show her affection and to exercise sufficient firmness in her dealings with her son. Both parents agreed that if marked improvement should not be evident within a reasonable length of time, the family as a group—father, mother, and son—would seek the services of a counselor.

SELECTED BIBLIOGRAPHY

CHAPTER ONE
DISADVANTAGED YOUTH AND THE PROBLEM OF DISCIPLINE

Cutts, Norma E., and Nicholas Moseley, *Teaching the Disorderly Pupil in Elementary and Secondary School.* New York: Longmans, Green and Co., 1959.

Farmer, James, "Stereotypes of the Negro and Their Relationship to His Self-Image," in Herbert C. Rudman and Richard L. Featherstone (eds.), *Urban Schooling.* New York: Harcourt, Brace & World, Inc., 1968.

Frost, Joe L., and Glenn R. Hawkes (eds.), *The Disadvantaged Child (Issues and Innovations).* Boston: Houghton Mifflin Company, 1966.

Green, Robert L., "Intellectual Development Among Disadvantaged Youth," in Herbert C. Rudman and Richard L. Featherstone (eds.), *Urban Schooling.* New York: Harcourt, Brace & World, Inc., 1968.

Haubrich, Vernon F., "Successful Educational Programs for Disadvantaged Youth," in Herbert C. Rudman and Richard L. Featherstone (eds.), *Urban Schooling.* New York: Harcourt, Brace & World, Inc., 1968.

Keach, Everett T. Jr., Robert Fulton, and William E. Gardner (eds.), *Education and Social Crisis (Perspectives on Teaching Disadvantaged Youth).* New York: John Wiley & Sons, Inc., 1967.

Noar, Gertrude, *Teaching the Disadvantaged.* Washington, D. C.: National Educational Association (Department of Classroom Teachers), 1967.

Rose, Arnold M., "Characteristics of Socio–Economic Status Among Whites and Nonwhites," in Herbert C. Rudman and Richard L. Featherstone (eds.), *Urban Schooling.* New York: Harcourt, Brace & World, Inc., 1968.

Schmidt, Ted H., "Remaking the Reading Program," *Teacher,* Vol. 91, No. 5, January, 1974, pp. 40–43.

Taba, Hilda, and Deborah Elkins, *Teaching Strategies for the Culturally Disadvantaged.* Chicago: Rand McNally & Company, 1966.

Thompson, Daniel C., "Our Wasted Potential," in Gordon J. Klopf and
Israel A. Laster (eds.), *Integrating the Urban School.* New York: Bureau
of Publications--Teachers College, Columbia University, 1963.

CHAPTER TWO
DISCIPLINING DISADVANTAGED YOUTH THROUGH EFFECTIVE TEACHING

Cohn, Stella M., and Jack Cohn, *Teaching the Retarded Reader (A Guide
for Teachers, Reading Specialists, and Supervisors).* New York: The
Odyssey Press, Inc., 1967.
Elkins, Deborah (with the assistance of Thelma Hickerson and George
Krieger), *Reading Improvement in the Junior High School.* New York:
Bureau of Publications -- Teachers College, Columbia University, 1963.
Green, Robert L. "Intellectual Development Among Disadvantaged Youth,"
in Herbert C. Rudman and Richard L. Featherstone (eds.), *Urban
Schooling.* New York: Harcourt, Brace & World, Inc., 1968.
Keach, Everett T. Jr., Robert Fulton, and William E. Gardner (eds.), *Educa-
tion and Social Crisis (Perspectives on Teaching Disadvantaged Youth).*
New York: John Wiley & Sons, Inc., 1967.
Mitchell, Joanne R., "Getting Poor Readers Ready To Read," *Teaching
Exceptional Children,* Vol. 6, No. 2, Winter, 1974, pp. 103–110.
Monserrat, Joseph, "School Integration: A Puerto Rican View," in Gordon J.
Klopf and Israel A. Laster (eds.), *Integrating the Urban School.* New
York: Bureau of Publications--Teachers College, Columbia University,
1963.
Neff, Monroe C. Dr., Elaine T. Paterno, and Dr. Curtis Ulmer (Editor),
Using Real Life Materials for the Culturally Disadvantaged. Englewood
Cliffs, N. J.: Prentice-Hall, Inc., 1972.
Storen, Helen F., *The Disadvantaged Early Adolescent: More Effective
Teaching.* New York: McGraw-Hill Book Company, 1968.
Taba, Hilda, and Deborah Elkins, *Teaching Strategies for the Culturally
Disadvantaged.* Chicago: Rand McNally & Company, 1966.
Vukelich, Carol V., and Margaret Matthias, "A Language Process for Use
with Disadvantaged Children," *Elementary English,* Vol. 51, No. 1,
January, 1974, pp. 119–124+.
Ward, Pearl L., and Robert Beacon, *The School Media Center: (A Book of
Readings).* Metuchen, N. J.: The Scarecrow Press, Inc., 1973.

CHAPTER THREE
SPECIAL HANDLING OF THE DISADVANTAGED CHILD

Attwell, Arthur A., *The School Psychologist's Handbook.* 12031 Wilshire
Boulevard, Los Angeles, California 90025: Western Psychological
Services (Publishers and Distributors)–A Division of Manson Weston
Corporation, 1972.
Cutts, Norma E., and Nicholas Moseley, *Teaching the Disorderly Pupil in
Elementary and Secondary School.* New York: Longmans, Green and
Co., 1959.
Drayer, Adam M., *Problems and Methods in High School Teaching.* Boston:
D. C. Heath & Company, 1963.

Hymes, James L. Jr., *Behavior and Misbehavior (A Teacher's Guide to Action)*. New York: Prentice-Hall, Inc., 1955.

Inlow, Gail M., *Maturity in High School Teaching*. Englewood Cliffs, N. J.: Prentice-Hall, Inc., 1963.

Noar, Gertrude, *The Teacher and Integration*. Washington, D. C.: National Educational Association, 1966.

Noar, Gertrude, *Teaching the Disadvantaged*. Washington, D. C.: National Educational Association (Department of Classroom Teachers), 1967.

Redl, Fritz, *When We Deal With Children (Selected Writings)*. New York: The Free Press (Collier-Macmillan Limited, London), 1966.

Sheviakov, George V., and Fritz Redl, *Discipline for Today's Children and Youth*. Washington, D. C.: Association for Supervision and Curriculum Development (A Department of the National Education Association of the United States), 1956.

Storen, Helen F., *The Disadvantaged Early Adolescent: More Effective Teaching*. New York: McGraw-Hill Book Company, 1968.

Taba, Hilda, and Deborah Elkins, *Teaching Strategies for the Culturally Disadvantaged*. Chicago: Rand McNally & Company, 1966.

CHAPTER FOUR
MANAGERIAL ANTIDOTES FOR DISCIPLINARY PROBLEMS

Bany, Mary A., and Lois V. Johnson, *Classroom Group Behavior (Group Dynamics in Education)*. New York: The Macmillan Company, 1964.

Carnot, Joseph B., "Dynamic and Effective School Discipline," *The Clearing House*, Vol. 48, No. 3, November, 1973, pp. 150–153.

Fisher, Eleanore, "The First Day of School," *Today's Education*, Vol. 61, No. 5, May, 1972, p. 35.

Getting Started in the Elementary School. Board of Education of the City of New York, 1967.

Green, Arthur S., *The Elementary School Classroom Discipline Manual*. Minneapolis: T. S. Denison & Co., Inc., 1963.

Hurlock, Elizabeth B., *Developmental Psychology*. New York: McGraw-Hill Book Company (3rd ed.), 1968.

Hymes, James L. Jr., *Behavior and Misbehavior (A Teacher's Guide to Action)*. New York: Prentice-Hall, Inc., 1955.

Inlow, Gail M., *Maturity in High School Teaching*. Englewood Cliffs, N. J.: Prentice-Hall, Inc., 1963.

Kounin, Jacob S., *Discipline and Group Management in Classrooms*. New York: Holt, Rinehart and Winston, Inc., 1970.

Sheviakov, George V., and Fritz Redl, *Discipline for Today's Children and Youth*. Washington, D. C.: Association for Supervision and Curriculum Development (A Department of the National Educational Association of the United States), 1956.

Veatch, Jeannette, "Learning, Training and Education," *Young Children*, Vol. 29, No. 2, January, 1974, pp. 83–88.

Vest, Lucy S., and Vera M. Summers, *Procedures on Classroom Organization for the Primary Teacher*. New York: Exposition Press, Inc., 1971.

CHAPTER FIVE
AFFECTIVE ANTIDOTES FOR PROBLEMS IN DISCIPLINE

Cutts, Norma E., and Nicholas Moseley, *Teaching the Disorderly Pupil in Elementary and Secondary School.* New York: Longmans, Green and Co., 1959.

Drayer, Adam M., *Problems and Methods in High School Teaching.* Boston: D. C. Heath & Company, 1963.

Gesell, Arnold, and Frances L. Ilg, *The Child from Five to Ten.* New York: Harper & Brothers, Publishers, 1946.

Gesell, Arnold, Frances L. Ilg, and Louise Bates Ames, *Youth, the Years from Ten to Sixteen.* New York: Harper & Row, 1956.

Hawkes, Glenn R., and Demaris Pease, *Behavior and Development from 5 to 12.* New York: Harper & Brothers, Publishers, 1962.

Hurlock, Elizabeth B., *Developmental Psychology.* New York: McGraw-Hill Book Company (3rd ed.), 1968.

Inlow, Gail M., *Maturity in High School Teaching.* Englewood Cliffs, N. J.: Prentice-Hall, Inc., 1963.

Kounin, Jacob S., *Discipline and Group Management in Classrooms.* New York: Holt, Rinehart and Winston, Inc., 1970.

Riccio, Anthony C., and Frederick Cyphert (eds.), *Teaching in America.* Columbus, Ohio: C. E. Merrill Books, 1962.

Public Affairs Committee (381 Park Ave. South, New York, N. Y. 10016) *Enjoy Your Child—Ages 1, 2, and 3,* by James L. Hymes, Jr., 1969.

———. *Three to Six: Your Child Starts to School,* by James L. Hymes, Jr., 1970.

———. *Understanding Your Child—from 6 to 12,* by Clara Lambert, 1969.

———. *Parents and Teenagers,* by Margaret Hill, 1973.

———. *Coming of Age: Problems of Teen-Agers,* by Paul H. Landis, 1970.

———. *Parent—Teen-Ager Communication (Bridging the Generation Gap),* by Millard J. Bienvenu, Sr., 1971.

U. S. Government Printing Office (Department of Public Documents, Washington, D. C. 20402). *Your Child from One to Six.*

———. *Your Child from Six to Twelve.*

———. *An Adolescent in Your Home.*

CHAPTER SIX
COGNITIVE ANTIDOTES FOR BEHAVIOR PROBLEMS

Bany, Mary A., and Lois V. Johnson, *Classroom Group Behavior (Group Dynamics in Education).* New York: The Macmillan Company, 1964.

Drayer, Adam M., *Problems and Methods in High School Teaching.* Boston: D. C. Heath & Company, 1963.

Galloway, Charles G., and Norma I. Mickelson, "Improving Teachers' Questions," *The Elementary School Journal,* Vol. 74, No. 3, December, 1973, pp. 145-148.

Good, Thomas L., and Jere E. Brophy, *Looking in Classrooms.* New York: Harper & Row, Publishers, 1973.

Morine, Greta, "Planning Skills: Paradox and Parodies," *Journal of Teacher Education,* Vol. XXIV, No. 2, Summer, 1973, pp. 135-143.

Redl, Fritz, *When We Deal With Children (Selected Writings)*. New York: The Free Press (Collier–Macmillan Limited, London), 1966.

Shavelson, Richard J., "What Is The Basic Teaching Skill?" *Journal of Teacher Education*, Vol. XXIV, No. 2, Summer, 1973, pp. 144–151.

Skillful Teaching Practices in the Elementary Schools. Bureau of Curriculum Development–Board of Education of the City of New York, 1969.

Sussna, Frances E.; Joel Goodman, Sidney B. Simon, Ron Witort; Frances E. Svensson; Sidney Dorros and John R. Browne; and Sara Goodman Zimet; "Human Relations in the Classroom," *Today's Education*, Vol. 62, No. 1, January, 1973, pp. 30–32.

Veatch, Jeannette, "Learning, Training and Education," *Young Children*, Vol. 29, No. 2, January, 1974, pp. 83–88.

CHAPTER SEVEN
LESSON PLANNING AND PRESENTATION AS THEY RELATE TO DISCIPLINE

The Association of Teachers of Social Studies of the City of New York, *Handbook for Social Studies Teaching*. New York: Holt, Rinehart and Winston, Inc. (Third Edition), 1967.

Bernstein, Abraham A., *Teaching English in High School*. New York: Random House, 1961.

Chesler, Mark, and Robert Fox, *Role–Playing Methods in the Classroom*. Chicago: SRA (Science Research Associates, Inc., A Subsidiary of IBM), 1966.

Getting Started in Elementary School. Board of Education of the City of New York, 1967.

Inlow, Gail M., *Maturity in High School Teaching*. Englewood Cliffs, New Jersey: Prentice–Hall, Inc., 1963.

Pearson, Neville P., and Lucius A. Butler (eds.), *Learning Resource Centers (Selected Readings)*. Minneapolis, Minnesota: Burgess Publishing Company, 1973.

Rivlin, Harry N., *Teaching Adolescents in Secondary Schools (The Principles of Effective Teaching in Junior and Senior High Schools)*. New York: Appleton-Century-Crofts, Inc., (Second Edition), 1961.

Shavelson, Richard J., "What Is the Basic Teaching Skill?" *Journal of Teacher Education*, Vol. XXIV, No. 2, Summer, 1973, pp. 144–151.

Skillful Teaching Practices in the Elementary Schools. Bureau of Curriculum Development–Board of Education of the City of New York, 1969.

Social Studies (Grade 4)–American People and Leaders: How the United States Began and Grew. Bureau of Curriculum Development–Board of Education of the City of New York, 1968.

Veatch, Jeannette, "Learning, Training and Education," *Young Children*, Vol. 29, No. 2, January, 1974, pp. 83–88.

Ward, Pearl L., and Robert Beacon, *The School Media Center: (A Book of Readings)*. Metuchen, N. J.: The Scarecrow Press, Inc., 1973.

CHAPTER EIGHT
HANDLING YOUTH THROUGH QUESTIONING

Drayer, Adam, M., *Problems and Methods in High School Teaching.* Boston: D. C. Heath & Company, 1963.

Enokson, Russell, "A Simplified Teacher Question Classification Model," *Education,* Vol. 94, September, 1973, pp. 27–29.

Galloway, Charles G., and Norma I. Mickelson, "Improving Teachers' Questions," *The Elementary School Journal,* Vol. 74, No. 3, December, 1973, pp. 145–148.

Getting Started in the Elementary School. Board of Education of the City of New York, 1967.

Good, Thomas L., and Jere E. Brophy, *Looking in Classrooms.* New York: Harper & Row, Publishers, 1973.

Groisser, Philip, *How To Use the Fine Art of Questioning.* New York: Teachers Practical Press, Inc., 1964.

Inlow, Gail M., *Maturity in High School Teaching.* Englewood Cliffs, New Jersey: Prentice-Hall, Inc., 1963.

Loughlin, Richard L., "On Questioning," *The Educational Forum,* Vol. XXV, May, 1961, pp. 481–482.

Reading–Grades 7, 8, 9. (A Teacher's Guide to Curriculum Planning). Board of Education of the City of New York, 1961.

Rivlin, Harry N., *Teaching Adolescents in Secondary Schools (The Principles of Effective Teaching in Junior and Senior High Schools).* New York: Appleton–Century–Crofts, Inc., (Second Edition), 1961.

Skillful Teaching Practices in the Elementary Schools. Bureau of Curriculum Development—Board of Education of the City of New York, 1969.

Social Studies (Grade 4)—American People and Leaders: How the United States Began and Grew. Bureau of Curriculum Development—Board of Education of the City of New York, 1968.

CHAPTER NINE
WAYS OF DEALING WITH DISCIPLINARY PROBLEMS

Carnot, Joseph B., "Dynamic and Effective School Discipline," *The Clearing House,* Vol. 48, No. 3, November, 1973, pp. 150–153.

Cranford, Peter G., *Disciplining Your Child the Practical Way.* Englewood Cliffs, N. J.: Prentice-Hall, Inc., 1963.

Cutts, Norma E., and Nicholas Moseley, *Teaching the Disorderly Pupil in Elementary and Secondary School.* New York: Longmans, Green and Co., 1959.

Drayer, Adam M., *Problems and Methods in High School Teaching.* Boston: D. C. Heath & Company, 1963.

Garner, Girolama, "Modifying Pupil Self-concept and Behavior," *Today's Education,* Vol. 63, No. 1, January, 1974, pp. 26–28.

Green, Arthur S., *The Elementary School Classroom Discipline Manual.* Minneapolis: T. S. Denison & Co., Inc., 1963.

Redl, Fritz, and William W. Wattenberg, *Mental Hygiene in Teaching.* New York: Harcourt, Brace and Company, Inc. (Second Edition), 1959.

Redl, Fritz, *When We Deal With Children (Selected Writings)*. New York: The Free Press (Collier-Macmillan Limited, London), 1966.

Sheviakov, George V., and Fritz Redl, *Discipline for Today's Children and Youth*. Washington, D. C.: Association for Supervision and Curriculum Development (A Department of the National Education Association of the United States), 1956.

Woody, Robert H., *Behavioral Problem Children in the Schools (Recognition, Diagnosis, and Behavioral Modification)*. New York: Appleton-Century-Crofts, 1969.

CHAPTER TEN
SPECIFIC PROBLEMS AND HOW TO HANDLE THEM

Attwell, Arthur A., *The School Psychologist's Handbook*. 12031 Wilshire Boulevard, Los Angeles, California 90025: Western Psychological Services (Publishers and Distributors)—A Division of Manson Weston Corporation, 1972.

Blair, Glenn Myers, R. Stewart Jones, and Ray H.Simpson, *Educational Psychology*. New York: The Macmillan Company (Third Edition), 1968.

Cutts, Norma E., and Nicholas Moseley, *Teaching the Disorderly Pupil in Elementary and Secondary School*. New York: Longmans, Green and Co., 1959.

Dmitriev, Valentine, and Jeanni Hawkins, "Susie Never Used To Say a Word," *Teaching Exceptional Children*, Vol. 6, No. 2, Winter, 1974, pp. 68–76.

Green, Arthur S., *The Elementary School Classroom Discipline Manual*. Minneapolis: T. S. Denison & Co., Inc., 1963.

Hurlock, Elizabeth B., *Developmental Psychology*. New York: McGraw-Hill Book Company (3rd ed.), 1968.

Hymes, James L. Jr., *Behavior and Misbehavior (A Teacher's Guide to Action)*. New York: Prentice-Hall, Inc., 1955.

Jersild, Arthur T., *Child Psychology*. Englewood Cliffs, N. J.: Prentice-Hall, Inc. (Third Edition), 1960.

Mikesell, William H., and Gordon Hanson, *Psychology of Adjustment*. New York: D. Van Nostrand Company, Inc., 1952.

Redl, Fritz, and David Wineman, *The Aggressive Child (A One Volume Edition, Containing "Children Who Hate" and "Controls from Within")*. Glencoe, Illinois: The Free Press, 1957.

Redl, Fritz, *When We Deal With Children (Selected Writings)*. New York: The Free Press (Collier-Macmillan Limited, London), 1966.

Woody, Robert H., *Behavioral Problem Children in the Schools (Recognition, Diagnosis, and Behavioral Modification)*. New York: Appleton-Century-Crofts, 1969.

CHAPTER ELEVEN
CASE STUDIES IN DISCIPLINE

Attwell, Arthur A., *The School Psychologist's Handbook*. 12031 Wilshire Boulevard, Los Angeles, California 90025: Western Psychological Services (Publishers and Distributors)—A Division of Manson Weston Corporation, 1972.

Braceland, Francis, Daniel Freedman, Karl Rickels, et al., *Drug Abuse: Medical and Criminal Aspects (Papers)*. New York: MSS Information Corporation (19 East 48th Street), 1972.

Cutts, Norma E., and Nicholas Moseley, *Teaching the Disorderly Pupil in Elementary and Secondary School*. New York: Longmans, Green and Co., 1959.

Gesell, Arnold, and Frances L. Ilg, *The Child from Five to Ten*. New York: Harper & Brothers, Publishers, 1946.

Gesell, Arnold, Frances L. Ilg, and Louise Bates Ames, *Youth, the Years from Ten to Sixteen*. New York: Harper & Row, 1956.

Green, Arthur S., *The Elementary School Classroom Discipline Manual*. Minneapolis: T. S. Denison & Co., Inc., 1963.

Hawkes, Glenn R., and Demaris Pease, *Behavior and Development from 5 to 12*. New York: Harper & Brothers, Publishers, 1962.

Hurlock, Elizabeth B., *Developmental Psychology*. New York: McGraw-Hill Book Company (3rd ed.), 1968.

Noar, Gertrude, *The Teacher and Integration*. Washington, D. C.: National Educational Association, 1966.

Sussna, Frances E.; Joel Goodman, Sidney B. Simon, Ron Witort; Frances E. Svensson; Sidney Dorros and John R. Browne; and Sara Goodman Zimet; "Human Relations in the Classroom," *Today's Education*, Vol. 62, No. 1, January, 1973, pp. 30–32.

Woody, Robert H., *Behavioral Problem Children in the Schools. (Recognition, Diagnosis, and Behavioral Modification)*. New York: Appleton-Century-Crofts, 1969.

INDEX

Aggressiveness, 147-48
Anecdotal records: consulting of, 124; explanation of, 143-45
Antidotes, affective, 65-84; being concerned for all, 84; being fair, grading fairly, 74-76; being friendly, not familiar, 68-69; building healthy atmosphere, 77-79; curbing competition, 79-81; granting recognition, rewards, and praise, 81-83; injecting sense of humor, 69; keeping students alert, 83-84; knowing your students, 70-73; maintaining firm control, 66-68; setting limits, 65-66; showing interest in students, 73-74; taming the "ringleaders," 76-77
Antidotes, cognitive, 85-91; being well prepared, 87; gearing pace and subject matter to class, 90; providing constructive activities, 90-91; selling your subject, 85-86; showing enthusiasm, 87; stimulating interest, 87-89
Antidotes, managerial, 54-64; announcing expectations, 55-56; assigning seats, 57-58; beginning classwork, 58-59; behaving with decorum, 64; being alert and observant, 61; formulating rules, 56-57; keeping room attractive, 64; learning names, 58; managing movement and transition, 60-61; requiring notebooks, 62-63; requiring preclass work, 59; scheduling varied activity, 63
Apologies, requiring, 142
Audiovisual aids: a need in class, 45; buffer against boredom, 63; inherent motivation, 20; lesson plan category, 93; list and discussion, 99-100; need for frequent use, 88-89; potential for underprivileged, 19-20; use of the chalkboard, 89

Behavioral modification, explained, 135
Behavior problems, emotional reactions and how handle, 47-53; corporal punishment beggar, 48-49; feeling of being picked on, 47-48; fighting, 52-53; obscenity and profanity, 50-51; running away, 49; stealing, 49-50
Behavior problems, specific ones and how handle, 146-59; aggressiveness, 147-48; being substitute teacher, 157-59; boisterous class, 156-57; cheating, 155-56; chip on shoulder, 149-50; class show-off, 148-49; constant talker, 152-53; restless student, 153-54; temper tantrum, 154; withdrawing student, 150-52
Black child, background of, 5-7

Black youth, ingredients in handling, 42
Boisterous class, 156-57

Case studies in discipline, 160-191; eleven cases of, 160-84; recommended solutions, 184-91
Characteristic behavior of young people, 71-73
Cheating, 155-56
Chip on shoulder, student with, 149-50
Class assistance with disciplinary problems, 134-35
Comparison, disadvantaged black child versus middle-class white child, 7-16; force vs. reason, 15; immediate aims vs. long-range goals, 15-16; inadequate parent attention vs. substantial parent attention, 12; insecurity vs. security, 9; insufficient general conversation vs. interesting conversation, 14-15; insufficient help with homework vs. substantial help from parents, 12-13; low expectations vs. high expectations, 10-11; meager exposure to books vs. being read to, 13-14; moving vs. stability, 9; poor self-image vs. favorable self-image, 11-12; uneducated parents vs. educated parents, 10; unwholesome surroundings vs. nice neighborhoods, 9-10
Conditioning process, 135, 140
Conferences, a basic technique, 124-28; parent-teacher conference, 126-28; student-teacher conference, 124-26
Corporal punishment, 48-49
Cumulative folder, consulting of, 124; explanation and discussion of, 70
Curing lateness through praise, 40-41

Deductive method, 98
Desensitization, 136; an explanation of, 136; three types of inhibitory responses used in, 136
Difficult class, launching of, 44-46
Disadvantaged black child's capacity to learn, 8
Disadvantaged blacks and speech, 27
Disadvantaged child, 3-53; disadvantaged youth and the problem of discipline, 3-22; disciplining through effective teaching, 23-39; identification of, 4-7; learning capacity of, 19; need for filling gaps of, 3, 8, 16; need for teacher knowledge and understanding of, 3-4, 7-8; reluctance to

DATE DUE

2.28 '83	
8.18 '83	
7.12 '84	
7.11 '85	
10.16. '85	
8.27. '86	
DEC 1 5 '93	